Doors

Into

Poetry

PRENTICE-HALL ENGLISH LITERATURE SERIES
Maynard Mack, Editor

CHAD WALSH

Beloit College

Doors

Into

Poetry

SECOND EDITION

PRENTICE-HALL, INC. *Englewood Cliffs, New Jersey*

PRENTICE-HALL INTERNATIONAL, INC., *London*
PRENTICE-HALL OF AUSTRALIA, PTY., LTD., *Sydney*
PRENTICE-HALL OF CANADA, LTD., *Toronto*
PRENTICE-HALL OF INDIA PRIVATE LIMITED, *New Delhi*
PRENTICE-HALL OF JAPAN, INC., *Tokyo*

13–218727–2

Library of Congress Catalog Card No. 75–97927

Current printing (last digit):

10   9   8   7   6   5   4   3

Printed in the United States of America

for
ROBERT GLAUBER
friend and fellow founder of
THE BELOIT POETRY JOURNAL

Acknowledgments

Acknowledgment is made to the following publishers, agents, and individuals who have granted permission to reprint selections included in this book.

CONRAD AIKEN
"The Fountain."

THE AMERICAN FOLKLORE SOCIETY, INC.
"Stagolee."

THE BELOIT POETRY JOURNAL
"Parting Song" by Peter Ferguson; "A Wife's Lament" by Jascha Kessler; "Good Boy" by Maude Totten.

JOHN BENNETT
"On D. H. Lawrence and His Snake."

THE CAXTON PRESS
"Sestina" from *The Fallen House*, by James K. Baxter.

CITY LIGHTS BOOKS
"Sunflower Sutra" and portion of "Howl" from *Howl and Other Poems*, copyright © 1959 by Allen Ginsberg.

CLARENDON PRESS
"All women born are so perverse" by Robert Bridges.

CORINTH BOOKS, INC.
"Letter 3" from *The Maximus Poems*, copyright © 1960 by Charles Olson Jargon Books/Corinth Books. "The Way" by Robert Creeley, from *A Form of Women*, published by Jargon Books in association with Corinth Books.

HILARY CORKE
"Hierosulem."

CRESSET PRESS, LTD.
"The Watch" from *Collected Poems*, by Frances Cornford, 1954.

UNIVERSITY OF DETROIT PRESS
"A Canticle to the Waterbirds" from *The Crooked Lines of God* by Brother Antoninus. Copyright © 1959 by the University of Detroit Press.

DOUBLEDAY & COMPANY, INC.
"Root Cellar" copyright 1943 by Modern Poetry Association, Inc.; "I Knew a Woman" copyright © 1955 by Theodore Roethke; "The Sequel" and "In a Dark Time" copyright © 1960 by Beatrice Roethke as Administratrix of the Estate of Theodore Roethke; "Journey to the Interior" copyright © 1961 by Beatrice Roethke as Administratrix; "Her Longing," "The Meadow Mouse," and "Wish for a Young Wife," copyright © 1963 by Beatrice Roethke as Administratrix; all from *The Collected Poems of Theodore Roethke*.

"Poor White" from *The Ballad of Catfoot Grimes and Other Verses*, copyright ⓒ 1964 by Hodding Carter.

ALAN DUGAN
"Love Song: I and Thou" from *Poems*, 1961.

EUGENE EOYANG
"In Memory."

EPOS
Suzanne Gross, "Vine."

FARRAR, STRAUS & GIROUX, INC.
"Winter Landscape" from *The Dispossessed*, copyright 1940 by New Directions, 1948 by John Berryman. "Man and Wife" from *Life Studies*, copyright ⓒ 1956, 1959 by Robert Lowell. "For the Union Dead" from *For the Union Dead*, copyright ⓒ 1960 by Robert Lowell. "Mutinous armed & suicidal grand" from *Sonnets*, copyright ⓒ 1952, 1967 by John Berryman.

FAWCETT PUBLICATIONS, INC.
"The Death of Jesse James" from *American Ballads: Naughty, Ribald and Classic.*

PETER FERGUSON
"Parting Song."

MRS. JOHN GOULD FLETCHER
"Evening Sky" by John Gould Fletcher.

ISABELLA GARDNER
"The Accomplices."

ALLEN GINSBERG
"Howl" and "The Shrouded Stranger."

ROBERT GRAVES
"The Florist Rose" from *Collected Poems of Robert Graves*. Reprinted by permission of Roturman S. A.

JOHN J. GROSS
"Hietaniemi."

SUZANNE GROSS
"Vine."

GROVE PRESS, INC.
"The Way" by Robert Creeley, from *The New American Poetry 1945–1960*.

HARCOURT, BRACE & WORLD, INC.
"in Just-spring" from *Poems 1923–1954*, copyright 1923, 1951 by E. E. Cummings. "maggie and milly and molly and may" and "that melancholy" from *95 Poems*, copyright ⓒ 1958 by E. E. Cummings. "my father moved through dooms of love," copyright 1940 by E. E. Cummings, renewed 1968 by Marion Morehouse Cummings; "pity this busy monster manunkind," copyright 1944 by E. E. Cummings; "somewhere I have never travelled," copyright 1931, 1959 by E. E. Cummings; "anyone lived in a pretty how town," copyright 1940 by E. E. Cummings, renewed 1968 by Marion Morehouse Cummings; all from *Poems 1923–1954*. "Burnt Norton" from *Four Quartets*, copyright 1943 by T. S. Eliot. "Gerontion," "The *Boston Evening Transcript*,"

"The Love Song of J. Alfred Prufrock," "Preludes" from *Collected Poems 1909–1962* by T. S. Eliot, copyright 1936 by Harcourt, Brace & World, Inc.; copyright © 1963, 1964 by T. S. Eliot. "Johann" from *Once*, © 1968 by Alice Walker. "Love Calls Us to the Things of This World" from *Things of This World*, © 1956 by Richard Wilbur. "Elephants Are Different to Different People" from *Home Front Memo*, copyright 1943 by Carl Sandburg. "Then" from *Ceremony and Other Poems*, copyright 1948, 1949, 1950 by Richard Wilbur.

HARPER & ROW, PUBLISHERS

"Hierosulem" by Hilary Corke. From *Harper's Magazine*, copyright © 1960 by Harper and Row, Publishers. "The Ballad of Rudolph Reed" from *Selected Poems*, copyright © 1960 by Gwendolyn Brooks Blakely. "Her Husband" from *Wodwo*, copyright © 1961 by Ted Hughes. "The Applicant" from *Ariel* by Sylvia Plath, copyright © 1963 by Ted Hughes. "The Examination" from *After Experience*, copyright © 1961 by W. D. Snodgrass.

WILLIAM HEINEMANN LTD.

"The Loss of the *Eurydice*" from *The Collected Poems of Edmund Gosse*.

HOLT, RINEHART AND WINSTON, INC.

"Design," "Moon Compasses," "Out, Out—," and "The Witch of Coös," from *Complete Poems of Robert Frost*. Copyright 1916, 1923 by Holt, Rinehart and Winston, Inc. Copyright 1936, 1944, 1951 by Robert Frost. Copyright 1964 by Lesley Frost Ballantine. "After Apple-Picking," "Birches," "Departmental: or My Ant Jerry," "The Pasture," "The Road Not Taken," and "The Secret Sits," from *Complete Poems of Robert Frost*. Copyright 1916, 1921 by Holt, Rinehart and Winston, Inc. Copyright 1936, 1942, 1944 by Robert Frost. "Stopping by Woods on a Snowy Evening," from *Complete Poems of Robert Frost*. Copyright 1923 by Holt, Rinehart and Winston, Inc. Copyright 1951 by Robert Frost. "I Did Not Lose My Heart," and "Loveliest of Trees," from *Complete Poems* by A. E. Housman. Copyright © 1959, 1924 by Holt, Rinehart and Winston, Inc. Copyright 1936 by Barclays Bank, Ltd. "Prayers of Steel," from *Cornhuskers* by Carl Sandburg. Copyright 1918 by Holt, Rinehart and Wiston, Inc. Copyright 1946 by Carl Sandburg.

HOUGHTON MIFFLIN COMPANY

"You, Andrew Marvell" from *The Collected Poems of Archibald MacLeish, 1917–1952*. Copyright 1952 by Archibald MacLeish.

INDIANA UNIVERSITY PRESS

"AD" from *New and Collected Poems*, copyright 1938, 1956 by Kenneth Fearing.

MARGOT JOHNSON AGENCY

"Sarajevo" from *The Blue Swallows*, copyright 1967 by Howard Nemerov.

SY KAHN

"Poet on Tour." This poem originally appeared in *Quixote*.

JASCHA KESSLER

"A Wife's Lament."

DON L. LEE

"The Death Dance" from *Black Pride*.

LITTLE, BROWN & COMPANY
"A bird came down the walk," and "I like to see it lap the miles," from *The Complete Poems of Emily Dickinson*.

LITTLE, BROWN & COMPANY, ATLANTIC MONTHLY PRESS, AND ALASTAIR REID
"Calenture" from *Oddments Inklings Omens Moments*, copyright © 1958 by Alastair Reid. This poem first appeared in *The New Yorker Magazine*.

LOUISIANA STATE UNIVERSITY PRESS
"Faulkner" from *Driving to Biloxi* by Edgar Simmons, 1968.

THE MACMILLAN COMPANY (NEW YORK)
"Coole and Ballylee," copyright 1933 by The Macmillan Company, renewed 1961 by Bertha Georgia Yeats; "Easter 1916," "A Prayer for My Daughter," and "The Second Coming," copyright 1924 by The Macmillan Company, renewed 1952 by Bertha Georgie Yeats; "The Wild Swans at Coole," copyright 1919 by The Macmillan Company, renewed 1947 by Bertha Georgie Yeats; "The Pity of Love," and "When You Are Old," copyright 1906 by The Macmillan Company, renewed 1934 by William Butler Yeats; "Sailing to Byzantium," copyright 1928 by The Macmillan Company, renewed 1956 by Georgie Yeats; all from *Collected Poems* by William Butler Yeats. "The Mill," and "Mr. Flood's Party" from *Collected Poems* by Edwin Arlington Robinson, copyright 1920, 1921 by Edwin Arlington Robinson, renewed 1948, 1949 by Ruth Nivison.

ELVA McALLASTER
"The Dinner."

CHARLES F. MADDEN
"The Fall of Icarus."

THE MARVELL PRESS
"Church Going" by Philip Larkin is reprinted from *The Less Deceived*, copyright © 1965, 1969, by permission of The Marvell Press, Hessle, Yorkshire, England.

MERRILL MOORE
"Warning to One" from *The Dance of Death in the 20th Century*. Reprinted by permission of I. E. Rubin Inc. and Mrs. Moore.

THOMAS NELSON & SONS
Corinthians 13: *1–3, 11–13*, from *The Revised Standard Version of the Holy Bible*. Copyright 1946, 1952 by the Division of Christian Education of the National Council of Churches.

NEW DIRECTIONS
"Life at War" from *The Sorrow Dance*, © 1966 by Denise Levertov Goodman. This poem was first published in *Poetry*. "The River-Merchant's Wife: a Letter," from *Personae*, copyright 1926 by Ezra Pound. "Ballad for Gloom," from *A Lume Spento and Other Early Poems*, © 1965 by Ezra Pound and New Directions Publishing Corporation. "A Marriage Ritual" and "The Poor" from *Collected Earlier Poems*, copyright 1938, 1951 by William Carlos Williams.

THE NEW YORKER MAGAZINE, INC.
"On D. H. Lawrence and His Snake" by John Bennett, © 1967 by The New Yorker Magazine, Inc. "Calenture" by Alastair Reid, copyright © 1958 by the New Yorker Magazine, Inc.

NORTHWEST REVIEW, UNIVERSITY OF OREGON
"The Fall of Icarus" by Charles F. Madden.

OCTOBER HOUSE INC.
"The Ballad of Sue Ellen Westerfield" and "The Web" by Robert Hayden from *Selected Poems*. Copyright © 1966 by Robert Hayden.

OXFORD UNIVERSITY PRESS
"Boston" from *Shifts of Being* by Richard Eberhart, copyright © 1968 by Richard Eberhart. "On the Industrial Highway" from *Striking the Stones* by Daniel Hoffman, copyright © 1968 by Daniel Hoffman. The six selections by Gerard Manley Hopkins are from *Poems of Gerard Manley Hopkins*.

RANDOM HOUSE, INC.
Lines from *The Age of Anxiety*, copyright 1946, 1947 by W. H. Auden. Lines from "In Time of War," copyright 1945 by W. H. Auden, from *The Collected Poetry of W. H. Auden*. Lines from "Kairos and Logos," copyright 1941 by W. H. Auden, from *The Collected Poetry of W. H. Auden*. "Musée des Beaux Arts," copyright 1940, 1968 by W. H. Auden, from *The Collected Poetry of W. H. Auden*. "Shine, Perishing Republic," copyright 1925, renewed 1953 by Robinson Jeffers, from *The Selected Poetry of Robinson Jeffers*. "The Express," "Landscape Near an Aerodrome," and "The Pylons," copyright 1934 by The Modern Library, Inc., renewed 1962 by Stephen Spender, from *Collected Poems 1928–1953* by Stephen Spender. Lines from "The Dome of Sunday," copyright 1941 by Karl Shapiro, from *Poems 1940–1953* by Karl Shapiro. "Before the Monkeys Came," from *Stanyan Street and Other Sorrows*, by Rod McKuen, copyright 1954 © 1960–1966 by Rod McKuen. "I'm Writing This Poem for Someone to See," copyright © 1964 by Karl Shapiro, from *Selected Poems* by Karl Shapiro. "Golden Bough," copyright 1932 by Alfred A. Knopf, Inc., renewed 1960 by Edwina C. Rubenstein, from *Collected Poems of Elinor Wylie*. "The Eagle and the Mole," copyright 1921 by Alfred A. Knopf, Inc., renewed 1949 by William Rose Benet, from *Collected Poems of Elinor Wylie*. "Peter Quince at the Clavier," copyright 1923, renewed 1951 by Wallace Stevens, from *The Collected Poems of Wallace Stevens*. "Morning After," copyright 1942 by Alfred A. Knopf, Inc., from *Selected Poems* by Langston Hughes.

ALASTAIR REID
"Calenture."

SAGAMORE PRESS, INC.
"The Fountain," from *Sheepfold Hill* by Conrad Aiken, copyright © 1958 by Sagamore Press, Inc.

SIEGFRIED SASSOON
"Base Details."

CHARLES SCRIBNER'S SONS
"The Way," copyright © 1959 by Robert Creeley, from *For Love* by Robert Creeley. The final paragraph from *A Farewell to Arms* by Ernest Hemingway,

copyright 1929 Charles Scribner's Sons; renewal copyright © 1957 Ernest Hemingway. "Views of the Oxford Colleges," copyright © 1960 Paris Leary, from *Views of the Oxford Colleges and Other Poems* by Paris Leary (*Poets of Today VII*). "Ode to the Confederate Dead" from *Poems* by Allen Tate, 1960.

SIMON & SCHUSTER, INC.
"Size of Breasts is of no Importance" from *Pop Poems* by Ronald Gross. Copyright © 1967 by Ronald Gross.

KNUTE SKINNER
"When Immanuel."

THE SOCIETY OF AUTHORS
As literary representatives of the estate of the late A. E. Housman. "I Did Not Lose My Heart" and "Loveliest of Trees," from A. E. Housman, *Collected Poems*. "The Widow in the Bye Street" by John Masefield.

STEPHEN SPENDER
"The Express," "The Landscape Near an Aerodrome," and "The Pylons."

MAUDE TOTTEN
"Good Boy."

PETER VIERECK
"To a Sinister Potato" from *New and Selected Poems*, Bobbs-Merrill Co., 1967; originally in *Terror and Decorum*, Scribner, 1948.

THE VIKING PRESS, INC.
Short prose passage from *Finnegans Wake* by James Joyce. "The Ballad of Persse O'Reilly," from *Finnegans Wake* by James Joyce. Copyright 1939 by James Joyce, copyright © renewed 1967 by George Joyce and Lucia Joyce. "Base Details," from *Collected Poems* by Siegfried Sassoon. Copyright 1918 by E. P. Dutton & Co., renewed 1946 by Siegfried Sassoon. "Combat Cultural," from *The Complete Poems of Marianne Moore*. Copyright © 1959 by Marianne Moore. Originally appeared in *The New Yorker*.

CHAD WALSH
"Ode to the Finnish Dead" from *The Unknowing Dance* (Abelard-Schuman). Copyright © 1964 by Chad Walsh.

WESLEYAN UNIVERSITY PRESS
"Cherrylog Road," copyright © 1963 by James Dickey, from *Helmets*, by James Dickey. This poem first appeared in *The New Yorker*.

RICHARD WILBUR
"Then."

DAVID WINTER & SONS, LTD.
"Attempted Assassination of the Queen" by William McGonagall.

YALE UNIVERSITY PRESS
"Coming Down Cleveland Avenue" from *The Lost Pilot* by James Tate, copyright © 1967 by Yale University.

Preface

This second edition of *Doors into Poetry*, like the first, is intended for college students undertaking their first systematic study of poetry. There is enough material for a full semester without the use of supplementary texts. At the same time, the book lends itself to those Freshman and Sophomore courses in which only a few weeks can be devoted to poetry. The explanatory material is compressed into eleven short chapters; the instructor can enrich them as much as time permits by use of the Additional Poems at the end.

The most important innovation is that the section of Additional Poems has been greatly expanded. It now constitutes an anthology in its own right, ranging from the early Elizabethans to the present, though with strongest emphasis on the twentieth century. Another change is that eight poets have been singled out for especially full representation, so that they may be studied individually: Donne, Dickinson, Hopkins, Yeats, Frost, Eliot, Cummings, Roethke.

A number of important changes have been made in the eleven chapters, all with the aim of producing a more concise, interesting, and usable book. To meet a particular need that seemed to be widespread, a short Glossary of Terms has also been added.

The underlying philosophy of *Doors into Poetry* remains unchanged. I have gone on the assumption that too much high seriousness or too exclusive an emphasis on mastery of technical matters can be deadly. The aim of a poetry course is not to turn out students who recite verse in a hushed tone or are programmed to chatter knowledgeably about the more esoteric reaches of analysis and criticism. Rather, one hopes to lead students, through a series of highly varied and individual experiences, to encounter poetry "from the inside," so that they will discover the delight of poetry and get into a lifelong habit of reading it.

With this goal in mind, the following approaches have been observed:

1. The material is presented more in psychological than in logical order. Thus the primitive or sensory elements are introduced first. The predominantly intellectual aspects gradually receive fuller treatment in the later chapters.

2. The method is primarily inductive. Whenever possible, the student is given a chance though various "experiments" to discover for himself the principles of poetry. The great variety of experiments—the most novel feature of *Doors into Poetry*—makes it possible to hold outright exposition to a minimum, though not of course to eliminate it altogether. By the time the student finishes at least the first eight chapters he should have an adequate command of analysis and criticism, *based mostly on his own encounters with individual poems.*

3. Though no attempt is made to provide a systematic coverage of periods, the poems in the main part of the book, together with those in the Additional Poems section, should ensure some familiarity with the development of poetry from the sixteenth century to the present.*

In undertaking this revision, I found myself endebted to many instructors and students who will observe how often I have incorporated their suggestions. I am particularly grateful to Professor Maynard Mack, an understanding and wise counselor at all stages of the work.

CHAD WALSH
Beloit College

---

*A *Teacher's Manual*, based upon this second edition, is available from the publishers. It contains suggestions for classroom use on each chapter, and a list of titles from Additional Poems suitable for comparative study.

Contents

Doors

Into

Poetry

Among those who have not read much poetry a vague impression prevails that prose is down-to-earth whereas poetry is peculiarly refined or "spiritual." The opposite is closer to the truth. Poetry has more in common with a primitive tribal dance than with an uplifting sermon.

Certainly the language of poetry tends toward the concrete and sensory. No matter what the poet wants to "say," he picks his words so as to stir the senses into imaginative action. Take, for instance, T. S. Eliot's "Preludes."

PRELUDES

I

The winter evening settles down
with smell of steaks in
           passageways.
Six o'clock.
The burnt-out ends of smoky
           days.
And now a gusty shower wraps   5
The grimy scraps
Of withered leaves about your
           feet
And newspapers from vacant
           lots;
The showers beat
On broken blinds and
           chimney-pots,   10
And at the corner of the street
A lonely cab-horse steams and
           stamps.
And then the lighting of the
           lamps.

The

Essential

Senses

1

II

The morning comes to consciousness
Of faint stale smells of beer   15
From the sawdust-trampled street
With all its muddy feet that press
To early coffee-stands.
With the other masquerades
That time resumes,   20
One thinks of all the hands
That are raising dingy shades
In a thousand furnished rooms.

III

You tossed a blanket from the bed,
You lay upon your back, and waited;   25
You dozed, and watched the night revealing
The thousand sordid images
Of which your soul was constituted;
They flickered against the ceiling.
And when all the world came back   30
And the light crept up between the shutters,
And you heard the sparrows in the gutters,
You had such a vision of the street
As the street hardly understands;
Sitting along the bed's edge, where   35
You curled the papers from your hair,
Or clasped the yellow soles of feet
In the palms of both soiled hands.

IV

His soul stretched tight across the skies
That fade behind a city block,   40
Or trampled by insistent feet
At four and five and six o'clock;
And short square fingers stuffing pipes,
And evening newspapers, and eyes
Assured of certain certainties,   45
The conscience of a blackened street
Impatient to assume the world.

I am moved by fancies that are curled
Around these images, and cling:
The notion of some infinitely gentle   50
Infinitely suffering thing.

Wipe your hand across your mouth, and laugh;
The worlds revolve like ancient women
Gathering fuel in vacant lots.

T. S. Eliot

Suppose you were to list the five senses, *sight, hearing, smell, taste,* and *touch,* and add at least two others that should be included—the *thermal sense* (ability to distinguish differences in temperature) and the *kinesthetic sense* (ability to feel muscular tensions, as when you lift a heavy weight). Eliot's poem, aided by the reader's imagination, calls all seven senses into play in section I:

> *Sight:* winter evening, passageways, smoky, gusty shower, grimy scraps, withered leaves, etc.
>
> *Hearing:* gusty shower, withered leaves about your feet, showers beat, etc.
>
> *Smell:* smell of steaks, burn-out, smoky days, etc.
>
> *Taste:* steaks, burnt-out, etc.
>
> *Touch:* scraps of withered leaves about your feet, showers beat.
>
> *Thermal sense:* winter, chimney pots, cab-horse steams.
>
> *Kinesthetic sense:* cab-horse steams and stamps, the lighting of the lamps (if one assumes that they are gas lights being lit, one by one).

This quiet poem assaults all seven senses, stirring up memories of sensory experience, and combining the memories into the new pattern created by the poem. The experience that the reader brings to the poem is essential. For instance, if he has grown up on a rice and fish diet and never eaten steak, the effect of "smell of steaks in passageways" loses much of its suggestive power. A modern reader whose acquaintance with horses is confined to television westerns must exercise his imagination if his senses are to respond to the motions of the cab-horse. But, though the reader may never have seen a cab-horse stamping to keep warm, he has probably done it himself, and can readily transfer his muscular experience to the horse.

A.   Read section II of "Preludes." List the seven senses, and under each include the words or phrases from Section II that evoke each sense.

B.   Reread sections I and II. Does the poem appeal to and stimulate one particular sense more than the others? If so, can you think of any particular reason why the poet chose to do this?

In large part "Preludes" is a mood poem, with smells, sounds, and muscular sensations, as well as colors, used to evoke the mood. What of poetry dealing with abstract subjects—the growth of conformity, for instance, and loss of individualism? One can imagine the following editorial in one of the more dignified dailies:

America used to be the land of rugged individualism. No more. The cult of conformity, of "social adjustment," of following the path of least resistance, is quietly turning us into a nation of standardized, interchangeable ciphers . . .

The language is relatively abstract. The few appeals to the senses are mild ("rugged" has a faint muscular implication). If the writer had wished to make the passage more vivid and impassioned, he might have begun something like this:

America used to be a land of square pegs, round pegs, hexagonal pegs, and any other kind of peg you care to name. There was a time when a man was proud to be what he was, and when he carved out a hole to fit his own shape and dimensions, instead of letting society sand him down to fit a standardized hole . . .

In this second version, the appeal to the senses is stronger. There is visual stimulation in the picture of various kinds of pegs and assorted holes. Touch and hearing are stirred up imaginatively by the allusion to carving and sanding. The writing is still rather pallid, but has at least moved away from the flat language of the original passage.

Poetry usually assails the senses more directly, even when the poem is "about" some abstract subject. Take, for instance, Robinson Jeffers' poem, "Shine, Perishing Republic":

SHINE, PERISHING REPUBLIC

While this America settles in the mould of its vulgarity,
          heavily thickening to empire,
And protest, only a bubble in the molten mass, pops and
          sighs out, and the mass hardens,

I sadly smiling remember that the flower fades to make fruit,
          the fruit rots to make earth.
Out of the mother; and through the spring exultances,
          ripeness and decadence; and home to the
          mother.

You making haste, haste on decay: not blameworthy; life is
          good, be it stubbornly long or suddenly

> A mortal splendor: meteors are not needed less than moun-
> tains: shine, perishing republic.
>
> But for my children, I would have them keep their distance
> from the thickening center; corruption
> Never has been compulsory, when the cities lie at the mon-
> ster's feet there are left the mountains.
>
> And boys, be in nothing so moderate as in love of man, a
> clever servant, insufferable master.
> There is the trap that catches noblest spirits, that caught—they
> say—God, when he walked on earth.   10
>
>   *Robinson Jeffers*

Note first of all that this poem is written much in the manner of a prose essay or editorial. Some things are stated quite directly and abstractly:

> life is good
> corruption   /   Never has been compulsory
> And boys, be in nothing so moderate as in love of man,
> a clever servant, insufferable master.

But the poet reinforces these matter-of-fact statements with language to invoke the senses. The prosaic "life is good" is followed by " be it stubbornly long or suddenly a mortal splendor: meteors are not needed less than mountains." "Meteors" suggest transient brilliance; "mountains" call up memories of things solid and lasting. Again, "corruption / Never has been compulsory" is an expository way of saying "when the cities lie at the monster's feet there are left the mountains." Corruption has now been transformed into a vivid picture, the monster, and the reference to mountains suggests not merely solidity but the smell and feel of fresh air (contrasted with the corruption of the cities). The admonition, "And boys, be in nothing so moderate as in love of man, a clever servant, insufferable master" is straightforward and didactic, like a father giving good advice to his children, but it is followed by "There is the trap that catches noblest spirits, that caught—they say—God, when he walked on earth." A powerful visual image now reinforces the plain statement. The reader summons up his own picture of the Crucifixion, perhaps a composite of half a dozen religious paintings.

Often the failure of a reader and a poem to make contact is caused by wrong anticipations on the reader's part. He is looking for something rarified and spiritual; he finds a welter of sense stimuli. He is sure the "real poem" must be concealed behind a shimmering curtain of descriptive language. But the "real poem" is a will-o'-the-wisp. There is only the *whole poem*, as it stands on the printed page or is read aloud. If the reader finds himself assailed by sensory images, it is because the poem is intended to stir the reader's smell and touch, as well as his mind. Take "The Pity of Love":

THE PITY OF LOVE

A pity beyond all telling
Is hid in the heart of love:
The folk who are buying and selling,
The clouds on their journey above,
The cold wet winds ever blowing,   5
And the shadowy hazel grove
Where mouse-grey waters are flowing,
Threaten the head that I love.

W. B. Yeats

One could say this is a poem about a lover's realization of the fragility of his beloved and his inability to shield her from all dangers. But it is also the chatter and clatter of the market place, the unpredictable movements of clouds in the sky, the touch of a cold wind, a mysterious hazel grove, a dim brook flowing steadily. It is the feeling toward the beloved exprienced and expressed in terms of things seen and touched.

The sensory stimuli in a poem do not have to be blatant. Sometimes they are so subdued as to be almost subliminal. All the same, they set to work on the subconscious level and make the reader's response more than a purely mental one. The poem below is an example. Its language seems starkly void of anything to make the nose twitch or the fingers tingle. Such is the first impression, but a rereading reveals that it is quietly engaged in setting several of the senses to work:

THE WAY

My love's manners in bed
are not to be discussed by me,
as mine by her
I would not credit comment upon gracefully.

But I ride by that margin of the lake in   5
the wood, the castle,

and the excitement of strongholds;
and have a small boy's notion of doing good.

Oh well, I will say here,
knowing each man,   10
let you find a good wife too,
and love her as hard as you can.

Robert Creeley

   C. Which two of the seven senses seem to be dominant here? List the words and phrases appealing to each of the two. In what way do these two lists point toward the over-all mood of the poem?

The next poem begins with sights, and then shifts to an emphasis on sounds.

LONDON

I wander through each charter'd street,
Near where the charter'd Thames does flow,
And mark in every face I meet
Marks of weakness, marks of woe.

In every cry of every Man,   5
In every Infant's cry of fear,
In every voice, in every ban
The mind-forg'd manacles I hear.

How the chimney-sweeper's cry
Every black'ning church appalls;   10
And the hapless soldier's sigh
Runs in blood down palace walls.

But most through midnight streets I hear
How the youthful harlot's curse
Blasts the new-born infant's tear,   15
And blights with plagues the marriage hearse.

William Blake

   D. (1) Make a list of all images of sight, and another of images of sound. (2) Take several of the images of sound and try to make up equivalent images of sight, e.g., change "chimney-sweeper's cry" to "chimney-sweeper's anguished eyes." (3) Change several of the images of sight into images of sound. (4) Do you have any theory as to why Blake chose to appeal to both sight and sound, but predominantly to the latter?

The point of all this is simply to recognize that poetry, however civilized it may appear, has savage or at least primitive ancestral roots. And it never outgrows them. No matter to what intellectual and spiritual heights a poem may soar, it keeps its permanent links with the things of the earth, the things of the body, the seven senses.[1]

The trouble is that in ordinary life the senses—especially if they belong to urban man—get lazy. He may see and hear effectively while in his car—his safety depends on that—but except for such practical uses, his senses grow rusty. Have you ever noticed what color eyes the child next door has? Can you distinguish four separate bird-calls? Do you know the difference between the smell of honeysuckle and that of sweet peas? The difference in texture between cotton and linen?

The more the reader can develop a primitive delight in the possession of various senses, the more he will be able to respond to poetry. The nose and taste buds need as much training as the mind if poetry is to be something more than a way of saying what could be more simply said in direct prose.

E.   Describe each of the following as vividly and accurately as possible in one sentence: (1) The color of dead oak leaves on a tree. (2) The shape of a dachshund. (3) The smell of a room the next morning after many people have been smoking in it. (4) The taste of the skin of baked potatoes. (5) The feeling when you lean against a tree with rough bark. (6) The feel of a cat's fur. (7) The sound of an ambulance siren. (8) The feeling of a snowball or a piece of ice in your hand. (9) Your reaction when you stretch before getting up in the morning. (10) The feeling when you sit down after hard exercise.

F.   Select a subject for a short poem. Then choose one of the senses (not sight) and write the poem, letting imagery involving this one sense carry the weight of the poem as much as possible. For example, write a poem about a walk through the woods in terms of touch, or a poem about a street fight in terms of sound.

---

[1]Other primitive aspects of poetry will be discussed in subsequent chapters. *E.g.*, the rhythm of poetry has a close relation with the motions of the body, such as walking and breathing.

W. H. Auden wrote in *Poets at Work* (Harcourt, Brace & World, Inc., 1948):

"Why do you want to write poetry?" If the young man answers, "I have important things I want to say," then he is not a poet. If he answers, "I like hanging around words listening to what they say," then maybe he is going to be a poet.

Prose, typically, is a way of putting words to work. Poetry is the art of teaching them to play and sing at the same time that they do the work the poet has assigned them. In poetry, words are not merely a means to an end, but an end in themselves.

The poet is the specialist who is concerned with more than the dictionary meaning of words. He wants to know their nuances of meaning and implication, the associations they carry with them, the subtleties of aura and mood.

Denotation and Connotation

2

Poets of course are not the only specialists of this sort. The lowliest writer of TV commercials is aware that the choice of the right adjective can make a 20 per cent difference in the sale of soap or lipstick. He knows, as does the poet, that words carry more than literal meaning (*denotation*). They also carry emotional overtones (*connotation*).

Below are four sentences that say practically the same thing, so far as literal meaning is concerned. A movie camera might record four identical scenes:

(1) The slim girl with the yellow hair walked down the street, and every one looked at her.
(2) The svelte girl with the golden hair glided down the street, and everyone stared at her.
(3) The skinny girl with the corn-colored hair came down the street, and everyone glanced at her.
(4) The slender maiden with tresses of gold proceeded down the street, and everyone gazed upon her.

The difference between one sentence and another is not in the girl but the spectator. The changes in key words indicate how the bystanders inwardly respond to her presense.

To take another example, consider three *synonyms* that describe the same objective state, but convey a different impression. If you say that a man is *intoxicated*, it sounds as though you are pronouncing a legal or scientific judgment. If you call him *inebriated*, the tone instantly becomes more indulgent, and the mental picture is perhaps a mellow gentleman in one of the better clubs. To call a person *drunk* suggests crudity and a convenient ditch nearby.

A.   List three current slang terms that are used to describe someone who has drunk too much. Make up a sentence for each to illustrate the different connotations of the three words.

In the chart below is another group of words which largely overlap in meaning. The dictionary will give you the literal meaning, but you must depend mostly on your own sense of language when it comes to the connotations.

B.   Examine the words at the head of the chart in relation to the phrases to the right, and indicate by a check mark which phrases apply to each word. Are any two of the words exact synonyms, in connotation as well as denotation?

Moan, wail, lament, and *whimper* are equally poetic as words, but it is the poet's task to choose *the* right word to use in the particular poem and line of poetry that he is writing. Of the four words just given, only the last could achieve the exact effect T. S. Eliot desired in the concluding lines of "The Hollow Men":

> This is the way the world ends
> Not with a bang but a whimper.

moan	groan	keen	sob	weep	wail	cry	lament	bawl	whimper	mourn	
											Applied mostly to children
											Applied mostly to adults
											Applied mostly to men
											Applied mostly to women
											A sympathetic word
											An unsympathetic word
											Suggests physical pain
											Suggests a trivial cause
											Suggests a loud noise
											Suggests deep grief
											Suggests physical motion
											Used especially in informal speech
											Used especially in formal speech or writing
											Produces comic effect

Many words have multiple and almost contradictory connotations, and only the surrounding words will determine which connotation is operative. The word *dusk*, a synonym for twilight, can be either pleasant or unpleasant—"The lovers strolled through the dusk" as contrasted with "Strange shapes moved through the dusk." The word "white" is equally many sided. By itself it suggests purity, brightness, cleanliness, splendor. But it can take on implications of sickness or unnaturalness—"Whited sepulchres" or "She turned white with fear."

The poet writing in English has an extraordinary number of synonyms and near-synonyms from which to choose. English has the largest vocabulary of any language in the world. This is due to its easy-going habit of borrowing words wholesale from other languages, including Eskimo (*igloo*) and Malay (*amuck*). The three largest sources have been Latin, Greek, and French.

English belongs to the same group of languages as Dutch, German,

Swedish, Danish, and Norwegian. The native Teutonic stock is reflected in words that express everyday ideas: *bread, wife, tree, house, love, father, mother.* They are often monosyllabic, and are frequently charged with powerful and direct emotional associations. For example, the native word, *brotherly,* has a heavier emotional charge than the Latin equivalent, *fraternal. Brotherly love* means more than *fraternal affection.*

Some Latin words, like *mile* and *wine,* seeped into the language while the Angles, Saxons, and Jutes were still on the European continent. But most of the words derived from the classical languages came later, partly through the Church, and partly through scholarship in general. Philosophic and theological ideas, and—more recently—the concepts of science are usually expressed by words taken from Latin or Greek. In general, the Latin and Greek derivatives have a more formal and learned flavor than those which come from the native Teutonic.

Words of French origin produce an intermediate effect. William the Conqueror overwhelmed the English in 1066, and for more than two hundred years the rulers of the country spoke French as their first and sometimes their only language. A very large part of the French vocabulary passed into English. French words are likely to be found whenever the topics discussed involve government (the very word is French), the Church, military affairs, law, medicine, the arts, society, food on the table (but not on the hoof—the native "pig" becomes the French "pork" when cooked), clothing and sports.

C.   Below are several sets of synonyms or near-synonyms. Pick out one set and write three sentences (one for each word), so phrased that they will illustrate the difference in connotation or degree of formality.

Native Teutonic	French	Latin
ask	inquire	interrogate
wretched	miserable	infelicitous
kingly	royal	regal
earthly	mundane	terrestrial
watery	humid	aqueous
empty	void	vacuous

(Note carefully that these words are not interchangeable in all circumstances. For example, one may speak of an "empty smile" or a "vacuous smile," but not of a "void smile." One may "ask" or "inquire" the way, but not "interrogate" the way; one interrogates a person as to the way.)

This enormous richness of the English vocabulary is a challenge and an opportunity to the writer. He may, if he wishes, aim at the absolute simplicity that comes from choosing short, native words. The famous ending of Ernest Hemingway's *A Farewell to Arms* is a good example. The narrator's sweetheart has just died. He has evicted the nurses and is in the hospital room:

> But after I had got them out and shut the door and turned off the light it wasn't any good. It was like saying good-by to a statue. After a while I went out and left the hospital and walked back to the hotel in the rain.

It would be possible to rewrite the passage with a greater use of French and Latin derivatives (*e.g.*, "extinguished" instead of "turned off") and the rewritten version might be good in itself—if it fitted with the rest of the book and contributed to the total effect the author was seeking. But the whole novel builds up toward this final paragraph. The ending gives the feeling of plain and stark finality to which the book has been pointing. The simplicity of the diction is right. There are only three words not of native origin—*statue*, *hospital*, and *hotel*—and all three have been so thoroughly assimilated in English that they "feel" almost like native words.

As an example of the powerful effects that the native part of the English vocabulary can achieve, consider A. E. Housman's poem, "Loveliest of Trees." The only foreign derivative in the twelve lines is *cherry*, an ancient borrowing from French. This poem demonstrates that the native English vocabulary has a down-to-earth familiarity, and at the same time is capable of a highly poetic quality. The effect, when the poet handles the words properly, is a sense of the beauty and poetry of ordinary things. If *bloom* and *bough* were replaced with the French-derived *flowers* and *branch*, something indefinable but perceptible would be lost. This does not mean that "native words" are always best, but simply that in this poem they best convey the absolute simplicity and beauty of simplicity that Housman intends.

LOVELIEST OF TREES

Loveliest of trees, the cherry now
Is hung with bloom along the bough,
And stands about the woodland ride,
Wearing white for Eastertide.

Now, of my threescore years and ten,   5
Twenty will not come again,

And take from seventy springs a score,
It only leaves me fifty more.

And since to look at things in bloom
Fifty springs are little room,   10
About the woodlands I will go
To see the cherry hung with snow.

A. E. Housman

Shakespeare could work a similar magic with the plainest words
in the language. In Sonnet 73, all the words are native Teutonic except
the few italicized:

SONNET 73

That time of year thou mayst in me behold
When yellow leaves, or none, or few, do hang
Upon those boughs which shake against the cold,
Bare ruined *choirs* where late the sweet birds sang.
In me thou see'st the twilight of such day   5
As after sunset *fadeth* in the west,
Which by-and-by black night doth take away,
Death's second self, that *seals* up all in rest.
In me thou see'st the glowing of such fire   10
That on the ashes of his youth doth lie,
As the deathbed whereon it must *expire*,
Consumed with that which it was *nourished* by.
This thou *perceiv'st*, which makes thy love more strong,
To love that well which thou must leave ere long.   15

William Shakespeare

It is interesting to note that the frequency of loan-words increases
slightly toward the end, as pure description fades into a more explicit
statement of thought.

In Shakespeare's Sonnet 106, the percentage of derived words sharply
increases, and they are used to evoke a splendor and richness which the
more homespun vocabulary of Sonnet 73 might not be able to express:

SONNET 106

When in the *chronicle* of wasted time
I see *descriptions* of the fairest wights,
And *beauty* making *beautiful* old *rime*

In *praise* of ladies dead and lovely knights,
Then, in the *blazon* of sweet *beauty's* best,   5
Of hand, of foot, of lips, of eye, of brow,
I see their *antique* pen would have *expressed*
Even such a *beauty* as you *master* now.
So all their *praises* are but *prophecies*
Of this our time, all you *prefiguring;*   10
And, for they looked but with *divining* eyes,
They had not skill enough your worth to sing;
For we, which now behold these *present* days,
Have eyes to wonder, but lack tongues to *praise.*

William Shakespeare

But what about highly technical words? It is a mistake to assume they are necessarily "prosaic" and unsuitable for poetry. As always, it is the context that is crucial. Shakespeare's Sonnet 87 is full of foreign derivatives (*italicized*). Many of them are legal and commercial terms, which, standing alone, would evoke few associations except of the courts and counting house. Yet in the context of the poem, they become highly charged with emotion:

SONNET 87

Farewell! thou art too dear for my *possessing,*
And like enough thou know'st thy *estimate.*
The *charter* of thy worth gives thee *releasing;*
My *bonds* in thee are all *determinate.*
For how do I hold thee but by thy *granting,*   5
And for that *riches* where is my *deserving?*
The *cause* of this fair gift in me is wanting,
And so my *patent* back again is swerving.
Thyself, thou gav'st, thy own worth then not knowing,
Or me, to whom thou gav'st it, else mistaking;   10
So thy great gift, upon *misprision* growing,
Comes home again, on better *judgment* making.
Thus have I had thee as a dream doth *flatter—*
In sleep a king, but waking no such *matter.*

William Shakespeare

Look up *charter, determinate, patent, misprision* in the *Oxford Dictionary* to learn the technical meanings they have in the poem.

It would be misleading to imply that only poetry is concerned with the use of connotative language. Prose, particularly in its more imaginative and emotional uses, has almost but not quite as great a vested interest. There is, of course, a type of prose (such as strictly scientific writing) that strives to avoid connotation altogether. This is a difficult if not impossible task. When Dr. Kinsey wrote his famous work, he called it not *Sexual Behavior of Men* but *Sexual Behavior of the Human Male*, presumably in order to set the work in a dispassionate biological framework. But his choice of title actually created a special set of connotations, conjuring up mental images of the ape in the zoo.

The language of totalitarian ideology provides a striking illustration of the way that seemingly objective and denotative language can create new connotations. Consider this simple sentence:

The antisocial elements were liquidated.

The sentence sounds scientific and antiseptic as though some chemical process had taken place in a laboratory. It suggests that human beings are not of significance in and of themselves, that they are merely part of a vast social process, and are as interchangeable and replaceable as the elements in any other compound. A whole theory of society and of the individual's place in it is implied by the coolly impersonal language of the sentence.

If the statement is translated into more familiar and human language—"The rebellious people were killed" or "The Secret Police shot the antigovernment leaders"—the literal meaning is still the same, but a different set of associations is created. Now the individual human beings come into focus.

Poetry and other forms of imaginative writing tend to avoid apparently colorless sentences like "The antisocial elements were liquidated." But not always. Sometimes a flat sentence, *in the right context*, can create very powerful poetic effects. In Thomas Hardy's poem, given below, the line "The Great Adjustment is taking place!" sounds like a report on economic conditions, but its very bareness and flatness, in the setting of the poem, makes it strong and evocative.

THERE SEEMED A STRANGENESS
A PHANTASY

There seemed a strangeness in the air,
Vermilion light on the land's lean face;

I heard a Voice from I knew not where:—
"The Great Adjustment is taking place!

"I set thick darkness over you   5
And fogged you all your years therein;
    At last I uncloud your view,
Which I am weary of holding in.

"Men have not heard, men have not seen
Since the beginning of the world   10
    What earth and heaven mean;
But now their curtain shall be furled,

"And they shall see what is, ere long,
Not through a glass, but face to face;
And Right shall disestablish Wrong: 15
The Great Adjustment is taking place."

Thomas Hardy

Hardy's poem is an example of intentionally flat diction, used for
the purposes of poetry. Occasionally (though less frequently than in
earlier periods) a poet will deliberately employ a stylized poetic language.
Often this includes the use of *archaisms*. Thus Spenser imitated the lan-
guage of Chaucer, and Keats imitated Spenser. In the following poem
by Ezra Pound we see a modern instance of archaism both in vocabulary
and grammar:

BALLAD FOR GLOOM

For God, our God is a gallant foe
That playeth behind the veil.

I have loved my God as a child at heart
That seeketh deep bosoms for rest,
I have loved my God as a maid to man—   5
But lo, this thing is best:

To love your God as a gallant foe that plays behind the veil;
To meet your God as the night winds meet beyond Arcturus'
    pale.

I have played with God for a woman,
I have staked with my God for truth,   10
I have lost to my God as a man, clear-eyed—
    His dice be not of ruth.

For I am made as a naked blade,
    But hear ye this thing in sooth:

Who loseth to God as man to man   15
    Shall win at the turn of the game.
I have drawn my blade where the lightnings meet
    But the ending is the same:
Who loseth to God as the sword blades lose
    Shall win at the end of the game.   20

For God, our God is a gallant foe that playeth behind the veil.
Whom God deigns not to overthrow hath need of triple mail.

Ezra Pound

D. Read Pound's poem aloud and underline each word or phrase that sounds archaic. Also underline any grammatical endings or constructions that seem old fashioned. Then try to modernize the poem by changing the words you have underlined. What happens to the tone and "feel" of the poem?

Chapter 1 suggested that the reader who wants to get inside poetry must arouse his senses from hibernation—teach them to respond to the sensory stimuli in poetry, so that in imagination at least he learns to see, hear, taste, with a new vividness and subtlety.

A parallel conclusion is implied by the present chapter. To read poetry with insight it is not enough to know the dictionary meaning of words. The reader needs to be aware at all times that poetry gets "extra mileage" out of words, by exploiting their power of implication and suggestion—in short, their connotations.

To develop a sensitivity to words, the best procedure is simply to read a variety of poetry with this possibility in mind, and to be alert for instances of effective connotative language. A sixth sense for words then gradually grows, parallel to the sense that the poet already has—otherwise he would not be a poet.

The concluding experiments are for the benefit of anyone who wishes a little further training in the art of "hanging around words listening to what they say."

E. The various English translations of the Bible provide a good opportunity to study the connotations of words. The King James Bible dates from the early seventeenth century, though its language was conservative even then. *The Revised Standard Version was published in the mid-twentieth century. Below are two versions of verses from* I Corinthians 13. *Study the italicized words, trying in each case to sense the differences in connotation.*

King James	Revised Standard
Though I speak with the tongues of men and of angels, and have not charity, I am become as *sounding brass*, or a *tinkling* cymbal. And though I have the *gift of prophecy*, and understand all mysteries, and all knowledge; and though I have all faith, so that I could remove mountains, and have not charity, I am nothing. . . . When I was a child, I *spake* as a child, I understood as a child, I *thought* as a child; but when I became a man, I *put away* childish things. For now we see through a glass, *darkly;* but then face to face; now I know in part; but then shall I *know* even as also I am *known*. And now abideth faith, hope, *charity*, these three; but the greatest of these is charity.	If I speak in the tongues of men and of angels, but have not love, I am a *noisy gong* or a *clanging* cymbal. And if I have *prophetic powers*, and understand all mysteries and all knowledge, and if I have all faith, so as to remove mountains, but have not love, I am nothing. . . . When I was a child, I *spoke* like a child, I thought like a child, I *reasoned* like a child; when I became a man, I *gave up* childish ways. For now we see in a mirror *dimly*, but then face to face. Now I know in part; then I shall *understand* fully, even as I have been fully *understood*. So faith, hope, *love* abide, these three; but the greatest of these is love.

F.   *Below is the first stanza of John Keats' The Eve of St. Agnes. In each case the correct reading has been given first. Can you explain why it is preferable to the theoretical alternative?*

St. Agnes' Eve—Ah/oh, bitter chill/cold it was!
The owl, for all his feathers/plumage, was a-cold;
The hare limped trembling/shaking through the frozen/frigid
       grass,
And silent/quiet was the flock in woolly fold:
Numb were the Beadsman's fingers, while he told   5
His rosary, and while his frosted/steaming breath,
Like pious/fragrant incense from a censor old,
Seemed taking flight/off for heaven, without a death,
Past the sweet/dear Virgin's picture/image, while his prayer
       he saith.

G.   *Study the alternative readings in the following poem. Decide in each case which you consider best. Underline it. Explain briefly why you chose each one.*

A BIRD CAME DOWN THE WALK

A bird came down the walk:
He did not know I saw;
He bit/tore an angle-worm in halves
And ate the fellow/creature raw.

And then he gulped/drank a dew   5
From a convenient/handy grass,
And then hopped sidewise to the wall
And let a beetle pass.

He glanced with rapid/speedy eyes
That hurried all abroad—   10
They looked like frightened pearls/beads, I thought
He stirred his velvet/satin head

Like one in danger; cautious,
I offered him a crumb,
And he unrolled/unwrapped his feathers   15
And rowed him softer home

Than oars divide the sea/ocean,
Too silver for a seam,
Or butterflies, off banks of noon,
Leap/jump, plashless, as they swim.   20

Emily Dickinson

H. *Below is an apparently simple poem. Underline the adjectives in it and see whether you can determine why the poet picked the particular ones that she used. Is there anything that they have in common? What is the over-all mood that they help create?*

GOOD BOY

The Hunter's Moon hung huge and queer that night
As the boy walked up the rutted road;
It mocked at his misery and stirred strange thoughts
Thoughts of flying like bats and frightening folks.
The car braked to a stop, the old man spoke,   5
"Can I give you a ride to some place, Son?"

Wind sounds moaned past the boy's tense face and he flew,
Flew up the hills and down on his great black horse.
Shadowy things, like worms, crossed the moon's face.
Fear gripped him, "What if the old man is dead?"   10
"I am a good boy" he thought, "So I must return
To the place where I left the kind old man."

The horse was gone, the car rattled up the hill
Up to the top, by the big black rock and the bush,
Big black rock and the bush which hid the precipice.   15

Maude Totten

    I.   In the following poem, the verbs seem to contribute a great deal of vividness and power. Underline all of them, then pick out four or five that seem to fit together in giving life to the poem. What do they have in common?

I KNEW A WOMAN

I knew a woman, lovely in her bones,
When small birds sighed, she would sigh back at them;
Ah, when she moved, she moved more ways than one:
The shapes a bright container can contain!
Of her choice virtues only gods should speak,   5
Or English poets who grew up on Greek
(I'd have them sing in chorus, cheek to cheek).

How well her wishes went! She stroked my chin,
She taught me Turn, and Counter-turn, and Stand;
She taught me Touch, that undulant white skin;   10
I nibbled meekly from her proffered hand;
She was the sickle; I, poor I, the rake,
Coming behind her for her pretty sake
(But what prodigious mowing we did make).

Love likes a gander, and adores a goose: 15
Her full lips pursed, the errant note to seize;
She played it quick, she played it light and loose;
My eyes, they dazzled at her flowing knees;
Her several parts could keep a pure repose,
Or one hip quiver with a mobile nose   20
(She moved in circles, and those circles moved).

Let seed be grass, and grass turn into hay:
I'm martyr to a motion not my own;

What's freedom for? To know eternity.
I swear she cast a shadow white as stone.   25
But who would count eternity in days?
These old bones live to learn her wanton ways:
(I measure time by how a body sways).

Theodore Roethke

J.   Something can be learned about the suggestive power of even the simplest words by restricting yourself to a very limited vocabulary. Try writing a short poem (serious and effective) in words of one syllable.

K.   Translating from a foreign language is a useful way of developing a feeling for the nuances of words. Often a foreign word has no exact English equivalent, and may have to be rendered by a phrase or figure of speech. If you have a reading knowledge of some other language, translate a poem into English, striving to keep the same tone and mood.

The preceding chapter dealt with the rather obvious ways that poetry utilizes the evocative power of language—in particular, the connotative function of words. The present chapter is concerned with more elaborate methods of making language yield an extra intensity and richness of implication.

For example, the poet may wish to introduce a particular kind of tension into the very structure of thought and feeling. He wants to express simultaneously two thoughts or emotions that seem to contradict each other, and leave it to the reader to perceive how they are both valid parts of a larger truth. The statement, "He won every battle and lost the war" is nonsense on the surface. But perhaps the implication may be that the victorious battles so devastated the country that victory was as ruinous as defeat. It is up to the reader to make the missing connection, to grasp the larger meaning or *paradox* by which the contradictions are reconciled.

There is a familiar prayer with the phrase, referring to God, "whose service is perfect freedom." Again, here is apparently a nonsense statement for it is saying that the person who is completely a servant to God is at the same time the truly free man. But by the paradox, a new dimension is introduced: the idea that ultimate freedom is not just "doing your thing" but fulfilling one's nature and destiny by a particular kind of relationship.

An effectively used paradox can thus reveal complexities of thought

Multiple Meanings

3

and feeling. The paradox contained in the above prayer is developed by John Donne in "Holy Sonnet 14":

HOLY SONNET 14

Batter my heart, three personed God, for you
As yet but knock, breath, shine, and seek to mend;
That I may rise and stand, o'erthrow me, and bend
Your force to break, blow, burn and make me new.
I like an usurped town, to another due,   5
Labor to admit you, but Oh, to no end;
Reason, your viceroy in me, me should defend,
But is captived and proves weak or untrue.
Yet dearly I love you and would be loved fain,
But am betrothed unto your enemy.   10
Divorce me, untie, or break that knot again;
Take me to you, imprison me, for I,
Except you enthrall me, never shall be free,
Nor ever chaste, except you ravish me.

John Donne

A. Examine this poem as an expansion of the phrase, "Whose service is perfect freedom." List all the ways in which the poem paradoxically develops the idea that servitude to God is the road to freedom.

A near neighbor of the paradox is the lowly *pun*, which is not lowly at all so far as the poets are concerned. It is a means of saying quite different things simultaneously, and compelling the reader to recognize an unsuspected relation. It plays on words to produce a kind of illumination. When Hamlet (Act III, Scene i) tells Ophelia, "Get thee to a nunnery," any Elizabethan groundling knew that he was commanding two opposite courses of action. The word "nunnery" meant a convent, then as now. Hamlet was telling Ophelia to leave the corrupt world of court life and go to a place of retirement and purity. But "nunnery" was also a slang term for a house of prostitution. Hamlet was thus contemptuously suggesting, "Go where you belong." The pun is here a deeply moving device, for it reveals the ambivalence of Hamlet's attitude toward Ophelia. To him she is simultaneously an image of purity and a strumpet.

Donne's "Holy Sonnet 14," which we have just examined, develops its paradox by the verbal device of puns. The speaker imparts a feminine personality to himself; God and the "enemy" both sound masculine. The poem is a prayer to God that he will "enthrall" and "ravish" the suppliant, so as to liberate him. The original meaning of *enthrall* was "enslave." It can also mean "captivate" or "enchant." All of these meanings are implied here. *Ravish* originally meant "seize and carry away forcibly." But it can also mean "to rape" or "to enrapture." Again, all the meanings seem to be present. God is being addressed (in terms of male-and-female imagery) as a rightful lord, a figure both of power and delight, a being who, by exercising complete domination, liberates the suppliant from himself.

   B.   *Why do you think the pun occupies a higher status in poetry than in polite conversation? (Does any point made in chapter 1 or 2 have a bearing on this?)*
   C.   *Collect half a dozen puns from friends. Choose one that seems to have a "dimension" to it, as though it opened unexpected vistas of insight. Write a poem in which it functions poetically.*

   We come now to another aspect of poetry where the choice of words is crucial. Every poem has a particular *tone*—the attitude (usually implied, rather than stated) of the poet toward his subject and the reader. It may, for example, be lighthearted or solemn, intimate or formal, humorous or serious, personal or impersonal. The poems already discussed provide examples of a variety of tones, and it will be seen in each case that the selection of words is the main factor in creating and controlling the tone.

   D.   *Reread Housman's "Loveliest of Trees" (p. 13) and Shakespeare's Sonnet 73 (p. 14). Both poets convey a strong sense of the passing of time, the coming of age and death. In what ways does the* tone *of one poem differ from that of the other? Can you point out how words are chosen in order to establish the tone of each poem?*

   One tone frequently employed in poetry deserves special attention: *irony*. In using irony, the poet sets up a special kind of tension within the tone of the poem. He expresses one attitude on the literal level, while simultaneously implying a different attitude underneath. The next poem is a simple example:

AD

Wanted: Men;
Millions of men are *wanted at once* in a big new field;
New, tremendous, thrilling, great.

If you've ever been a figure in the chamber of horrors,
If you've ever escaped from a psychiatric ward,   5
If you thrill at the thought of throwing poison into wells, have
                heavenly visions of people, by the thou-
                sands, dying in flames—

You are the very man we want
We mean business and our business is *you*
Wanted: A race of brand-new men.

Apply: Middle Europe;   10
No skill needed;
No ambition required; no brains wanted and no character
                allowed;

Take a permanent job in the coming profession
Wages: *Death.*

Kenneth Fearing

This poem was written in the 1930's when it seemed likely that
Nazism would engulf all of Europe. The language is deliberately chosen
to be as flat as possible, as though the poem were an advertisement for
mundane and harmless door-to-door canvassers: "Millions of men
are *wanted at once* in a big new field ... *You are the very man we want*
... No skill needed ... *Take a permanent job in the coming profession.*"
The banality of these phrases is set in ironic contrast with further details
of the "job": "If you thrill at the thought of throwing poison into wells,
have heavenly visions of people, by the thousands, dying in flames ...
Wanted: A race of brand-new men ... no brains wanted and no character
allowed ..."

The irony in this poem has no very great finesse. It serves simply to
make the horror of Nazism more evident, by treating it as though it
were as ordinary and acceptable as the daily activities of any legitimate
occupation. The ironical tone is created by talking of ghastly things
as if they were normal.

A somewhat less obvious use of irony occurs in T. S. Eliot's "The
Boston Evening Transcript":

THE BOSTON EVENING TRANSCRIPT

The readers of the *Boston Evening Transcript*
Sway in the wind like a field of ripe corn.

    When evening quickens faintly in the street
Wakening the appetites of life in some
And to others bringing the *Boston Evening Transcript*,   5
I mount the steps and ring the bell, turning
Wearily, as one would turn to nod good-bye to Rochefou-
        cauld,
If the street were time and he at the end of the street,
And I say, "Cousin Harriet, here is the *Boston Evening
        Transcript*."

                                T. S. Eliot

    Eliot has chosen language that suggests a romantic landscape, and contrasted it with the readers of the *Boston Evening Transcript*, a now defunct newspaper celebrated for its arid sedateness. "The readers of the *Boston Evening Transcript* / Sway in the wind like a field of ripe corn," he states, and goes on to another ironical contrast—"When evening quickens faintly in the street, / Wakening the appetites of life in some / And to others bringing the *Boston Evening Transcript*." The poem reaches a mock-climax when the narrator triumphantly deposits the newspaper in the hands of Cousin Harriet. Taking the poem as a whole, the hints of vitality and natural beauty serve only to emphasize, by ironical contrast, all that is symbolized by the *Transcript* and its devotees.

    Eliot and Fearing have created what might be called *irony of statement*. The irony lies in a tension between the actual words of the poem and the implied attitude and judgment. There is also *irony of situation or event*. John Crowe Ransom's "Bells for John Whiteside's Daughter" is a particularly successful example:

BELLS FOR JOHN WHITESIDE'S DAUGHTER

There was such speed in her little body,
And such lightness in her footfall,
It is no wonder that her brown study
Astonishes us all.

Her wars were bruited in our high window.   5

We looked among orchard trees and beyond,
Where she took arms against her shadow,
Or harried unto the pond

The lazy geese, like a snow cloud
Dripping their snow on the green grass,   10
Tricking and stopping, sleepy and proud,
Who cried in goose, Alas,

For the tireless heart within the little
Lady with rod that made them rise
From their noon apple-dreams, and scuttle   15
Goose-fashion under the skies!

But now go the bells, and we are ready;
In one house we are sternly stopped
To say we are vexed at her brown study,
Lying so primly propped.   20

John Crowe Ransom

The reader surmises that the little girl has been very active—perhaps too much so for her harried family. Often they must have exclaimed, "Can't you ever be quiet five minutes?" Now she is quiet; she is in a "brown study." She is lying "so primly propped" instead of pursuing the tormented geese. The irony is that the family now has its wish, but not in the way they desired. She is quiet, but she is also dead. The pathos of the poem is powerfully intensified by the irony of this kind of fulfillment. Except for the irony, the poem could easily have slipped into a soft and sloppy pathos.

E.   *Irony of situation or event is not confined to poetry. Can you think of an example from history? From today's newspaper? From your personal experience?*

So far we have been looking at somewhat specialized poetic devices: paradox, pun, tone, various kinds of irony. We come now to a cluster of important figures of speech, all of which have one thing in common: they involve *comparisons.*

Conversation itself is full of such uses of language. If you say that "John is like a dynamo," you are not proposing that he supply you with electrical power, but merely stating in a vivid way that he is a vigorous, active person. You are using a *simile*—a comparison introduced by a word such as *like* or *as*. You can go a step further and say "John is a dynamo," and your simile has changed into a *metaphor*.

You can go yet another step and start composing a poem in which a dynamo is central:

> Dynamo
> Never sleeping
> Hidden heart of all lighted paths of night
> Dynamo
> Death and light   5
>
> Death to the touch
> In the beginning and the end
> Dynamo
> The soft hum
> Of a universe wheeling in shrunken space.   10

Your dynamo is not a simple simile or metaphor, for there is nothing explicitly compared with it. It has become a *symbol:* it points beyond itself to a meaning, or cluster of meanings. Perhaps in the fragment of poetry the dynamo stands for the forces that move the galaxies and keep the planets on their courses; perhaps it symbolizes evolution; perhaps God. Perhaps all three. The exact symbolic force of *dynamo* would depend on the whole poem, rather than on a few lines of it. In fact, if you were actually writing this poem, one of your challenges would be precisely this: to reach at least an intuitive if not analyzed concept of what *dynamo* actually stands for *in this particular poem* so that you could shape the poem accordingly.

This hypothetical example of symbolism is murkier than many actual uses of a symbol. Sometimes the symbol is a "natural" one—*i.e.*, the meaning is almost self-evident. A spider web automatically suggests a prison or trap. The following poem makes telling use of this universal symbolism:

THE WEB

> My hand by chance
> brushed and tore
> a spider's web;
>
> The spider dangled,
> aerialist hanging   5
> by a thread,

Then fled the ruin,
fit snare for nothing
now but my

Embittered thoughts   10
of a web
more intricate,

More fragile—and
the stronger for
its fragileness.   15

Its iron gossamer
withstands the blows
that would destroy.

Caught in that filmy
trap, who shall   20
contrive escape?

                    Robert Hayden

Often, when a symbol dominates a whole poem, the meaning of
the symbol (what it points to beyond itself) is *not* self-evident. The reader
may be compelled to seek the meaning by an intensive study of the poem,
and on occasion he will find himself visiting the reference room of the
library. Take William Butler Yeats' "Sailing to Byzantium" for illus-
tration:

SAILING TO BYZANTIUM

I

That is no country for old men. The young
In one another's arms, birds in the trees
—Those dying generations—at their song,
The salmon-falls, the mackerel-crowded seas,
Fish, flesh, or fowl, commend all summer long   5
Whatever is begotten, born, and dies.
Caught in that sensual music all neglect
Monuments of unageing intellect.

II

An aged man is but a paltry thing,
A tattered coat upon a stick, unless   10
Soul clap its hand and sing, and louder sing

For every tatter in its mortal dress,
Nor is there singing school but studying
Monuments of its own magnificence;
And therefore I have sailed the seas and come   15
To the holy city of Byzantium.

III

O sages standing in God's holy fire
As in the gold mosaic of a wall,
Come from the holy fire, perne in a gyre,
And be the singing-masters of my soul.   20
Consume my heart away; sick with desire
And fastened to a dying animal
It knows not what it is; and gather me
Into the artifice of eternity.

IV

Once out of nature I shall never take   25
My bodily form from any natural thing,
But such a form as Grecian goldsmiths make
Of hammered gold and gold enamelling
To keep a drowsy Emperor awake;
Or set upon a golden bough to sing   30
To lords and ladies of Byzantium
Of what is past, or passing, or to come.

W. B. Yeats

Byzantium is rich in poetic implications. On the most literal level, the word is simply an ancient name for the city once called Constantinople and now Istanbul. Depending upon its particular moment in history, Byzantium might suggest, among other things: (1) Long survival (as the second capital of the Roman Empire, it remained powerful for centuries after Rome fell.) (2) The Greek Orthodox Church and all its practices and traditions. (3) A lonely outpost of western culture. (4) Civilization threatened by barbarism. (5) Cruelty (if one can believe the annals of its internal conflicts.) (6) A particular kind of art and spirituality.

In "Sailing to Byzantium" the poet is not actually going to a city. His Byzantium is a reality of the mind and the spirit, not a dot on the map. The question is: What does this symbol point toward? Its significance may not be one clear-cut idea; it can be a cluster of ideas and emotions. A careful rereading of the poem suggests that this is the case.

The first stanza pictures a world of instinct, caught in the "sensual music" of the life cycle, oblivious to intellect and age. In the second stanza the focus shifts from youth to age, and from nature to soul. Only the soul can redeem the ravages of time and physical decline. This leads to mention of "the holy city of Byzantium."

The third stanza suggests a Byzantine mosaic, an unearthly splendor that eludes the ravages of time and creates or reveals a spiritual reality manifesting eternity. The poet renounces the world of nature ("Whatever is begotten, born, and dies") and prays that he will be taken into "the artifice of eternity."

The last stanza emphasizes a realm at once of spirit and "artifice." Freed from nature and time, the poet yearns not to be clothed with another mortal body, but to take "such a form as Grecian goldsmiths make / Of hammered gold and gold enamelling / To keep a drowsy Emperor awake." Perfect and eternal in the form of artifice, he can "sing / To lords and ladies of Byzantium / Of what is past, and passing, or to come."

Of the six possible "meanings" of Byzantium, listed earlier, numbers (1) and (6) seem the closest. But it is best to forget the list and look at the poem once again. It now appears that the fundamental contrast in the whole poem is not between youth and age but between nature and nonnature. This can be expressed in several ways: body and soul, instinct and intellect, nature and art, time and eternity. In any case, Byzantium stands as a complex symbol for whatever is set over against nature. It suggests all this with a special nuance: the art associated with medieval Byzantium was peculiarly spiritualized and "artificial." It embodied an escape from time and nature into the eternity of art and spirit.

Hayden's "web" was a self-explanatory symbol, with a clear-cut significance—trap, prison. Yeats' "Byzantium" can be grasped in its full meaning only by careful analysis of the entire poem, supplemented by some background information on the historical Byzantium. Finally understood in all its richness, the symbol Byzantium expresses an interrelated group of concepts and feelings with an economy, accuracy, and impact that would be hard to achieve in any other way.

F. *Try to find some other city to take the place of Byzantium. It must suggest eternity, artifice, splendor, the nonnatural, the other-worldly. Is what ways, if any, would your new city, now used as the symbol, change the poem?*

33

"Why doesn't the poet come right out and say it?" This is the anguished or angry question asked by readers who want a poem to convey a clear-cut "message." The answer is that the poet—if he is any good—does "say it." But he says it with as much fidelity to thought and feeling as he can express. In order to "say it" honestly, to say it the way it really is, he uses the capacities of language discussed in these last two chapters —thus he makes language do what otherwise might be beyond its capacity.

Take for example the following poem. Is there any way Blake could have said in straightforward language what the poem expresses?

I SAW A CHAPEL ALL OF GOLD

I saw a chapel all of gold
That none did dare to enter in,
And many weeping stood without,
Weeping, mourning, worshipping.

I saw a serpent rise between   5
The white pillars of the door,
And he forced and forced and forced,
Down the golden hinges tore.

And along the pavement sweet,
Set with pearls and rubies bright,   10
All his slimy length he drew,
Till upon the altar white

Vomiting his poison out
On the bread and on the wine.
So I turned into a sty,   15
And laid me down among the swine.

William Blake

G. *Conventionally, a serpent symbolizes evil or temptation. Is that true in this poem? Study the references to the serpent in relation to the chapel and the sty, and determine what you believe the symbolic meaning (or meanings) of the serpent to be.*

Who is speaking in a poem? And who is listening? The obvious answer: the poet and the reader.

Too simple an answer. Poets put on a variety of masks. Furthermore, a poem often has an "internal audience" in addition to the reader.

One of the most important things to look for in a poem is the "speaker"— is it the poet himself, or does he fade away, or even replace himself by other "voices"? And what about the audience? Does the poem perhaps imply listeners inside the poem itself?

This is easier illustrated than described. So far as the relation between the poet and the speaker is concerned, you can think of a range of possibilities, all the way from the poet as speaker to his complete replacement by one or more masks—speakers of his own invention:

Poet as speaker	Poet disappears	Poet is replaced
(Personal)	(Impersonal)	(Dramatic)

Speakers, Masks, and Audiences

4

To start with the poet as speaker, take William Wordsworth. In most of his poems he gives the impression of sharing his thoughts and feelings, as though the reader were invited to a leisurely monologue. Wordsworth seems to wear no mask, to employ no simulated voice.

Wordsworth's sister, Dorothy, kept a journal during the period they lived in the English lake country, and on April 15, 1802, she wrote of a stroll they took by Grasmere Lake:

I never saw daffodils so beautiful. They grew among the mossy stones about and above them; some rested their heads upon these stones as on a pillow for weariness; and the rest tossed and reeled and danced, and seemed as if they verily laughed with the wind, that blew upon them over the lake; they looked so gay, ever glancing, ever changing.

William Wordsworth expressed the same experience:

I WANDERED LONELY AS A CLOUD

I wandered lonely as a cloud
That floats on high o'er vales and hills,
When all at once I saw a crowd
A host of **golden** daffodils;
Beside the lake, beneath the trees,   5
Fluttering and dancing in the breeze.

Continuous as the stars that shine
And twinkle on the milky way,
They stretched in never-ending line
Along the margin of a bay: 10
Ten thousand saw I at a glance,
Tossing their heads in sprightly dance.

The waves beside them danced, but they
Outdid the sparkling waves in glee—
A poet could not but be gay   15
In such a jocund company:
I gaz'd—and gaz'd—but little thought
What wealth the shew to me had brought:

For oft when on my couch I lie
In vacant or in pensive mood,   20
They flash upon that inward eye
Which is the bliss of solitude,
And then my heart with pleasure fills,
And dances with the daffodils.

William Wordsworth

A. *William's presence and personality seems more central in his poem than Dorothy's in the journal. This is especially true of the fourth stanza. Suppose it were omitted—would the poem be significantly changed? In what way?*

Often the poet remains the speaker, but addresses himself to an implied "you," who then becomes the internal audience. The reader finds himself overhearing an implied conversation, as in:

JOHANN

You look at me with children
In your eyes,
        Blond, blue-eyed
Teutons
Charmingly veiled   5
In bronze
        Got from me.

What would Hitler say?

I am brown-er
Than a jew   10
Being one step
Beyond that Colored scene.
You are the Golden Boy,
Shiny but bloody
And with that ancient martial tune   15
Only your heart is out of step—
You love.

But even knowing love
I shrink from you. Blond
And Black; it is too charged a combination.   20
Charged with past and present wars,
Charged with frenzy
and with blood
Dare I kiss your German mouth?
Touch the perfect muscles   25
Underneath the yellow shirt
Blending coolly
With your yellow
Hair?

I shudder at the whiteness   30
Of your hands.

Blue is too cold a color
For eyes.

But white, I think, is the color
Of honest flowers,   35

And blue is the color
Of the sky.

Come closer then and hold out to me
Your white and faintly bloodied hands.
I will kiss your German mouth   40
And will touch the helpless
White skin, gone red,
Beneath the yellow shirt.
I will rock the yellow head against
My breast, brown and yielding.   45

But I tell you, love,
There is still much to fear.
We have only seen the
First of wars
First of frenzies   50
First of blood.

Someday, perhaps, we will be
Made to learn
That blond and black
Cannot love.   55

But until that rushing day
I will not reject you.
I will kiss your fearful
German mouth.
And you—   60
Look at me boldly
With surging, brown-blond teutons
In your eyes.
                              Alice Walker

    B.   *Imagine that you want to turn this poem into a full conversation. Rewrite the poem. Leave all the present lines, but write additional lines for places where you imagine Johann speaking. Now read the original poem and your new version aloud. What has happened to the poem?*

So far we have looked at poems in which the poet is unmistakably the speaker. He may, however, choose to fade out, to become almost invisible. For example:

CONCORD HYMN
SUNG AT THE COMPLETION OF THE BATTLE MONUMENT, JULY 4, 1837

By the rude bridge that arched the flood,
   Their flag to April's breeze unfurled,

Here once the embattled farmers stood,
And fired the shot heard round the world.

The foe long since in silence slept;   5
Alike the conqueror silent sleeps;
And Time the ruined bridge has swept
Down the dark stream which seaward creeps.

On this green bank, by this soft stream,
We set to-day a votive stone;   10
That memory may their dead redeem,
When, like our sires, our sons are gone.

Spirit, that made those heroes dare
To die, and leave their children free,
Bid Time and Nature gently spare   15
The shaft we raise to them and thee.

Ralph Waldo Emerson

Who is the speaker here? Not Emerson, at least not in any intimate
way. His personality seems deliberately excluded. Does anyone step on
the stage to take his place? No one that has a name. It is rather as though
the American people collectively are speaking, and the poet is simply
the one who supplies words for the collective speaker.

The poem also implies a different audience from the reader. The
actual audience was presumably the crowds gathered to see the dedication
of the battle monument that Fourth of July, 1837. The broader audience
is the American people. Thus, in terms of the poem itself, we have
America speaking to America.

*C. Suppose Wordsworth had been commissioned to write the poem
for this occasion, and had chosen the same basic subject matter. In what ways
would you expect his poem to be different from Emerson's? (If you are ambitious,
try writing the poem that Wordsworth might have composed.)*

The poet can go one step further. He not only renounces his own
personality; he puts on an individualized mask, creating a totally different
speaker. In so doing, he moves into the territory of dramatic monologue
or outright drama. The following poem, when read by itself, seems a
dramatic monologue, but is actually part of a play:

From UNDER MILK WOOD
POLLY GARTER'S SONG

I loved a man whose name was Tom
He was strong as a bear and two yards long
I loved a man whose name was Dick
He was big as a barrel and three feet thick
And I loved a man whose name was Harry   5
Six feet tall and sweet as a cherry
But the one I loved best awake or asleep
Was little Willy Wee and he's six feet deep.

O Tom Dick and Harry were three fine men
And I'll never have such loving again   10
But little Willy Wee who took me on his knee
Little Willy Wee was the man for me.

Now men from every parish round
Run after me and roll me on the ground
But whenever I love another man back   15
Johnnie from the Hill or Sailing Jack
I always think as they do what they please
Of Tom Dick and Harry who were tall as trees
And most I think when I'm by their side
Of little Willy Wee who downed and died.   20

O Tom Dick and Harry were three fine men
And I'll never have such loving again
But little Willy Wee who took me on his knee
Little Willy Weazel is the man for me.

                                                Dylan Thomas

D.   Suppose the speaker in the poem were an elderly moralistic lady of the community who is talking about Polly Garter. *Rewrite the poem (in prose if you must) from that point of view.*

E.   Can you think of any poem from an earlier chapter that would become essentially a different poem if the "speaker" were changed? Explain what changes might be made and how the effect of the poem would be transformed.

In poetic drama, the poet not merely disappears but replaces himself with many masks—the characters he creates become the speakers, and the less the audience is aware of the poet, the more he has succeeded.

Take a brief passage from Shakespeare's *Antony and Cleopatra* (from Act V, Scene ii). Antony is dead, and the Egyptian queen, in the presence of her attendants, Charmian and Iras, prepares for suicide:

> *Cleopatra:* Give me my robe, put on my crown; I have
> Immortal longings in me. Now no more
> The juice of Egypt's grape shall moist this lip.
> Yare, yare, good Iras; quick. Methinks I hear
> Antony call; I see him rouse himself   5
> To praise my noble act; I hear him mock
> The luck of Caesar, which the gods give men
> To excuse their after wrath. Husband, I come!
> Now to that name my courage prove my title!
> I am fire and air; my other elements   10
> I give to baser life. So; have you done?
> Come then, and take the last warmth of my lips.
> Farewell, kind Charmian; Iras, long farewell.
>
> *(Kisses them. Iras falls and dies.)*
>
> Have I the aspic in my lips? Dost fall?
> If thou and nature can so gently part,   15
> The stroke of death is as a lover's pinch,
> Which hurts, and is desir'd. Dost thou lie still?
> If thus thou vanishest, thou tell'st the world
> It is not worth leave-taking.
>
> *Charmian:* Dissolve, thick cloud, and rain; that I may say   20
> The gods themselves do weep!
>
> *Cleopatra:*   This proves me base.
> If she first meet the curled Antony,
> He'll make demand of her, and spend that kiss
> Which is my Heaven to have. Come, thou mortal wretch,
>
> *(To an asp, which she applies to her breast.)*
>
> With thy sharp teeth this knot intrinsicate   25
> Of life at once untie.

Where is Shakespeare? Nowhere, except as the writer who could call this Cleopatra and her attendants into being. He is replaced by the speakers he has created: the queen, Charmian, and Iras here, and Antony, Caesar, and all the other characters in the play.

The question of audience can become complex. Clearly, the unfailing audience of any play is the people sitting in a theater watching it. But on the stage there is an internal audience. Each character is audience to the other characters. In the passage given above, the attendants are an audience for Cleopatra. And yet they are not her sole audience. She speaks to the dead Antony—"Husband, I come!"—and to the living snake, "Come, thou mortal wretch." These two are also part of the internal audience.

F.   Shakespearean drama involved a clear distinction between the spectators and the actors. Many contemporary forms of drama are attempting to break down this distinction, and to involve the spectators more intimately in the action of the play. Can you imagine how this might be done, perhaps with some rewriting, in the passage just given? How would it change the impact of the scene?

Finally, one particular point is worth making. If a poem has an ironical tone, this is a clear signal that the poet is wearing some kind of mask. For example, Kenneth Fearing's "Ad" in the preceding chapter (p. 26). The real Kenneth Fearing was inclined to the Left in politics, but here he speaks with the voice of a Nazi propaganda minister, to an audience that presumably consists of paranoids who "thrill at the thought of throwing poison into wells." The poet has turned himself upside down for purposes of the poem, and has invited the sane reader to overhear an implied conversation between a lunatic leader and his insane disciples.

G.   Below are three poems. Study them and in each case ask yourself: (1) Does the poet himself seem to be the speaker? (2) Does the poet withdraw without being replaced as speaker? (3) Is the poet replaced by a generalized or abstract speaker? (4) Is the poet replaced by an individualized speaker—or perhaps by a number of them? (5) Is there an internal audience of one or more persons?

CARELESS LOVE

When I wore my apron low,
When I wore my apron low,
When I wore my apron low,
You'd pass my door and say hello.

Refrain: Love, oh love, oh careless love,   5
Love, oh love, oh careless love,
Love, oh love, oh careless love,
Love someone that don't love me.

Now my apron string won't pin,
Now my apron string won't pin,   10
Now my apron string won't pin,
You pass my door and won't come in.

    Refrain: Love, oh love, etc.

Mama, oh Mama, oh yonder he goes,
Mama, oh Mama, oh yonder he goes,   15
Mama, oh Mama, oh yonder he goes,
With brand new shoes and a suit of clothes.

    Refrain: Love, oh love, etc.

You pass my door and you pass my gate,
You pass my door and you pass my gate,   20
You pass my door and you pass my gate,
But you shan't pass my thirty-eight.

    Refrain: Love, oh love, etc.

                                        Anonymous

PROUD MAISIE

Proud Maisie is in the wood,
Walking so early;
Sweet Robin sits on the bush
Singing so rarely.

"Tell me, thou bonny bird,   5
When shall I marry me?"
"When six braw gentlemen
Kirkward shall carry ye."

"Who makes the bridal bed,
Birdie, say truly?"   10
"The gray-headed sexton
That delves the grave duly.

The glow-worm o'er grave and stone
Shall light thee steady.
The owl from the steeple sing,   15
'Welcome, proud lady.'"

                                    Sir Walter Scott

THE BISHOP ORDERS HIS TOMB AT SAINT PRAXED'S
CHURCH
ROME, 15—

Vanity, saith the preacher, vanity!
Draw round my bed; is Anselm keeping back?
Nephews—sons mine . . . ah, God, I know not! Well—
She, men would have to be your mother once,
Old Gandolf envied me, so fair she was!   5
What's done is done, and she is dead beside,
Dead long ago, and I am Bishop since,
And as she died so must we die ourselves,
And thence ye may perceive the world's a dream.
Life, how and what is it? As here I lie   10
In this state-chamber, dying by degrees,
Hours and long hours in the dead night, I ask
"Do I live, am I dead?" Peace, peace seems all.
Saint Praxed's ever was the church for peace;
And so, about this tomb of mine. I fought   15
With tooth and nail to save my niche, ye know—
Old Gandolf cozened me, despite my care;
Shrewd was that snatch from out the corner South
He graced his carrion with, God curse the same!
Yet still my niche is not so cramped but thence   20
One sees the pulpit o' the epistle-side,
And somewhat of the choir, those silent seats,
And up into the aery dome where live
The angels, and a sunbeam's sure to lurk:
And I shall fill my slab of basalt there,   25
And 'neath my tabernacle take my rest,
With those nine columns round me, two and two,
The odd one at my feet where Anselm stands:
Peach-blossom marble all, the rare, the ripe
As fresh-poured red wine of a mighty pulse.   30
—Old Gandolf with his paltry onion-stone,
Put me where I may look at him! True peach,
Rosy and flawless: how I earned the prize!
Draw close: that conflagration of my church
—What then? So much was saved if aught were missed!   35
My sons, ye would not be my death? Go dig
The white-grape vineyard where the oil-press stood,
Drop water gently till the surface sink,
And if ye find . . . ah, God I know not, I! . . .
Bedded in store of rotten fig-leaves soft,   40

And corded up in a tight olive-frail,
Some lump, ah God, of *lapis lazuli*,
Big as a Jew's head cut off at the nape,
Blue as a vein o'er the Madonna's breast . . .
Sons, all have I bequeathed you, villas, all,   45
That brave Frascati villa with its bath,
So, let the blue lump poise between my knees,
Like God the Father's globe on both his hands
Ye worship in the Jesu Church so gay,
For Gandolf shall not choose but see and burst!   50
Swift as a weaver's shuttle fleet our years:
Man goeth to the grave, and where is he?
Did I say basalt for my slab, sons? Black—
'Twas ever antique-black I meant! How else
Shall ye contrast my frieze to come beneath?   55
The bas-relief in bronze ye promised me,
Those Pans and Nymphs ye wot of, and perchance
Some tripod, thyrsus, with a vase or so,
The Saviour at his sermon on the mount,
Saint Praxed in a glory, and one Pan   60
Ready to twitch the Nymph's last garment off,
And Moses with the tables . . . but I know
Ye mark me not! What do they whisper thee,
Child of my bowels, Anselm? Ah, ye hope
To revel down my villas while I gasp   65
Bricked o'er with beggar's mouldy travertine
Which Gandolf from his tomb-top chuckles at!
Nay, boys, ye love me—all of jasper, then!
'Tis jasper ye stand pledged to, lest I grieve.
My bath must needs be left behind, alas!   70
One block, pure green as a pistachio-nut,
There's plenty jasper somewhere in the world—
And have I not Saint Praxed's ear to pray
Horses for ye, and brown Greek manuscripts,
And mistresses with great smooth marbly limbs?   75
—That's if ye carve my epitaph aright,
Choice Latin, picked phrase, Tully's every word,
No gaudy ware like Gandolf's second line—
Tully, my masters? Ulpian serves his need!
And then how I shall lie through centuries,   80
And hear the blessed mutter of the mass,
And see God made and eaten all day long,
And feel the steady candle-flame, and taste
Good strong thick stupefying incense-smoke!

For as I lie here, hours of the dead night,   85
Dying in state and by such slow degrees,
I fold my arms as if they clasped a crook,
And stretch my feet forth straight as stone can point,
And let the bedclothes, for a mortcloth, drop
Into great laps and folds of sculptor's -work: 90
And as yon tapers dwindle, and strange thoughts
Grow, with a certain humming in my ears,
About the life before I lived this life,
And this life too, popes, cardinals and priests,
Saint Praxed at his sermon on the mount,   95
Your tall pale mother with her talking eyes,
And new-found agate urns as fresh as day,
And marble's language, Latin pure, discreet,
—Aha, ELUCESCEBAT quoth our friend?
No Tully, said I, Ulpian at the best!   100
Evil and brief hath been my pilgrimage.
All *lapis*, all, sons! Else I give the Pope
My villas! Will ye ever eat my heart?
Ever your eyes were as a lizard's quick,
They glitter like your mother's for my soul,   105
Or ye would heighten my impoverished frieze,
Piece out its starved design, and fill my vase
With grapes, and add a vizor and a Term,
And to the tripod ye would tie a lynx
That in his struggle throws the thyrsus down,   110
To comfort me on my entablature
Whereon I am to lie till I must ask
"Do I live, am I dead?" There, leave me, there!
For ye have stabbed me with ingratitude
To death—ye wish it—God, ye wish it! Stone—   115
Gritstone, a-crumble! Clammy squares which sweat
As if the corpse they keep were oozing through—
And no more *lapis* to delight the world!
Well, go! I bless ye. Fewer tapers there,
But in a row: and, going, turn your backs   120
—Ay, like departing altar-ministrants,
And leave me in my church, the church for peace,
That I may watch at leisure if he leers—
Old Gandolf—at me, from his onion-stone,
As still he envied me, so fair she was!   125

Robert Browning

Words are useful, workaday things. With them you order a hamburger, spread propaganda, present a scientific theory, or yell a warning to someone in the path of a truck. Words are also rich in layers of meaning and frequently say more than one thing at a time.

Words, however, can do still more. When put together they can create interesting patterns of sound, much as colors on a canvas can produce an unlimited number of designs.

Often a special kind of pattern is created in poetry by repeating certain sounds. Children are fascinated by this possibility, as seen in their counting games—"Eenie, meenie, miney, mo"—and verses that don't *mean* much but have a liveliness of sound—"A tisket, a tasket, a green and yellow basket." The poet is not too far removed from the child at this point. He is likely to be fascinated with the effects he can get by repeating sounds, and he uses the device for a variety of poetic purposes. In fact, some kind of rhyme is found in poetic traditions as widely separated as the Chinese and the European.

Patterns of sound repetition (ordinary rhyme is the most familiar type) appeal to the poet for at least three reasons. One is simply the richness of acoustic effect that the repetitions make possible. Imagine you have written the first line of a poem:

Ah low and deep with rest of languid

Words and Sounds

5

and then you begin playing with the sounds and change it to:

> Oh low and deep with sleep of slow

what you have mainly done is to create several patterns of sound repetition—the $\bar{o}$ and $\bar{e}$—sounds. You may or may not like the almost sensuous effect of the repetitions, so close to the rhymes that children delight in. You will have to decide whether this richness of pattern is desirable on the basis of what you are trying to do in the whole poem.

A second use of sound repetitions is to give an extra emphasis to words. In the above example, as it was first written, there is nothing to call attention to the word *rest*. When the line is rewritten, *rest* is changed to *sleep* and the new word stands out more sharply simply because it rhymes with *deep*. Sound repetition is therefore one device, among many others, that the poet can use to give special prominence to certain words.

The third use of sound repetitions is the most important—it is a means of linking various lines of a poem so as to create stanzas. This is a large subject in itself, and will be discussed in chapter seven, *The Architecture of Poetry*.

Ordinary rhyme is not the only type of sound repetition that one finds in poetry. In the history of English poetry, *alliteration* preceded rhyming. Usually from two to four of the stressed syllables in each line began with the same sound. As a basic structural element, alliteration is rarely used today, though it is often employed for incidental enrichment. For example, note the constant repetition of *m* in a line from Allen Ginsberg's "Howl":

> Moloch! Moloch! Nightmare of Moloch! Moloch the
>   loveless! Mental Moloch! Moloch the heavy
>   judger of men!

Ordinary rhyme is so familiar it hardly needs illustration or discussion. The spelling of words has nothing to do with it: the actual pronunciation counts. Rhyme involves identity of sound in the stressed vowels of two or more words, and in all the sounds that follow. For example, *write, knight, indict*. In English poetry, rhymes like *redeem* and *deem* or *see* and *sea* are usually avoided, though the French cultivate such rhymes under the name of *rime riche*.

A rhyme can involve one or more syllables:

(1) Single rhyme ("masculine rhyme"): cat—rat
(2) Double rhyme ("feminine rhyme"): snappy—happy
(3) Triple rhyme: easily—breezily

Triple and longer rhymes rarely occur outside nonsense or humorous verse, such as the limerick:

> A tiger, by taste anthropophagous,
> Felt a yearning within his œsophagus;
>   He spied a fat Brahmin,
>   And growled, "Where's the harm in
> A peripatetic sarcophagus?"

Several types of near-rhymes need to be mentioned, since they are common in modern poetry. One of the most frequent is *slant rhyme*.[1] It is like ordinary rhyme in that the final consonants, if any, after the stressed vowel have to be identical. But the vowels are not the same. For example, *hill* and *still* rhyme; *hill* and *ball* are slant rhymes. Any two words ending in stressed vowels are also considered slant rhymes: *me, day, construe, ago*. For a good example of the skillful use of slant rhyme, read Emily Dickinson's "I Like to See it Lap the Miles" (p. 129).

Orthographical rhyme is a "spelling rhyme"—words that rhyme to the eyes but not to the ears. The hymnal is full of them: *God, road; heaven, even; come, home;* etc. In older poetry these were often perfect rhymes: *food, good,* and *blood* once rhymed precisely, but no longer do. In most cases, an orthographical rhyme is the same as slant rhyme.

The opposite of slant rhyme is *assonance*, in which the stressed vowels are the same but the final consonants different—such as *seem* and *Queen* in William McGonagall's "Attempted Assassination of the Queen":

> There's a divinity that hedgeth a king,
>   And so it does seem,
> And my opinion is, it has hedged
>   Our most gracious Queen.

Common in folk poetry, assonance in literary verse most often takes the form of an occasional variation of straight rhyme, though sometimes it will be used throughout an entire poem.

---

[1] The terminology for various types of near-rhyme is still unsettled. You may find different terms used in other books.

One of the most unusual sorts of near-rhyme is *consonance*. In this the consonants before and after the stressed vowels are identical, but the stressed vowels are not: *mile, mull; retain, ton; seeing, saying*. It functions as a powerful, almost blatant type of rhyme, and is used to good effect in the poem below:

WHEN IMMANUEL
I

When Immanuel came to our town,
it changed its tone.
Men passed the word to their wives
and everyone went to church in waves.
Everyone left his shop   5
without putting it in shape.
Even the Negroes were admitted,
and we listened, muted.

II

After the meeting was done
store prices came down,   10
money piled in the Community Chest
and high-school girls were chaste.
We scraped off old manners like rust.
But some of us did not rest
with being good.   15
Something had to be done for God.

III

So Mr. Woodward wrote a rule book,
Jane Hoyt whipped her naked back,
and there were five or six
who gave up sex.   20
Quite a few left home
to go abroad and hymn,
suggesting that they may have been called.
Many of them have been killed.

Knute Skinner

The most important by far of the formal sound patterns used to link words together is ordinary rhyme, but the reader—or poet—needs to be aware of the others. Perhaps a chart will make them easier to keep straight.

	Identity of consonant before stressed vowel	Identity of stressed vowel	Identity of sounds after stressed vowel
Alliteration[2]	×		
Assonance		×	
Rhyme		×	×
Rime riche	×	×	×
Slant rhyme			×
Consonance	×		×

A. Read the following poem to sense its tone. Then study the final words of the lines in the first three stanzas. List all the examples of strict rhyme and various kinds of near-rhyme. What effect does the poem achieve by modulating between rhyme and near-rhyme? In what way does this modulation contribute to the tone?

CHURCH GOING

Once I am sure there's nothing going on
I step inside, letting the door thud shut.
Another church: matting, seats, and stone,
And little books; sprawlings of flowers, cut
For Sunday, brownish now; some brass and stuff   5
Up at the holy end; the small neat organ;
And a tense, musty, unignorable silence,
Brewed God knows how long. Hatless, I take off
My cycle-clips in awkward reverence,

Move forward, run my hand around the font.   10
From where I stand, the roof looks almost new—
Cleaned, or restored? Someone would know: I don't.
Mounting the lectern, I peruse a few
Hectoring large-scale verses, and pronounce
"Here endeth" much more loudly than I'd meant.   15
The echoes snigger briefly. Back at the door
I sign the book, donate an Irish sixpence,
Reflect the place was not worth stopping for.

---

[2]Also—all stressed vowels at the beginning of words alliterate with one another.

Yet stop I did: in fact I often do,
And always end much at a loss like this,   20
Wondering what to look for; wondering, too,
When churches fall completely out of use
What we shall turn them into, if we shall keep
A few cathedrals chronically on show,
Their parchment, plate and pyx in locked cases,   25
And let the rest rent-free to rain and sheep.
Shall we avoid them as unlucky places?

Or, after dark, will dubious women come
To make their children touch a particular stone;
Pick simples for a cancer; or on some   30
Advised night see walking a dead one?
Power of some sort or other will go on
In games, in riddles, seemingly at random;
But superstition, like belief, must die,
And what remains when disbelief has gone?   35
Grass, weedy pavement, brambles, buttress, sky.

A shape less recognizable each week,
A purpose more obscure. I wonder who
Will be the last, the very last, to seek
This place for what it was; one of the crew   40
That tap and jot and know what rood-lofts were?
Some ruin-bibber, randy for antique,
Or Christmas-addict, counting on a whiff
Of gown-and-bands and organ-pipes and myrrh?
Or will he be my representative,   45

Bored, uninformed, knowing the ghostly silt
Dispersed, yet tending to this cross of ground
Through suburb scrub because it held unspilt
So long and equably what since is found
Only in separation—marriage, and birth,   50
And death, and thoughts of these—for which was built
This special shell? For, though I've no idea
What this accoutred frowsty barn is worth,
It pleases me to stand in silence here;

A serious house on serious earth it is,   55
In whose blent air all our compulsions meet,
Are recognized, and robed as destinies.
And that much never can be obsolete,
Since someone will forever be surprising
A hunger in himself to be more serious,   60

And gravitating with it to this ground,
Which, he once heard, was proper to grow wise in,
If only that so many dead lie round.

Philip Larkin

So much for ordinary rhyme and its near neighbors. There is, how-
ever, a great deal of poetry that does not employ any kind of rhyme.
Shakespeare's and Milton's blank verse was devoid of rhyme, or used
it only as an occasional ornament. Among the newer poets rhyme is a
"take it or leave it" possibility. Thus devices of sound repetition are not
an essential part of poetry.

A sensitivity to the sound of words and combinations of words
is essential. Consciously or unconsciously, the poet combines sounds
to create acoustic patterns. He can make a poem flow smoothly with
many vowels and few consonants; he can give it a resonant, sonorous
quality with certain vowels or a shriller (or gayer) quality with other
vowels. He can pick consonants that are abrupt or those that are gentle
and lingering. He can even control the speed of a line of poetry—slow
it down with long vowels, diphthongs, and complex clusters of con-
sonants, or speed it up with short vowels and quickly-pronounced
consonants.

It may be useful to classify the sounds of English—not in a strictly
scientific fashion but in terms of the impression they produce on the
hearer. First of all, most vowels can be ranged in a continuum. Those
at the beginning have a thin, bright, or shrill quality. As you go along
the list, the vowels become richer, darker, more resonant. Try pronounc-
ing each vowel aloud: ē (*eat*), ĭ (*it*), ā (*ate*), ĕ (*met*), ă (*cat*), ä (*art*), ŏ
(*hot*),³ ô (*law*), ō (*home*), ŏŏ (*good*), ōō (*food*).

There are also four other vowels with more of a muffled quality:
ŭ (*cut*), û (*hurt*), ē (*father*)⁴, ə (*sofa*)⁵.

And finally, four diphthongs—combinations of two vowels. They
slow down a line of verse: ī (*right*), oi (*boy*), ou (*out*), ū (*use*).

The above lists help to explain why Poe used as a refrain line,
"Quoth the Raven, Nevermore," instead of "Said the Raven, Never
again." He was exploiting the sonorous vowels to get a slow, resonant
effect. The alternative would have sounded "tinny."

---

³ In the speech of most Americans, this sound is replaced by ä.
⁴ The unstressed form of û.
⁵ The unstressed form of ŭ.

The most abrupt consonants are the three voiceless[6] stops: *p, t, k.*
Slightly less abrupt are their voiced equivalents: *b, d, g.*

Next comes a group of consonants that have a fricative, buzzing
or hissing quality. Most of these come in voiceless and voiced pairs:
ch (*j*), *f* (*v*), *h, s* (*z*), *sh* (*zh*),[7] *th* (*dh*).[8]

Finally, there is a group of very smooth consonants, almost with
a vowel-like quality: *l, m, n, ng, r, w, y.*

One way to become sensitive to the effects that different vowels
and consonants can produce is to make up lines of verse entirely in
nonsense words. For example:

Emifki stratisk tickilesks

Here the use of abrupt or hissing consonants (sometimes in difficult
combinations, like *fk* and *sks*) and shrill vowels produces a clattering,
rattling effect.

*B.   Make up several lines of verse in nonsense words. Try to choose
vowels and consonants in such a way that the effect will be smooth, sonorous,
rather slow and stately. Read your lines aloud and then read the line given
above. What mood is created by your lines? By the line given above?*

*C.   Below is a series of short poems or passages from poems. Read them
all, then pick out one for analysis. Do sonorous or thin vowels predominate?
What types of consonants are most frequent? Are vowels relatively frequent
or does the poem go in for heavy clusters of consonants? How would you de-
scribe the acoustic effect?*

First stanza of TO AUTUMN

Season of mists and mellow fruitfulness,
    Close bosom-friend of the maturing sun;
Conspiring with him how to load and bless
    With fruit the vines that round the thatch eaves run;
To bend with apples the mossed cottage-trees,   5
    And fill all fruit with ripeness to the core;
        To swell the gourd, and plump the hazel shells
    With a sweet kernel; to set budding more,

---

[6] A consonant is *voiced* when the vocal cords vibrate, *voiceless* when they do not.
[7] *zh*—the sound as in pleasure.
[8] *dh*—the sound as in ei*th*er (distinguished from the sound in e*th*er.)

And still more, later flowers for the bees,
Until they think warm days will never cease, 10
   For Summer has o'er-brimmed their clammy cells.

John Keats

THE WATCH

I wakened on my hot, hard bed,
Upon the pillow lay my head;
Beneath the pillow I could hear
My little watch was ticking clear.
I thought the throbbing of it went 5
Like my continual discontent,
I thought it said in every tick:
I am so sick, so sick, so sick;
O death, come quick, come quick, come quick.
Come quick, come quick, come quick, come quick. 10

Frances Cornford

From HOWL, beginning of Part II

What sphinx of cement and aluminum bashed open their
    skulls and ate up their brains and imagination?
Moloch! Solitude! Filth! Ugliness! Ashcans and unob-
    tainable dollars! Children screaming under the
    stairways! Boys sobbing in armies! Old men weep-
    ing in the parks!
Moloch! Moloch! Nightmare of Moloch! Moloch the
    loveless! Mental Moloch! Moloch the heavy judger
    of men!
Moloch the incomprehensible prison! Moloch the crossbone
    soulless jailhouse and Congress of sorrows! Moloch
    whose buildings are judgement! Moloch the vast
    stone of war! Moloch the stunned governments!
Moloch whose mind is pure machinery! Moloch whose 5
    blood is running money! Moloch whose fingers
    are ten armies! Moloch whose breast is a cannibal
    dynamo! Moloch whose ear is a smoking tomb!
Moloch whose eyes are a thousand blind windows! Moloch
    whose skyscrapers stand in the long streets like
    endless Jehovahs! Moloch whose factories dream

and croak in the fog! Moloch whose smokestacks
and antennae crown the cities!

Allen Ginsberg

From THE PRINCESS

The splendor falls on castle walls
    And snowy summits old in story;
The long light shakes across the lakes,
    And the wild cataract leaps in glory.
Blow, bugle, blow, set the wild echoes flying.   5
Blow, bugle; answer, echoes, dying, dying, dying.

O, hark, O, hear! how thin and clear,
    And thinner, clearer, farther going!
O, sweet and far from cliff and scar
    The horns of Elfland faintly blowing!   10
Blow, let us hear the purple glens replying,
Blow, bugle; answer, echoes, dying, dying, dying.

O love, they die in yon rich sky,
    They faint on hill or field or river;
Our echoes roll from soul to soul,   15
    And grow for ever and for ever.
Blow, bugle, blow, set the wild echoes flying,
And answer, echoes, answer, dying, dying, dying.

Alfred, Lord Tennyson

*Often the mood and feeling of a poem are partly created and sustained
by a careful selection of sounds. Few poets have been more conscious of this
than Dylan Thomas:*

FERN HILL

Now as I was young and easy under the apple boughs
About the lilting house and happy as the grass was green,
    The night above the dingle starry,
        Time let me hail and climb
        Golden in the heydays of his eyes,   5
And honored among wagons I was prince of the apple towns
And once below a time I lordly had the trees and leaves

Trail with daisies and barley
Down the rivers of the windfall light.

And as I was green and carefree, famous among the barns   10
About the happy yard and singing as the farm was home,
    In the sun that is young only once,
      Time let me play and be
    Golden in the mercy of his means,
And green and golden I was huntsman and herdsman, the
    calves   15
Sang to my horn, the foxes on the hills barked clear and cold,
      And the sabbath rang slowly
    In the pebbles of the holy streams.

All the sun long it was running, it was lovely, the hay-
Fields high as the house, the tunes from the chimneys, it was
    air   20
    And playing, lovely and watery
      And fire green as grass.
    And nightly under the simple stars
As I rode to sleep the owls were bearing the farm away,
All the moon long I heard, blessed among stables, the
    nightjars   25
    Flying with the ricks and horses
      Flashing into the dark

And then to awake, and the farm, like a wanderer white
With the dew, come back, the cock on his shoulder: it was all
    Shining, it was Adam and maiden,   30
      The sky gathered again
    And the sun grew round that very day.
So it must have been after the birth of the simple light
In the first, spinning place, the spellbound horses walking
    warm
    Out of the whinnying green stable   35
      On to the fields of praise.

And honored among foxes and pheasants by the gay house
Under the new-made clouds and happy as the heart was long
    In the sun born over and over,
      I ran my heedless ways,   40
    My wishes raced through the house-high hay
And nothing I cared, at my sky blue trades, that time allows
In all his tuneful turning so few and such morning songs
    Before the children green and golden
      Follow him out of grace.   45

Nothing I cared, in the lamb white days, that time would
    take me
Up to the swallow-thronged loft by the shadows of my hand,
    In the moon that is always rising,
        Nor that riding to sleep
    I should hear him fly with the high fields   50
And wake to the farm forever fled from the childless land.
Oh as I was young and easy in the mercy of his means,
        Time held me green and dying
      Though I sang in my chains like the sea.

Dylan Thomas

The whole poem is worth careful study. Take the second stanza, for example. Several phonetic characteristics stand out. There are a few words with difficult consonant clusters (like huntsman, herdsman, *and* streams) *but mostly the words abound in vowels. Note how many words end in vowels:* carefree, only, play, be, *and the like. In addition, numerous words contain "smooth" consonants at or near the end—the* n *in* green *and* barns, *the* ng *in* singing *and* rang, *the* m *in* farm *and* home, *the* l *in* hills *and* pebbles, *the* r *in a great number of words. A smooth, lingering effect is produced. This effect, of course, reinforces what the words are saying—the picture they paint of a happy, timeless, golden day in late summer or early fall.*

    D. (1) *Reread the first stanza, and list examples of the choice of sounds as we did with stanza two. Is it pretty much the same, or do you find important differences?* (2) *Stanza four seems to have a large number of "thin" vowels. What feeling or mood do they accentuate here?* (3) *Read the first stanza again, and then compare it with the rewritten version below (disregard the slight changes in meaning that the rewritten version occasionally requires):*

Now as I was young and easy under the apple *branches*
About the lilting house and *joyous* as the grass was green,
    The night above the *thicket* starry,
        Time let me *greet* and climb
    Golden in the heydays of his eyes,   5
And honored among wagons I was prince of the apple towns
And once below a time I lordly had the *limbs* and leaves
        Drift with daisies and barley
      Down the rivers of the windfall light.

Pick out two instances where the sound of the new words makes a definite difference in the effect of the poem. Explain the difference, referring back to the discussion of the English vowels and consonants. (4) Read the whole poem aloud. Is there anything else that strikes you about the sound of it?

One question often asked: Do words sound like what they mean? For the great majority, No. The exceptions are a small group of words, like *buzz, splash,* and *hiss,* that probably originated as imitations of sounds (*onomatopoeia*). For the rest, the sounds that make up a given word have no essential connection with the meaning; a word is a sign whose meaning exists by virtue of a kind of "social contract" among those who speak the language. If *love* is a word that sounds amorous and tender to an English speaker, this is because of the contexts in which he has heard the word used. An Italian would have similar reactions to *amore,* a Finn to *rakkaus.*

The poet is not much concerned with the impossible attempt to use only words that sound like their meaning. He *is* concerned with words as they are linked into phrases, lines, and longer units. Here he can think about the sound effects that are possible—smooth and flowing, rough and cacophonous, gay and tripping, solemn and stately. The poems in this chapter have illustrated some of these possibilities.

It is possible to imagine creating a new language in which each word sounds like its meaning. This parlor game at least helps the participant become somewhat more aware of all the consonants and vowels, and how they strike the ear in various combinations. For what it is worth, try the following:

E. Imagine you are creating a new language and want words to "sound like" their meaning. Create words for the following: (1) love; (2) hate; (3) the sound and feeling of walking in deep mud; (4) a crocodile; (5) an adjective meaning "beautiful" but suggesting something unwholesome or unnatural; (6) a confrontation between police and pickets; (7) a verb meaning "to run for the sheer joy of running"; (8) the hushed feeling in the air just before a storm breaks.

Little has been said so far about one of the most obvious characteristics that distinguish poetry from ordinary prose: rhythm. (The term *meter* is commonly used to designate the kind of rhythm that can be neatly analyzed and divided into feet: iambic, trochaic, etc. *Rhythm* is a broader term, embracing meter but including other and subtler ways of creating an ebb and flow or rise and fall. Since the meaning of the two terms overlaps, *rhythm* will ordinarily serve here as the general word, covering the territory of meter but going beyond it.)

Our very bodies are constantly engaged in rhythmic activities: the lungs inflate and deflate, the heart beats steadily. Walking is a rhythm, dancing a more complex one. Nor is rhythm confined to living things—any machine at work has its own characteristic pattern of movement and measure.

Much of poetry's mysterious power comes from its deliberate exploitation—sometimes obvious, sometimes camouflaged—of the omnipresent fact of rhythm.

English-speaking poets in more than a thousand years of experiment and experience have investigated four main ways of creating rhythm.[1] These are listed below in *ascending* order of importance:

(1) *Duration:* patterns based on "feet" involving a contrast between *long* and *short* syllables.

Measure

and

Motion

6

---

[1]Excluding free verse for the moment.

(2) *Syllable-counting:* patterns based on the number of syllables per line.

(3) *Stress-counting:* patterns based on the number of *stressed* syllables per line.

(4) *The "standard" system:* patterns based on "feet" involving a contrast between *stressed* and *unstressed* syllables.

The first system—based on duration—may be treated briefly, inasmuch as it has never struck deep roots in English prosody. It was characteristic of classical Greek poetry, and was somewhat artificially adopted by the Romans. Its basis can be illustrated by looking at a couple of Latin words. Take *fēmina.* The first syllable, with the long *ē* (indicated by the macron over it), is pronounced about twice as slowly as the next two syllables. In musical notation:

fē - mi - na

Usually, if two consonants came together, the syllable before them was considered long, because the consonants slowed down the rate of speech. For instance, in the word *potest*, the first syllable was counted as short, but the second was long, because of the *st*. On this fundamental basis— the contrast between long and short syllables—a system of metrical feet was created.

The difference between stress and unstress is so great in English that it obscures all other contrasts. In a word like *forest*, according to the classical rules of scansion, the first syllable should be regarded as short, the second as long because the latter is followed by the two final conso- nants, but the ear simply hears a stressed syllable followed by an un- stressed one. "Quantity" therefore is not an important basis for creating English rhythms. On the other hand, a sensitive poet is aware that some syllables take longer to pronounce than others, and he may utilize this distinction in order to speed up or slow down his lines, or to create particular effects—the short syllables lend themselves to lighter moods, the long ones to heavy or solemn moods.

The second type of rhythm—based on syllable-counting—is some- what more important in English poetry, but has never become the main system. It works best in a language where there is a rather even stress, such as Japanese and French. In that case, the number of syllables per line is very evident, and is not blurred by the distinction (as in English) between heavily stressed and unstressed syllables.

A couplet from Corneille's *Le Cid* will illustrate the French usage:

Réduit à te déplaire, ou souffrir un affront,
J'ai pensé qu'à son tour mon bras était trop prompt.

Each line has twelve syllables. The stress is so nearly even that the number of syllables is the thing that stands out. A definite system of patterning is quickly established. The reader's ear learns to expect twelve syllables per line. Any variations are achieved by secondary devices such as pauses in the line, the use of *end-stopped* as compared with *run-over* lines, etc. Rhythm, as the English ear ordinarily understands it (patterns of stress and unstress) is a subordinate device.

Now imagine you decided to write a poem in English based on the same principle, twelve syllables per line:

Through the city streets, where twilight settles like smog,
Lights grow in brightness and number. The name of night
Comes to be spoken. Deep dark and defiant spot
Of crude light deny the memory of dead day—

You have run into a problem. The reader will not be particularly aware of the fact that there are exactly twelve syllables to a line. The pattern created by the stressed and unstressed syllables is far more obvious.

Syllabically based rhythm has become better known recently, thanks to translations of Japanese *haiku*, which are three-line poems with 5, 7, and 5 syllables:

Never be a frog
Who opens his mouth so wide
He shows all inside.

Kaga no Chiyo (1703-1775)

An occasional poet has succeeded in creating effective English poetry on the syllabic basis. Marianne Moore's "Combat Cultural" is an example. (See p. 252 for the entire poem.) It begins:

One likes to see a laggard rook's high
speed at sunset to outfly the dark,
or a mount well schooled for a medal—
front legs tucked under for the barrier,
or team of leapers turned aerial.   5

Here the reader is less aware of any contrast between stressed and unstressed syllables than he is of the fact that each line seems a measured unit (of nine syllables, to be exact). Marianne Moore has approached the effect of French verse, but not many have succeeded as she has. Because of the enormous influence of French poetry over many centuries, a certain feeling for syllable count has indeed become part of the English rhythmic sense, but it usually remains secondary—a source of variations introduced into other types of rhythm, rather than a main basis for rhythm.

The third system of rhythm in English verse—and a very important one—is the native device of stress-counting. The original basis of English poetry, it was practiced before the Norman Conquest of 1066 and for several centuries thereafter. It was being revived as late as the time of Chaucer and even in modern times there are poets who have successfully experimented with it.

Usually there were four stressed syllables per line, with a varying number of unstressed syllables. A few lines from J. L. Hall's translation of *Beowulf* will illustrate this rugged but versatile rhythm:

> The men of the Weders made accordingly
> A hill on the height, high and extensive,
> Of sea-going sailors to be seen from a distance,
> And the brave one's beacon built where the fire was

If the lines are scanned, the result at first seems chaos. The number of unstressed syllables varies widely, as does their placement in relation to the stresses:

> ˘ ´ ˘ ˘ ´ ˘   ´ ˘ ´ ˘ ˘
> ˘ ´ ˘ ˘ ´   ´ ˘ ˘ ´ ˘
> ˘ ´ ˘ ˘ ´ ˘   ˘ ˘ ´ ˘ ˘ ´ ˘
> ˘ ˘ ´ ˘ ´ ˘   ´ ˘ ˘ ´ ˘

The beginning of Auden's *The Age of Anxiety* demonstrates a modern revival of the ancient meter:

> My deuce, my double, my dear image,
> Is it lively there, that land of glass
> Where song is a grimace, sound logic
> A suite of gestures? You seem amused.
> How well and witty when you wake up,
> How glad and good when you go to bed,
> Do you feel, my friend? What flavor has
> That liquor you lift with your left hand;

5

Is it cold by contrast, cool as this
To a soiled soul; does your self like mine   10
Taste of untruth? Tell me, what are you
Hiding in your heart, some angel face,
Some shadowy she who shares in my absence,
Enjoys my jokes? I'm jealous surely . . .

Sometimes, especially in folk poetry, the awareness of stressed
syllables still seems more important than any minute concern with the
traditional metrical feet of ordinary scansion. This is often seen in the
ballad, whose most common form involves four lines, the odd ones
having four heavy stresses, and the even ones three each—for example,
"The Death of Jesse James":

THE DEATH OF JESSE JAMES

It was on a Wednesday night, the moon was shining bright,
    They robbed the Glendale train.
And the people they did say, for many miles away,
    'Twas the outlaws Frank and Jesse James.

Jesse had a wife to mourn all her life,   5
    The children they were brave.
'Twas a dirty little coward shot Mister Howard,
    And laid Jesse James in his grave.

It was Robert Ford, the dirty little coward,
    I wonder how he does feel,   10
For he ate of Jesse's bread and he slept in Jesse's bed,
    Then he laid Jesse James in his grave.

It was his brother Frank that robbed the Galatin bank,
    And carried the money from the town.
It was in this very place that they had a little race,   15
    For they shot Captain Sheets to the ground.

They went to the crossing not very far from there,
    And there they did the same;
And the agent on his knees he delivered up the keys
    To the outlaws Frank and Jesse James.   20

It was on a Saturday night, Jesse was at home
    Talking to his family brave,
When the thief and the coward, little Robert Ford,
    Laid Jesse James in his grave.

How people held their breath when they heard of Jesse's death,   25

And wondered how he ever came to die.
'Twas one of the gang, dirty Robert Ford,
That shot Jesse James on the sly.

Jesse went to his rest with his hand on his breast.
The devil will be upon his knee.   30
He was born one day in the county of Clay,
And came from a solitary race.

Anonymous

Try reading the first few stanzas aloud (or better still, sing them), letting the stresses fall naturally. It is impossible to say that any of the traditional rhythms of ordinary scansion is the norm. Yet the feeling of rhythm is strong. This comes from a very definite pattern: 4 stresses—3 stresses—4 stresses—3 stresses. The number of light syllables doesn't seem to matter.

Submerged, but never completely forgotten, the Old English sense for heavily stressed syllables colors the poetry that almost any poet composes, and conditions the reader's response. This is even true of the upper reaches of poetry. Examine almost any passage of iambic pentameter in Shakespeare's plays and you will find that very frequently it modulates into an accentual rhythm, often with four stresses to a line, precisely as in Old English poetry.

It should be pointed out that not only have poets like W. H. Auden attempted with some success to revive the Old English system *in toto*, but that many other poets have adapted certain features of it. Coleridge's "Christabel" is one example. Gerard Manley Hopkins developed a type of poetry that scans on the basis of stressed syllables. In his "Spelt from Sibyl's Leaves" the rhythm is created by having seven heavily stressed syllables in each line:

> *Earn*est, *earth*less, *e*qual, at*tun*able, *vaul*ty, vo*lum*inous, stu-
>   *pend*ous
> *Eve*ning *strains* to be *time's* vast, *womb*-of-all, *home*-of-all,
>   *hearse*-of-all *night*.
> Her *fond* yellow *hornlight wound* to the *west*, her *wild* hollow
>   *hoar*light *hung* to the *height*.

Finally, the fourth—and most important—way the rhythm of English poetry can be analyzed is in terms of metrical *feet*, each of which consists usually of two or three syllables, arranged in a definite pattern of stressed and unstressed syllables. This type of rhythm was well established in English verse by the fourteenth century. Despite the continued influence of the Old English system, and experiments in newer approaches (such as free verse), it has never lost its dominance.

Historically speaking, what seems to have happened is this: after the Norman Conquest, French became the language of the upper classes. Something of the feeling for syllable-counting gradually permeated English verse. Still more important, Latin poetry (both hymns and secular verse) exerted a steady influence. Long before the Norman Conquest, poets had mostly abandoned the attempt to write qualitative Latin verse based on the relative duration of syllables. A shift had been made to a stress basis. Thus the Latin poetry of the Middle Ages retained the familiar rhythms of ancient times (iambic, trochaic, etc.) but based them (as in modern English poetry) on the patterns created by stressed and unstressed syllables. It thus provided English poets with a ready model for the evolution of a new rhythm based on metrical feet, each of which contains a fixed number of syllables arranged in a pattern of stressed and unstressed syllables.

The foregoing discussion is a simplification, indeed an oversimplification, of a highly complex subject. But the important fact is that until the eleventh century, English verse had been mostly of the *Beowulf* type in its metrical structure. By the time of Chaucer it had shifted to a basis almost identical to that of modern poetry. One can speak, without exaggeration, of the "standard" system: it has dominated for six hundred years or more.

A few experiments will show how naturally one can arrive at the most common rhythms in English poetry.

A. (1) Tap a pencil on the edge of a table six times. Tap it slowly and as evenly as possible. After each sixth tap, pause for several seconds, and then slowly tap six times again. Probably your tapping will unconsciously speed up, and you will discover you are tapping certain times harder than others. If you have unwittingly begun to create a particular pattern of taps, jot it down on a sheet of paper. Use ⌣ as a symbol for a light tap and ′ for a heavy one. (2) Now deliberately experiment with different combinations of light and heavy taps in each six-tap sequence. Jot down each new pattern as it is created, until you have recorded ten different patterns. (3) Is there one particular pattern that is somehow more appealing than the others? Practice tapping it out a number of times. Then try writing a short, unrhymed poem, using this rhythm. (Each line will have six syllables.) (4) Can your favorite rhythm be broken down into smaller groupings? For example, if your rhythm is ⌣ ⌣ ′ ⌣ ⌣ ′, it can be divided into two groups of ⌣ ⌣ ∕. (*This, incidentally, is one of the standard rhythms in English verse*—anapestic.) *If you arrive at a subgroup of two or three syllables, the chances are that it will be one of the common metrical feet. As such, it can be repeated as many times as you wish in a line of poetry. For instance, the small group* ⌣ ⌣ ∕, *when used four times in a line, is technically known as* anapestic tetrameter (*Greek for "four feet"*).

    B.   Examine the first lines of some of the poems at the back of this book. Read them aloud, tapping with your pencil to emphasize the rhythm. Can you find a poem that has the rhythm you have been working with? If so, how many feet does it have? In other words, how many times is the small rhythmic group repeated in one line?

If experiments like this are continued long enough, you will discover for yourself what the poets have learned through trial and error over the centuries—there are four rhythms that are particularly suitable for English poetry. These are:

Iambic	⌣ ∕
Trochaic	∕ ⌣
Anapestic	⌣ ⌣ ∕
Dactylic	∕ ⌣ ⌣

The great bulk of English poetry is written in one or another of these meters, or in a combination of them.[2]

The most important is the iambic. It is the rhythm of all work, suitable for nearly every type of poetry, from the simplest to the most complex. The most common line length is five feet (pentameter). The combination of the two, if no rhyme is employed, is called *blank verse.* From shortly before the time of Shakespeare it has been a favorite verse line for poetic dramas, epics, and long narrative or reflective poems, as well as for a large variety of other purposes.

The beginning of *Paradise Lost* illustrates blank verse:

⌣ ∕	⌣ ∕	⌣ ∕	⌣ ∕	⌣ ∕
Of Man's	first dis	obed	ience and	the fruit

⌣ ∕	⌣ ∕	⌣ ∕	⌣ ∕	⌣ ∕
Of that	forbid	den tree	whose mor	tal taste

---

    [2]A more extensive list of feet occasionally used in English poetry would include: *amphibrach* (⌣ ∕ ⌣), *amphimacer* (∕ ⌣ ∕), *antispast* (⌣ ∕ ∕ ⌣), and *choriamb* (∕ ⌣ ⌣ ∕).

| ⌣ ／ | ⌣ ／ | ⌣ ／ | ⌣ ／ | ⌣ ／ |
| Brought death | into | the World, | and all | our woe, |

| ⌣ ／ | ⌣ ／ | ⌣ ／ | ⌣ ／ | ⌣ ／ |
| With loss | of E | den, till | one great | er Man |

| ⌣ ／ | ⌣ ／ | ⌣ ／ | ⌣ ／ | ⌣ ／ |
| Restore | us, and | regain | the bliss | ful seat | . . .

Before going any further with a discussion of rhythm, it is important to point out that poets rarely use a perfectly regular rhythm. Take a few lines from *Macbeth.* Here there is almost constant tension, a sort of lover's quarrel, between the theoretical iambic rhythm (as given above each line) and the actual rhythm (as given below):

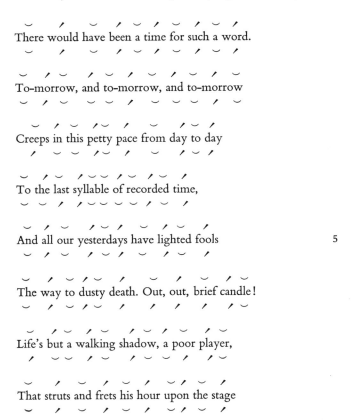

⌣ ／ ⌣ ／ ⌣ ／ ⌣ ／ ⌣ ／
There would have been a time for such a word.
⌣ ／ ⌣ ／ ⌣ ／ ⌣ ／ ⌣ ／

⌣ ／ ⌣ ／ ⌣ ／ ⌣ ／ ⌣ ／ ⌣
To-morrow, and to-morrow, and to-morrow
⌣ ／ ⌣ ⌣ ⌣ ／ ⌣ ⌣ ⌣ ／ ⌣

⌣ ／ ⌣ ／ ⌣ ／ ⌣ ／ ⌣ ／
Creeps in this petty pace from day to day
／ ⌣ ⌣ ／ ⌣ ／ ⌣ ／ ⌣ ／

⌣ ／ ⌣ ／ ⌣ ⌣ ／ ⌣ ／ ⌣ ／
To the last syllable of recorded time,
⌣ ⌣ ／ ／ ⌣ ⌣ ⌣ ⌣ ／ ⌣ ／

⌣ ／ ⌣ ／ ⌣ ／ ⌣ ／ ⌣ ／
And all our yesterdays have lighted fools   5
⌣ ／ ⌣ ／ ⌣ ／ ⌣ ／ ⌣ ／

⌣ ／ ⌣ ／ ⌣ ／ ⌣ ／ ⌣ ／
The way to dusty death. Out, out, brief candle!
⌣ ／ ⌣ ／ ⌣ ／ ／ ／ ／ ／ ⌣

⌣ ／ ⌣ ／ ⌣ ／ ⌣ ／ ⌣ ／ ⌣
Life's but a walking shadow, a poor player,
／ ⌣ ⌣ ／ ⌣ ／ ⌣ ⌣ ／ ／ ⌣

⌣ ／ ⌣ ／ ⌣ ／ ⌣ ／ ⌣ ／
That struts and frets his hour upon the stage
⌣ ／ ⌣ ／ ⌣ ／ ⌣ ／ ⌣ ／

68

˘ / ˘ / ˘ / ˘ / ˘ /
And then is heard no more. It is a tale
˘ / ˘ / / / ˘ ˘ ˘ /

˘ / ˘ / ˘ / ˘ / ˘ / ˘
Told by an idiot, full of sound and fury . . .   10
/ ˘ ˘ / ˘ / ˘ / ˘ / ˘

The shorter the poem, the more likely it is to have a relatively regular rhythm. But in general, the standard rhythms, such as the iambic, have been regarded by poets as norms but not as strait jackets. A great deal of the pleasure that poetry gives can come from the infinitely complex tug-of-war between the ostensible rhythms and the changes rung upon them by the poet.

Dramatic poetry is an extreme type. It is based, at least in part, on the rhythms of ordinary speech, especially as these are dislocated by strong feeling. Lyric poetry usually has a smoother rhythm, and properly so. One cannot expect to find in such a poet as A. E. Housman the extreme tensions between theoretical and actual rhythm that abound in Shakespeare. Housman's "I Did Not Lose My Heart" is almost perfectly regular iambic rhythm, and the regularity fits the tone of the poem:

I DID NOT LOSE MY HEART

I did not lose my heart in summer's even
    When roses to the moonrise burst apart:
When plumes were under heel and lead was flying,
    In blood and smoke and flame I lost my heart.

I lost it to a soldier and a foeman,   5
    A chap that did not kill me, but he tried;
That took the sabre straight and took it striking,
    And laughed and kissed his hand to me and died.

A. E. Housman

C. Robert Frost's supple, loose-jointed blank verse provides a good opportunity to observe the deliberate irregularities that a poet may introduce into his rhythm. Study this passage from "Birches" and underline all the places where strict iambic rhythm is abandoned. Pick out three or four of these instances and try to imagine why Frost varied the rhythm there:

From BIRCHES

Some boy too far from town to learn baseball,
Whose only play was what he found himself,
Summer or winter, and could play alone.
One by one he subdued his father's trees
By riding them down over and over again   5
Until he took the stiffness out of them,
And not one but hung limp, not one was left
For him to conquer. He learned all there was
To learn about not launching out too soon
And so not carrying the tree away   10
Clear to the ground. He always kept his poise
To the top branches, climbing carefully
With the same pains you use to fill a cup
Up to the brim, and even above the brim.

Robert Frost

The three other standard rhythms should now be briefly illustrated.
Trochaic rhythm at its most regular can be exemplified by a passage
from Longfellow's *Hiawatha:*

And the smoke rose slowly, slowly,
Through the tranquil air of morning,
From a single line of darkness,
Then a denser, bluer vapor,
Then a snow-white cloud unfolding,   5
Like the tree-tops of the forest . . .

Trochaic rhythm is simply iambic rhythm turned upside down.
It is ⁄ ‿ instead of ‿ ⁄. Often a very slight rewriting can quite easily turn
one rhythm into the other, as in this revision of the passage from
Hiawatha:

The smoke rose slowly, slowly up,
Through tranquil air of morning light,
Straight from a single line of dark,
And then a denser, bluer smoke . . . etc.

But though one rhythm may be easily replaced by the other, the effect
produced by each is quite different.

D. Read the following passage, which is basically iambic in rhythm. Then rewrite it in trochaic rhythm, making as few changes in choice of words as possible. Describe the difference in effect:

From THE DOME OF SUNDAY

With focus sharp as Flemish-painted face
In film of varnish brightly fixed
And through a polished hand-lens deeply seen,
Sunday at noon through hyaline thin air
Sees down the street,   5
And in the camera of my eye depicts
Row-houses and row-lives:
Glass after glass, door after door the same,
Face after face the same, the same,
The brutal visibility the same. . . .   10

Karl Shapiro

Inasmuch as the iambus and the trochee are simply the reverse of each other, either one is frequently substituted for the other as a passing variation. In the passage from *Macbeth* there are several instances where an iambus is replaced by a trochee.

The third standard rhythm, *anapestic* ($\smile \smile \prime$) is most common in light verse, but is occasionally used in serious poetry, especially if a fast-moving effect is desired (for entire poem, see p. 186):

From THE DESTRUCTION OF SENNACHERIB

For the Angel of Death spread his wings on the blast,
And breathed in the face of the foe as he passed;
And the eyes of the sleepers waxed deadly and chill,
And their hearts but once heaved, and for ever grew still!

George Gordon, Lord Byron

Since it differs from iambic rhythm only by having one extra unstressed syllable, an anapest is a frequent substitution for an iambus, and *vice versa*. (In the second line of the stanza above, the first foot is an iambus, not an anapest.)

The least common of the four standard rhythms is the dactylic ($\prime \smile \smile$). Longfellow's "Evangeline" is one of the few English poems of any length which consistently employ it. More often, dactylic rhythm is found as an occasional variation for other meters. Its smooth but often monotonous character can be shown by a few lines from Long-fellow's poem:

> It was the month of May. Far down the Beautiful River,
> Past the Ohio shore and past the mouth of the Wabash,
> Into the golden stream of the broad and swift Mississippi,
> Floated a cumbrous boat, that was rowed by Acadian
>   boatmen.

The four rhythms can be classified schematically by dividing them first of all into *rising* and *falling* meters. A rising meter is one in which the foot ends on a stressed syllable. A falling meter begins with a stressed syllable. In the second palce, rhythms are *double* or *triple*, depending whether the foot has two or three syllables:

	Rising	Falling
Double	Iambic ($\smile$ $/$)	Trochaic ($/$ $\smile$)
Triple	Anapestic ($\smile$ $\smile$ $/$)	Dactylic ($/$ $\smile$ $\smile$)

One other foot needs to be mentioned. It never constitutes an entire poem, but frequently serves as substitute for a different meter in a given foot. This is the *spondee*, which consists of two heavy syllables ($/$ $/$). In the passage from *Macbeth*:

> The way to dusty death. Out, out, brief candle!

"Out, out" is a spondee, replacing the normal iambus. In general, the use of spondees slows up the rhythm, imparting a heavier and more massive quality.

One might also add the *pyrrhic* ($\smile$ $\smile$), an occasional variant for other feet. The second foot in the last line quoted from Milton illustrates it:

> Restore us, and regain the blissful seat.

Neither *us* nor *and* is stressed; thus we have a pyrrhic in place of an iambic foot. The pyrrhic, being the opposite of a spondee, gives an effect of quickness and lightness.

One different type of rhythm remains to be mentioned: *free verse*. The term must be carefully distinguished from blank verse. Blank verse is unrhymed iambic pentameter. Free verse, on the contrary, is a convenient catch-all term for poetry which cannot be easily analyzed in terms of ordinary metric feet, syllabic count, duration or number of stresses. Ordinarily, though not necessarily, it is unrhymed.

The term is relatively new, but the thing itself is of long standing. It is impossible to draw any hard and fast line separating poetic prose from free verse. The Psalms of the Old Testament were written as poetry. The King James translators simply rendered them into English prose, and printed them as such. It is, however, very easy to take one of the psalms and divide it into lines according to the sense, and produce what would undoubtedly be considered free verse if written by a contemporary poet. For example, the beginning of Psalm 137:

> By the rivers of Babylon, there we sat down,
> Yea, we wept, when we remembered Zion.
> We hanged our harps upon the willows
> In the midst thereof.
> For there they that carried us away captive required of us a
>   song;   5
> And they that wasted us required of us mirth, saying
> Sing us one of the songs of Zion.
> How shall we sing the Lord's song
> In a strange land?
> If I forget thee, O Jerusalem,   10
> Let my right hand forget her cunning.

Free verse is especially associated with Walt Whitman, who did much to advocate and explore its possibilities. A good brief example is his "When I Heard the Learn'd Astronomer":

WHEN I HEARD THE LEARN'D ASTRONOMER

> When I heard the learn'd astronomer,
> When the proofs, the figures, were ranged in columns before
>   me,
> When I was shown the charts and diagrams, to add, divide,
>   and measure them,
> When I sitting heard the astronomer where he lectured with
>   much applause in the lecture room,
> How soon unaccountable I became tired and sick,   5
> Till rising and gliding out I wander'd off by myself,
> In the mystical moist night-air, and from time to time,
> Look'd up in perfect silence at the stars.

Walt Whitman

At first glance, this may look like prose which has been arbitrarily chopped into lines. But if one reads it aloud, a poetic rhythm is evident, though elusive. A few rereadings will reveal that an individual line does not tell much about the rhythm; it is the rhythm of the poem as a whole which is important. Some of the most important elements that help to create the feeling of rhythm are soon obvious:

(1) Though the poem cannot be analyzed in terms of any one metrical foot, it does tend toward a "rising rhythm" (iambic, anapestic) as opposed to a "falling rhythm" (trochaic, dactylic).
(2) The first four lines begin the same (*When . . .*).
(3) The poem breaks in two after the fourth line, and the focus of action shifts. This produces a kind of symmetry.
(4) The poem starts with a short line, goes into long lines, and ends with a short line.

It is for such features that one must look when analyzing the rhythm of free verse. Neither metrical feet nor the individual line can necessarily be regarded as the unit. One must search for breath groups, verse paragraphs, patterns formed by combinations of different length lines, special repetitions, and the like. Many contemporary poets write almost entirely in free verse, and anyone who reads widely will quickly discover how much the free verse, say, of an Allen Ginsberg differs from that of a Charles Olson.

To talk about rhythm requires technical terms, and is even facilitated by making pencil marks on paper. Fortunately, the human sense of rhythm is so inbuilt that most people can respond to it in poetry, even if they have never called an anapest by its right name. Reading poetry aloud is a surer way of appreciating its rhythm than any detailed analysis foot by foot.

Still, the analysis has a modest value in its own right, by making you more aware of the effects of rhythm. One useful thing is to take a short poem and squeeze it dry—analyze the rhythm as thoroughly as you can, trying to see not merely the reason for the basic rhythm but for the variations and irregularities.

E. *Read the following poem aloud several times to get the sense of the rhythm. Then determine whether the basic rhythm is primarily one of duration, syllable-counting, stress-count, the "standard system," or free verse. Next,*

*look for lines which seem to be based on some system other than the dominant
one. Finally, read the poem aloud again and try to describe the effect the poet
is creating by his basic and variant rhythms.*

MAN AND WIFE

Tamed by Miltown, we lie on Mother's bed;
the rising sun in war paint dyes us red;
in broad daylight her gilded bed-posts shine,
abandoned, almost Dionysian.
At last the trees are green on Marlborough Street,   5
blossoms on our magnolia ignite
the morning with their murderous five days' white.
All night I've held your hand,
as if you had
a fourth time faced the kingdom of the mad—   10
its hackneyed speech, its homicidal eye—
and dragged me home alive. . . . Oh my *Petite*,
clearest of all God's creatures, still all air and nerve:
you were in your twenties, and I,
once hand on glass   15
and heart in mouth,
outdrank the Rahvs in the heat
of Greenwich Village, fainting at your feet—
too boiled and shy
and poker-faced to make a pass,
while the shrill verve
of your invective scorched the traditional South.

Now twelve years later, you turn your back.
Sleepless, you hold   20
your pillow to your hollows like a child;
your old-fashioned tirade—
loving, rapid, merciless—
breaks like the Atlantic Ocean on my head.

Robert Lowell

The Architecture of Poetry

7

The building block in most poetry is the line. Some poems consist simply of a succession of lines, perhaps grouped into verse paragraphs of varying length. This is frequently true of blank verse and many kinds of free verse. More often, however, lines are grouped into stanzas, and stanzas become the larger units, to be grouped in turn into the complete poem. In still more complex instances, lines may be organized into one complex pattern, so that the entire poem is, in effect, one elaborate stanza.

For the enjoyment of poetry it is not necessary to have a complete knowledge of these matters; the reader may easily enough respond intuitively to the effect of poetic architecture without being able to give a technical name to the specimen before him. It does help, however, to have at least a passing familiarity with the most common stanza forms and whole poem forms and some understanding of why the poet chooses to subject himself to their complicated demands upon his skill.

In a good poem, the total form is not something arbitrarily imposed upon the poet's vision. The form should be so integral to the poem that one cannot think of "poem" and "form" separately. Rather, the form *is* the poem, as surely as the paraphrasable content, the multiple nuances of words, the mood, and everything else *are* the poem. The form should seem as inevitable and right—and as invisible—as a man's skeleton.

Starting with the simplest forms, one can simply write two lines of poetry and make them rhyme. This is a *couplet*, and when done in iambic pentameter it goes by the name of the *heroic couplet*.[1] Particularly cultivated by eighteenth-century poets, it is still used in a great variety of poems, ranging from the epigrammatic to the meditative. Its effect depends greatly on whether the lines are *end-stopped* (a natural pause at end of the line) or whether the poet practices *enjambement* (use of *run-on* lines, so that one line often flows into the next). For an example of end-stopped lines and run-on lines:

From AN ESSAY ON CRITICISM

Pride, where wit fails, steps into our defence,
And fills up all the mighty void of sense.
If once right reason drives that cloud away,
Truth breaks upon us with resistless day.
Trust not yourself; but your defects to know,   5
Make use of every friend—and every foe.

Alexander Pope

From HERO AND LEANDER

Leander strived; the waves about him wound
And pulled him to the bottom, where the ground
Was strewed with pearl, and in low coral groves
Sweet singing mermaids sported with their loves
On heaps of heavy gold, and took great pleasure   5
To spurn in careless sort the shipwreck treasure.

Christopher Marlowe

The distinction between end-stopped and run-on lines is important in any stanza form; it helps to determine whether the reader senses each line as a distinct entity, or responds to the stanza as primary, hardly noticing the separate lines.

The most common type of stanza is the *quatrain*, four lines. But there are quatrains and quatrains. None of the lines may rhyme, some

---

[1] Heroic couplets may be printed either with or without space between the couplets, depending on the poet's preference. In either case, they still constitute formal units of more than one line, and it seems convenient to apply the word "stanza" to them. This somewhat broad definition of stanza will be used throughout.

may, all may. The rhyme scheme can be, for instance, *xaxa, abab, abba, aaxa.* If the stanza is written in lines of uniform length, they may be whatever the poet chooses—in extreme cases, from one foot to seven or more. (Four or five feet is most common.) The line-length may vary systematically, either in keeping with the rhyme scheme, or running counter to it. The poet may employ various kinds of near-rhyme, either as substitutes for strict rhyme, or as occasional variations. In view of all these variables, to say that a poem is written in quatrains says very little.

One of the most versatile quatrain forms is the so-called *elegiac stanza* (iambic pentameter, rhyming *abab*) named for its use in Thomas Gray's "Elegy Written in a Country Churchyard." It lends itself to a leisurely, reflective tone:

> Perhaps in this neglected spot is laid
> Some heart once pregnant with celestial fire;
> Hands, that the rod of empire might have swayed,
> Or waked to ecstasy the living lyre.

Below is a short poem, "Golden Bough," by Elinor Wylie that uses this stanza form:

GOLDEN BOUGH

> These lovely groves of fountain-trees that shake
>   A burning spray against autumnal cool
> Descend again in molten drops to make
>   The rutted path a river and a pool.
>
> They rise in silence, fall in quietude,   5
>   Lie still as looking-glass to every sense
> Save where their lion-color in the wood
>   Roars to miraculous heat and turbulence.

Elinor Wylie

Anyone willing to play around with this poem can learn a great deal about the effect of various quatrains by rewriting it a number of times, trying (though not slavishly) to retain the general content and imagery.

A. Here are some possible ways of reshaping the stanza, while keeping it a quatrain: (1) *Change the rhyme scheme to* xaxa. (2) *Change it to* abba.

78

(*3*) *Change it to* aaba. (*4*) *Keep the rhyme scheme but work out some pattern for a contrast of long and short lines.* (*5*) *Change the iambic rhythm to one of the other rhythms.* (*6*) *Combine two of the suggestions given above.*

Another type of quatrain, but very different in its impact, is the traditional *ballad* stanza. Typically, the odd lines have four feet, the even three. The rhythm is most often a rough-hewn iambic, though frequently shading off into anapestic. The usual rhyme scheme is *xaxa*, though *abab* is found, as well as the device of internal rhyme (for some examples, see "The Death of Jesse James," p. 63). Here is a stanza from "John Henry," an American ballad:

> John Henry was a steel-driving man,
> He belonged to the steel-driving crew.
> And every time that hammer swung
> You could see that steel going through.

The overall rhythmic effect is elementary but effective. Each stanza is felt as two units of two lines each. The longer line combined with the short one produces an effect like the rise and fall of a wave. The broader rhythm might be diagrammed like this:

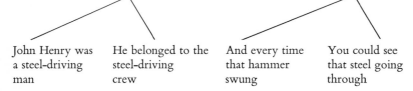

| John Henry was a steel-driving man | He belonged to the steel-driving crew | And every time that hammer swung | You could see that steel going through |

Thus lines 1 and 2 constitute a rhythmic unit, and lines 3 and 4 are a similar one. The rhyme at the end of lines 2 and 4 accentuates the division of the stanza into two smaller units.

The effect of the ballad stanza can be studied in the section of traditional poetry, at the end of Additional Poems. In general, it is suited for swift action and a stark directness of narration; it lends itself less easily to meditative introspections.

Stanza forms with more than four lines are so numerous that it is hopeless—and unnecessary for present purposes—to give a catalogue of them. New ones are being created all the time. Perhaps three forms should be mentioned, because of their great longevity. (1) *Rime royal* was first used by Chaucer and has been employed by many other poets, including Shakespeare in "The Rape of Lucrece," and in more recent times, John Masefield. The lines are iambic pentameter, the rhyme scheme *ababbcc*. (2) *Ottava rima* was imported from Italian poetry by the sixteenth century poet, Sir Thomas Wyatt, and has been used by poets as diverse as Byron and Longfellow. Written in iambic pentameter, it rhymes *abababcc*. (3) The Spenserian stanza, named for its inventor, has been employed by Burns, Keats, Byron, Tennyson, Joaquin Miller, and many others. It is written in iambic pentameter except for the last line, which is iambic hexameter. The rhyme scheme is *ababbcbcc*.

Below are examples of each:

From THE WIDOW IN THE BYE STREET

(1)   *Rime royal:*
        Sometimes she wandered out to gather sticks,
        For it was bitter cold there when it snowed.
        And she stole hay out of the farmer's ricks
        For bands to wrap her feet in while she sewed,
        And when her feet were warm and the grate glowed   5
        She hugged her little son, her heart's desire,
        With "Jimmy, ain't it snug beside the fire?"

                                                    John Masefield

From DON JUAN

(2)   *Ottava rima:*
        They look upon each other, and their eyes
            Gleam in the moonlight; and her white arm clasps
        Round Juan's head, and his around her lies
            Half buried in the tresses which it grasps;
        She sits upon his knee, and drinks his sighs,   5
            He hers, until they end in broken gasps;
        And thus they form a group that's quite antique,
        Half naked, loving, natural, and Greek.

                                                    George Gordon, Lord Byron

From THE EVE OF ST. AGNES

(3)   *Spenserian stanza:*
        Anon his heart revives: her vespers done,
        Of all its wreathèd pearls her hair she frees;
        Unclasps her warmèd jewels one by one;
        Loosens her fragrant bodice; by degrees

Her rich attire creeps rustling to her knees: 5
Half-hidden, like a mermaid in sea-weed,
Pensive awhile she dreams awake, and sees,
In fancy, fair St. Agnes in her bed,
But dares not look behind, or all the charm is fled.

John Keats

So far we have been talking as though a stanza were a bead, strung along with other similar beads, to make a poetic necklace. Often, indeed, this is the case. But there are some stanza forms in which each stanza links with the next, thus emphasizing the unbroken continuity of the poem. This can be done by having the rhymes overflow the stanza boundaries. The best known example is *terza rima*, which was used in Dante's *Divine Comedy*. The rhyme scheme is *aba, bcb, cdc, ded,* etc. Since English is poor in rhymes, this form has not been transplanted too successfully, though Shelley used it effectively in "Ode to the West Wind." (See pp. 187–188.) A shorter example by a contemporary poet is Peter Ferguson's "Parting Song." Note that the poem is brought to a definite end by a single line that rhymes with the middle line of the preceding stanza:

How easy to return, yet have no share
In what was once our own, to bring no vow,
To lose a God and leave a statue there.

So quietly they left us; even now
Chance could be miracle, an echo born 5
Of silence (as it seems) could so endow

Our voices, we would seem to praise, not mourn.
But, not to-night, or, not when I am here,
I say, though trusting always that a dawn

Must come, when they will silently draw near, 10
And when to one who waits by chance alone
An individual vision will appear.

But now, perhaps, it may be best to own
That they will never come, that all our care
Is not to summon them, but to atone: 15

Their very absence is a cause for prayer.

Another way of making stanzas flow into one another is to repeat certain words from stanza to stanza. A highly stylized form based on

this principle is the *sestina*, invented by the twelfth-century troubadour,
Arnaut Daniel. The poet selects six words for the ends of the lines, and
these six are repeated in each stanza. Usually the pattern of repetition
is symmetrically worked out, so that stanza 1: stanza 2 as stanza 2:
stanza 3. All six of the repeating words, or at least three of them, are
used in the tercet at the end.

An example by the New Zealand poet, James K. Baxter, will
make these technical matters clearer:

SESTINA
TO MY WIFE

Now as the nights lengthen and the placid season
Ages to decay, we can hear, my love
(Waiting with window flowers, a wood fire flaring across
The small safe room)—we can hear the rawhead
Elegies of winter in the wind striding perilous   5
From antarctic, ravening where our days lie tangled.

Against that ice colossus I recall now the tangled
Wild bush at Silverstream in the picnic season.
You bathed there laughing, where deep and perilous
Under clay banks the creek ran. With sharpened love   10
I saw the child swell under your dress: the fountainhead
Of our content was plain, Time's enmity no cross.

And under the bridge shaken where lorries cross
And stones are flood-scum white with briars tangled
Among them—kids had scrawled an ogre's head   15
And crooked thigh, graffiti of a season
More innocent than ours, whose adult love
Walks in the night, naked and perilous.

Like Bors we come to the Chapel Perilous
Torn arches, sunken tomb and ruined cross.   20
This is where our too-long-buried love
Festering waits renewal. Against night's terror tangled
No charm avails; here in a dry season
A generation stands, cloud thundering overhead.

For symbol take the maori coffinhead   25
Seen under glass, proclaiming perilous
The grief and horror of an older season
Purged perhaps long since by the mission cross;
Yet big with death, emerges from the tangled
Archaic night, dwarfing our human love.   30

So too in the small death of parting, love,
When the ferry stirred gigantic, turning her head
Seaward. My heart, my very breath entangled
With yours, drawn out to fragile perilous
Threads of longing stretching across   35
The darkened Strait and the autumnal season.

May Time season our too wincing love
With the humor of the Cross, sparing your fortunate head
And in a perilous age our skein of peace untangled.

James K. Baxter

B.   (1) *List the six repeated words. Why do you think the poet chose
them? Do the six have anything in common that makes them suitable? (2)
Can you find any places where some of the six words change meaning, though
spelled the same? What does this accomplish in the poem? (3) On the basis
of this poem, what would you say about the poetic possibilities—and disadvan-
tages—of the sestina?*

Another way of linking stanzas is to repeat not single words but
whole lines in the form of a *refrain.* This is common in folk ballads.
See "Stagolee," p. 328, in which the line O *dat man, bad man, Stagolee
done come* ends every stanza and seems like a kind of drum beat tying
the whole poem together.

Much more complicated uses of the same principle are found in
some of the so-called "French forms," intricate poetic inventions that
were revived in the nineteenth century and are occasionally used by
modern poets. Note the intricate pattern of repetition in the *triolet:*

ALL WOMEN BORN ARE SO PERVERSE

All women born are so perverse
No man need boast their love possessing.
If nought seem better, nothing's worse:
All women born are so perverse.

From Adam's wife, that proved a curse   5
Though God had made her for a blessing,
All women born are so perverse
No man need boast their love possessing.

Robert Bridges

Though these forms seem extremely artificial, in the hands of a good poet they can become effective vehicles for serious poetry, as in E. A. Robinson's *villanelle*, a still more complex form:

THE HOUSE ON THE HILL

They are all gone away,
   The House is shut and still,
There is nothing more to say.   5

Through broken walls and gray
   The winds blow bleak and shrill
They are all gone away.

Nor is there one to-day
   To speak them good or ill:
There is nothing more to say.

Why is it then we stray   10
   Around the sunken sill?
They are all gone away,

And our poor fancy-play
   For them is wasted skill:
There is nothing more to say.   15

There is ruin and decay
   In the House on the Hill:
They are all gone away,
There is nothing more to say.

E. A. Robinson

C. Does the use of the two repeating lines accomplish the same effect as the refrain in "Stagolee," or is there a difference?

Finally, there are whole-poem forms that do not make use of words or lines repeated throughout the entire poem. They may be illustrated by the modest *limerick* and the lofty *sonnet*.

The limerick is used almost exclusively for light, humorous, epigrammatic verse. It is a very strict form. The rhyming pattern is *aabba*, the basic rhythm is anapestic, and the *a* lines have three feet each, and the *b* lines two. Below is a sample:

There was a young lady of Malta,
Who strangled her aunt with a halter.
  She said, "I won't bury her,
  She'll do for my terrier:
She'll keep for a month if I salt her."   5

*D. Is there any reason why a limerick has to be humorous? Try writing
a serious limerick or perhaps a poem consisting of several limericks used as
stanzas. (Note that a limerick does not have to begin with "There was.")
What luck? Does this experiment throw any light on the relation between
form, content, and mood in poetry?*

The sonnet was introduced into England from Italy by Thomas
Wyatt in the early sixteenth century, and has proved a curiously versatile
and persistent whole poem form. Ordinarily the lines are iambic penta-
meter. There are two main varieties of the sonnet, different in their
impact. The older form is the *Petrarchan* (also called *Italian*) which empha-
sizes two big groupings: the *octave* (first eight lines) and *sestet* (last six
lines). The usual rhyme scheme is *abbaabba cdecde*, though variations in
the sestet are possible. The idea or theme is ordinarily stated in the octave,
and somehow resolved in the sestet:

From BERRYMAN'S SONNETS

Mutinous armed & suicidal grind
Fears on desires, a clutter humps a track,
The body of expectation hangs down slack
Untidy black; my love sweats like a rind;
Parrots are yattering up the cagy mind,   5
Jerking their circles . . . you stood, a week back,
By, I saw your foot with half my eye, I lack
You . . . the damned female's yellow head swings blind.

Cageless they'd grapple. O where, whose Martini
Grows sweeter with my torment, wrung on toward   10
The insomnia of eternity, loud graves!
Hölderlin on his tower sang like the sea
More you adored that day than your harpsichord,
Troubled and drumming, tempting and empty waves.

John Berryman

Sometimes the poet chooses to set up a contrast between the formal structure and the flow of idea and emotion. In the sonnet given below, the Petrarchan octave and sestet are retained, but the development of the thought disregards the formal distinction, thus creating a counterpoint between form and content:

WHEN I CONSIDER

When I consider how my light is spent,
Ere half my days in this dark world and wide,
And that one talent which is death to hide,
Lodged with me useless, though my soul more bent
To serve therewith my Maker, and present   5
My true account, lest He returning chide,
"Doth God exact day-labor, light denied?"
I fondly ask; but patience to prevent
That murmur soon replies, "God doth not need
Either man's work or His own gifts; who best   10
Bear His mild yoke, they serve Him best; His State
Is Kingly. Thousands at His bidding speed
And post o'er land and ocean without rest:
They also serve who only stand and wait."

John Milton

The *Shakespearean* (or *English*) sonnet is simpler to write. It consists of three elegiac stanzas, followed by a heroic couplet. Typically, the three quatrains correspond to three stages in the presentation of the thought or feeling, and the final couplet seems to "sew up" the poem, as in Shakespeare's Sonnet 138:

SONNET 138

When my love swears that she is made of truth
I do believe her, though I know she lies,
That she might think me some untutored youth,
Unlearnèd in the world's false subtleties.
Thus vainly thinking that she thinks me young,   5
Although she knows my days are past the best,
Simply I credit her false speaking tongue:
On both sides thus is simple truth suppressed.
But wherefore say I not she is unjust?
And wherefore say not I that I am old?   10
O, love's best habit is in seeming trust,
And age in love loves not to have years told.

Therefore I lie with her and she with me,
And in our faults by lies we flattered be.

William Shakespeare

The Shakespearean type of sonnet can also set up a contrast between form and the flow of thought and feeling. In the one below, note how the first quatrain slides into the second, and the third into the final couplet:

POOR WHITE

His five lean brats pollute the single room,
They breathe more sweetly since the young twins died.
In the south corner, where the tangled gloom
Obscures the bed, the slattern by his side
Lumps with the mattress. Then the tender mist   5
Tears into mottled crimson at the sun.
The man rolls over, tugs her by the wrist.
"Get up," he growls. "That snap-bean patch ain't done."

Pine-sweetened breezes sweep the barnyard smell
Away, and through the dusty, fly-specked panes   10
Gold atoms stream to tint the tired swell
Of arm and breast and thigh. A hot flush stains
His face and hands that grope in rough caress
Blot out the bean patch for a space . . . they dress.

Hodding Carter

A question at this point. Does there seem something inauthentic about the picture of a poet, in the agony or raptures of composition, taking time to count out the iambs in a line of verse or jotting down letters of the alphabet to indicate a rhyme scheme?

A poet is concerned with form not *as an end in itself*, but as a means by which he can more powerfully and accurately express what he wants to express. Often, when he begins a poem, he is not certain what form it will take. He may find himself experimenting with different possibilities, hoping to find the invisible skeleton that will surely and gracefully give shape to the visible flesh.

Imagine this hypothetical situation: You want to write a poem dealing with the evolution of various species of flora and fauna, and the way in which man differs from them. If you are lucky, the idea of the poem, the mood, and the inevitable form may come to you in one total movement of your imagination. But suppose you have the idea and the mood, but not the form. All you can do is experiment, trial and error. Perhaps you decide first to say it in free verse:

> The gifts were showered from the years;
> Each ran off with his own into his existence;
> Bees took the politics of the communal hive;
> Fish swam as fish, pears hardened into pears.
> All were successful from the start;   5
> The moment of birth, their college commencement;
> Their precocious knowledge was all they needed;
> They knew where they belonged; they were good forever.
> Till at last there came
> A childish being   10
> Whom the years could mold
> To leopard or lamb;
> Whom the lightest wind could shake;
> He looked for truth;
> He was always in error;   15
> The few friends he had, he envied;
> He chose his love.

Not bad. By some careful rewriting it might prove a successful free-verse poem. But you are not sure. You next decide to try blank verse. You keep the general idea and much of the language, but come up with this, which is pretty regular iambic pentameter:

> So from the years the gifts were showered; each
> Ran off with his at once into his life.
> Bee took the hive and communal politics.
> Fish swam as fish. Pears settled into pears.
> And were successful at the first attempt,   5
> The hour of birth their only college days.
> They were content with their precocious knowledge.
> They knew their station and were good forever.
> Till finally there came a childish being
> On whom the years could model any feature,   10
> And fake with ease a leopard or a lamb;
> Who by the lightest wind was changed and shaken,
> And looked for truth and often fell in error,
> And envied his few friends and chose his love.

This, too, has promising possibilities, with further revision to give greater variety—perhaps more variation in the rhythm and closer attention to the diction. But you decide to experiment with the effect of rhyme. So you rewrite the poem in rhymed couplets (long a favorite for poems that aim at an epigrammatic quality):

> So from the years the gifts were showered; each
> Ran off with his. Peach settled into peach.
> Bees took the politics that make a hive.
> Fish swam as fish. Each to his separate life.
> All were successful at the first endeavor.   5
> All knew their station and were good forever.
> They were content with their precocious knowledge,
> The hour of birth their only time at college.
> Then finally there came a childish creature
> On whom the years could model any feature,   10
> Who by the slightest wind was changed and shaken,
> And looked for truth and was continually mistaken.
> He faked with ease a leopard or a dove,
> And envied his few friends and chose his love.

Again, good possibilities for further revision. But rhymed couplets, though crisp and precise, have no natural stopping point. Since you happen to have fourteen lines, already in iambic pentameter, it occurs to you that another poetic work-horse, the sonnet, might be worth trying. Perhaps by a little shuffling of the lines, you can even keep the same rhymes. You experiment, and come up with this (if your name is W. H. Auden):

From IN TIME OF WAR

> So from the years the gifts were showered; each
> Ran off with his at once into his life:
> Bee took the politics that make a hive,
> Fish swam as fish, peach settled into peach.
>
> And were successful at the first endeavor;   5
> The hour of birth their only time at college,
> They were content with their precocious knowledge,
> And knew their station and were good forever.
>
> Till finally there came a childish creature
> On whom the years could model any feature,   10
> And fake with ease a leopard or a dove;
>
> Who by the lightest wind was changed and shaken,
> And looked for truth and was continually mistaken,
> And envied his few friends and chose his love.

W. H. Auden

This demonstration is of necessity an artificial one. There is no reason to believe that Auden's poem evolved in this fashion. In fact, we know it did not; it is the opening poem in a cycle of twenty-seven sonnets, entitled "In Time of War." But at least the experiment illustrates certain points about the relationship between form and content.

    E.   *Reread the four versions—free verse, blank verse, rhymed couplets, sonnet. What are the specific advantages and disadvantages of each* in this particular case?

To illustrate a real life situation, in which the poet is searching for a suitable form, read the two versions of the poem given below. The poet was born in China, came to the United States as a boy, and wrote the poem while a student at Harvard.

IN MEMORY (Version 1)

With infant's schoolbag strung across my slight
Four-year-old frame, I bowed, as was my rule,
Toward my mother, then into the light
Of day, I made my lonely way to school.

I had my choice of three separate routes—   5
Around the sides, or over the little pond,
Bordered on the edges with disordered shoots,
Which lay between home and the school beyond.

Strident and sure, I chose the middle way,
Bisecting by a sturdy wooden bridge   10
The muddy pool—on that still solemn day
Long ago in the inland Asian village.

Breaking the silence with clattering footfalls,
I marched intently forward, peering down,
Stopped momently to mark the muffled calls   15
But saw only a mound of mud-colored brown.

I proceeded on across, more quickly now,
Seized with fantastical fears of unseen
Evil, wiping the sweat off my brow—
On to the sanctuary of a school routine.   20

Coming home that day from lessons of rote
And memory—around the tiny lake,
I saw that form from further off, remote
Now, to a child's consciousness, hardly awake.

At home, my mother, sitting with a friend,   25
Questioned me casually about my day
And I, trying very hard to pretend
Said I had really nothing much to say.

Dismissing me abruptly she turned away,
And—thinking me safely out of earshot—   30
Spoke of a man found drunk and drowned, who lay
By the pond near Kweilin—but I was not.

IN MEMORY (Version 2)

With my school-bag strung diagonally
Across my four-year-old frame,
I bowed before my mother
Before leaving home for school
In Kweilin.   5

My mother nodded with Confucian severity
Acknowledging my filial piety
And turned to other things
In our pleasant little home
In Kweilin.   10

I had my choice of three different routes
Around or over the little pond
Which stood between home and school
On that day far inland
—In Kweilin.   15

Strident and sure, I chose the middle way
Bisecting the muddy pool
By a sturdy wooden bridge,
—On that still solemn morning.

As I clomped over the noisy boards   20
Leaning to one side, peering down,
I saw the still surface of the water
Disturbed by a ragged mound
—In Kweilin.

I proceeded on across the bridge   25
Unheeding—on to the schoolboy lessons
Of rote and memory
(Which I soon forgot)
—In Kweilin.

When I returned home later that day   30
I went another route out of whimsical
Preference for variety, and saw that
Form from further off with fainter consciousness
—In Kweilin.

At home, I bowed   35
Once again before my mother,
Now chatting busily with a friend.
I dared not intrude and said nothing.
She inquired about my day,
And I, not having noticed much   40
Said little.

    She resumed her talk
And spoke of a drunken man found dead
In the dusty pond
In Kweilin.   45

Eugene Eoyang

F. *As you read the two versions, try to determine what the poet hopes to accomplish—in particular, what feeling he wants of convey on the basis of his memories. Then closely examine both versions and decide which on the whole is more suitable for his purposes. Why?*

G. *Imagine you are planning to write poems on* three *of the following subjects:* (1) *a poem to be read aloud at the dedication of a new slum clearance project;* (2) *a poem about a police bust on your campus;* (3) *a poem intended as a half-serious, half-humorous birthday greeting to a friend;* (4) *a narrative poem about a space flight to Mars;* (5) *a quiet nature poem;* (6) *a poem intended as a personal attack on someone whose ideas you detest;* (7) *a long philosophic poem;* (8) *a poem describing a psychedelic experience. In each of the three cases, see whether one of the standard poetic forms would be suitable. If not, create one that would. Write the first stanza of the three poems.*

This is a grab-bag of a chapter, dealing with certain barriers that sometimes stand between a poem and a reader.

Nearly all of them arise because of the way poetry uses language—the extra compression, vividness, intensity, and intricate accuracy that the poet aims at. He has a way of leaving out the explanatory links that the prose writer usually provides.

Nonetheless, the difference between an "easy" and a "difficult" poem is not as self-evident as might seem. Sometimes a poem written in the simplest language and dealing with familiar sights is deceptive, and may pose as many challenges to the reader's analytic skill and imaginative insight as one that looks more formidable on the surface. For example:

THE PASTURE

I'm going out to clean the pasture
        spring;
I'll only stop to rake the leaves
        away
(And wait to watch the water
        clear, I may):
I shan't be gone long.—You
        come too.

I'm going out to fetch the
        little calf
That's standing by the mother.
        It's so young,
It totters when she licks it with
        her tongue.
I shan't be gone long.—You
        come too.

Robert Frost

Problems

8

5

It seems at first a simple vignette. But look at the things *not* told: (1) Who is *I*? (2) Who is *you*? (3) What kind of relation exists between them? (4) Is the speaker going to serve some useful purpose by watching the water clear, or does he have another motive? (5) Why the emphasis on *I shan't be gone long*? (6) Is there any reason why cleaning the pasture spring should be combined with fetching the little calf? (7) Why the emphasis on the cow-calf relation, and the extreme youth of the calf? (8) Is there some way in which the process of cleaning the spring, watching the water clear, and fetching the very young calf are all connected with the relation between the speaker and *you*?

The above are mostly flat-minded questions. A perceptive reader quickly supplies the missing gaps in the poem and recognizes a close human relationship (probably a man and woman, perhaps husband and wife—but this doesn't matter) in which there is a desire to share beauty (the spring) and tenderness (the young calf and its mother). There is also the hint of busy life, with little time available for esthetic contemplation or overt tenderness—"I shan't be gone long." Such a poem requires no visit to reference books, but simply a human openness on the part of the reader.

Sometimes, however, a poem presents problems that can be easily resolved by simply looking up words in the dictionary. Obviously unfamiliar words must be pinned down if the poem is to make much sense. A trickier situation arises when the reader knows one meaning of a word, but it doesn't seem to fit. For instance, in modern English the most common meaning of *charity* is a hand-out, but if you came on a phrase like "She lived in charity with all her neighbors," the statement would make no sense at all unless you looked up the baffling word and found that it used to mean, and can still mean, "love."

The problem of course is much more frequent in older poetry, where often the meanings of individual words have changed over the centuries. In such cases, the multi-volume *New English Dictionary* (commonly called the *Oxford Dictionary*) is invaluable. It traces the meaning of each English word from the earliest recorded use, and in-dicates the approximate date at which new meanings develop and old ones die out.

In the next chapter, the poem, "A Valediction: Forbidding Mourn-ing," will illustrate how changes in the meaning of words can throw the reader off the track. Meanwhile, a little experience with this aspect of poetry can be useful.

A. Look up the following words in the Oxford Dictionary and jot down their principal meanings, with an indication in each case of the earliest date of each meaning, and which meanings are now obsolete: clerk, mistress, nice, prevent, silly, sway, villain.

A more difficult problem arises—and a reference library is of less use—when the poet, delighted with the playful and plastic quality of language, begins to take liberties with it—twisting the normal grammar for his special purposes, or even creating new words. Often this is done for humorous purposes, as in Lewis Carroll's "Jabberwocky":

> 'Twas brillig, and the slithy toves
>   Did gyre and gimble in the wabe;
> All mimsy were the borogoves,
>   And the mome raths outgrabe.

This is nonsense for the sake of nonsense, but some of the newly coined words have enough resemblance to ordinary words to suggest glimmers of meaning. For instance, *slithy* looks very much like a "portmanteau word." It consists of *slimy* + *lithe*, just as the modern *smog* consists of *smoke* + *fog*. Because of its position in the sentence, *gimble* is obviously a verb, and its resemblance in sound to *gambol* suggests that it means to *frolic* or something of the sort.

More frequent and often more difficult are distortions of grammar and sentence structure. In the following poem the initial effect is a striking freshness, combined with considerable obscurity:

ANYONE LIVED IN A PRETTY HOW TOWN

anyone lived in a pretty how town
(with up so floating many bells down)
spring summer autumn winter
he sang his didn't he danced his did.

Women and men(both little and small)   5
cared for anyone not at all
they sowed their isn't they reaped their same
sun moon stars rain

children guessed(but only a few
and down they forgot as up they grew   10
autumn winter spring summer)
that noone loved him more by more

when by now and tree by leaf
she laughed his joy she cried his grief
bird by snow and stir by still   15
anyone's any was all to her

someones married their everyones
laughed their cryings and did their dance
(sleep wake hope and then)they
said their nevers they slept their dream   20

stars rain sun moon
(and only the snow can begin to explain
how children are apt to forget to remember
with up so floating many bells down)

one day anyone died i guess   25
(and noone stooped to kiss his face)
busy folk buried them side by side
little by little and was by was

all by all and deep by deep
and more by more they dream their sleep   30
noone and anyone earth by april
wish by spirit and if by yes.

Women and men(both dong and ding)
summer autumn winter spring
reaped their sowing and went their came   35
sun moon stars rain

E. E. Cummings

Notice, for instance, the two sets of four words each that create
a framework of nature: *spring summer autumn winter* and *sun moon stars
rain*. The words have no grammatical relation to anything; they are
not part of sentences, but more like exclamations. Each set is repeated
three times, with some variation in word order, as though to emphasize
the changing seasons and the fact that at one moment people are most
aware of a particular aspect of nature, and later of another.

The pattern of repetition in the list of seasons is particularly inter-
esting. On the first time around, *winter* concludes the list (line 3), and
on the third repetition the last word is *spring* (34). Does this suggest that
the poem moves from a death symbolism to a note of new life, rebirth?

The very first stanza poses problems of broken or twisted syntax.
What is a *pretty how town?* Does it suggest both "How pretty a town!"
and "The town is pretty, but how"? Then what a'   *ith up so floating*

many bells down? There is the sense of a stream, perhaps the stream of time. What are the bells? Do they imply bells that mark the passage of hours and days? Does *down* convey the idea of downstream, perhaps of the inevitable movement from youth to age and death?

The poem is striking for its use of what linguists call *functional shift*—employing one part of speech for another. In particular, verbs serve as nouns: *he sang his didn't he danced his did.* It would be extraordinarily hard to replace these verbs (*didn't, did*) with real nouns and achieve the same living impact.

The pronouns also behave unconventionally: *anyone, no one, someones* and *everyones* (these two inflected like nouns!). Is it possible that they provide a main key to the poem?

B.   Study the four pronouns and see which of them seem to refer to people in general, and which possibly to specific people. In the latter case, is any kind of double meaning involved? Do the pronouns lead you to believe that the poem is narrating a story as well as creating a mood? If so, what is the story?

Much more common than the dislocation of syntax is the obscurity that comes from *allusions.* Fortunately, this can usually be remedied by a trip to the library. Any poet is likely to draw on his background of reading: he quotes, paraphrases, makes oblique references—all frequently without the benefit of quotation marks. In earlier periods he usually shared a body of literature in common with educated readers: the Greek and Roman classics and the Bible. Thus no great problem was presented. In our more individualistic century, when people—even the most educated—vary widely in what they have read, the poet may make allusions, say, to the Buddhist scriptures and create a problem for the reader who makes a hobby of collecting the folktales of the southern Appalachians.

History itself is another rich source of allusions. Often a poet writes when events are recent and known to everyone, and the obscurity comes with the passage of time. Suppose you were reading a love poem, written a few decades ago, in which this line occurs: *The Omaha of all our hateful nights.*

Offhand, the line might suggest a rendezvous in a motel in the city of Omaha, but the poem, written at the time that the Allies invaded Fortress Europe toward the end of World War II, assumes everyone knows that Omaha Beach was the code name for the invasion site. *Omaha* therefore suggests the climax of a long struggle, the final "moment of truth" when hate and conflict enter their climactic phase.

Or to take an actual poem, the sonnet below is partially understandable without any great literary or historical background, but yields a richer meaning if the background is known:

ON THE LATE MASSACRE IN PIEDMONT

Avenge, O Lord, thy slaughtered saints, whose bones
Lie scattered on the Alpine mountains cold,
Ev'n them who kept thy truth so pure of old
When all our fathers worshipped stocks and stones.
Forget not: in thy book record their groans   5
Who were thy sheep and in their ancient fold
Slain by the bloody Piedmontese that rolled
Mother with infant down the rocks. Their moans
The vales redoubled to the hills, and they
To heaven. Their martyred blood and ashes sow   10
O'er all th' Italian fields where still doth sway
The triple tyrant: that from these may grow
A hundredfold, who having learnt thy way
Early may fly the Babylonian woe.

John Milton

The general historical background is the massacre in 1655 of the Piedmont Waldensians, a religious sect founded in the twelfth century and frequently persecuted as dissenters. "The triple tyrant" refers to the tiara worn by the Pope, and probably has the double meaning of "threefold tyrant." In the phrase, "the Babylonian woe," Milton is following the common Protestant practice of his time—identifying Babylon ("Babylon the great, the mother of harlots and abominations of the earth"— *Revelation* 17:5) with Roman Catholicism.

If historical and literary allusions are likely to be most troublesome in older poetry, the opposite is true of another complication: the particular kind of order or organization that prevails in a poem. Some poems, of course, are as systematically organized as a prose essay. The typical ballad moves in a straight chronological line, narrating events one after the other. Many sonnets, as we have seen, progress from a statement of particulars to a generalized conclusion.

The twentieth century, however, is a highly psychological period, much given to introspection and taking the unconscious mind with all due seriousness. Often a poem seems to correspond to a reverie or stream-of-consciousness. This kind of order—call it *free association*—is not devoid of logic, but is simply a different kind, based on the way thoughts and feelings ebb and flow and go off on tangents when the mind is not held in tight rein. If you close your eyes for a minute and try not to think of anything in particular, you quickly enough discover that the mind does not naturally function in syllogisms and coherent logical patterns.

Some poems, therefore, are based on free association, and reflect the apparently random workings of the unconscious. As an example of a poem that is moving toward psychological organization, without going all the way, take Robert Frost's "After Apple-Picking":

AFTER APPLE-PICKING

My long two-pointed ladder's sticking through a tree
Toward heaven still,
And there's a barrel that I didn't fill
Beside it, and there may be two or three
Apples I didn't pick upon some bough.   5
But I am done with apple-picking now.
Essence of winter sleep is on the night,
The scent of apples: I am drowsing off.
I cannot rub the strangeness from my sight
I got from looking through a pane of glass   10
I skimmed this morning from the drinking trough
And held against the world of hoary grass.
It melted, and I let it fall and break.
But I was well
Upon my way to sleep before it fell,   15
And I could tell
What form my dreaming was about to take.
Magnified apples appear and disappear,
Stem-end and blossom-end,
And every fleck of russet showing clear.   20
My instep arch not only keeps the ache,
It keeps the pressure of a ladder-round.
I feel the ladder sway as the boughs bend.
And I keep hearing from the cellar bin
The rumbling sound   25
Of load on load of apples coming in.

For I have had too much
Of apple-picking: I am overtired
Of the great harvest I myself desired.
There were ten thousand thousand fruit to touch,   30
Cherish in hand, lift down, and not let fall.
For all
That struck the earth,
No matter if not bruised, or spiked with stubble,
Went surely to the cider-apple heap   35
As of no worth.
One can see what will trouble
This sleep of mine, whatever sleep it is.
Were he not gone,
The woodchuck could say whether it's like his   40
Long sleep, as I describe its coming on,
Or just some human sleep.

Robert Frost

The speaker, about to go to bed, finds all kinds of thoughts running through his mind: apple-picking, consciousness of fatigue, longing for sleep, the memory of the film of ice and what he saw through it, confused speculations about desire and overfulfillment. The poet has, however, firmly imposed order upon these thoughts and the result is an essay-like presentation rather than a random selection in no very logical order or coherence.

C. To see that this is so, write down (in prose) the apple-picker's thoughts. Let one thought merge into another without any pretense at formal logic. Abandon any essay-like editorializing. If the poem were rewritten, using free-association as the principle, what would be the difference in effect? Would it really be the same poem or a different poem? What advantages and disadvantages, from both the poet's and the reader's viewpoints, is there in free-association poetry?

Often the recognition that a poem is based on free association provides a tool for getting inside of it. At first glance, T. S. Eliot's "Gerontion" seems uncompromisingly opaque, and so it remains if one insists that a poem must be organized like a freshman composition:

GERONTION

Thou hast nor youth nor age
But as it were an after dinner sleep
Dreaming of both.

Here I am, an old man in a dry month,
Being read to by a boy, waiting for rain.
I was neither at the hot gates
Nor fought in the warm rain
Nor knee deep in the salt marsh, heaving a cutlass,   5
Bitten by flies, fought.
My house is a decayed house,
And the Jew squats on the window sill, the owner,
Spawned in some estaminet of Antwerp,
Blistered in Brussels, patched and peeled in London.   10
The goat coughs at night in the field overhead;
Rocks, moss, stonecrop, iron, merds.
The woman keeps the kitchen, makes tea,
Sneezes at evening, poking the peevish gutter.
                        I an old man,   15
A dull head among windy spaces.

Signs are taken for wonders. "We would see a sign!"
The word within a word, unable to speak a word,
Swaddled with darkness. In the juvescence of the year
Came Christ the tiger   20

In depraved May, dogwood and chestnut, flowering judas,
To be eaten, to be divided, to be drunk
Among whispers; by Mr. Silvero
With caressing hands, at Limoges
Who walked all night in the next room;   25

By Hakagawa, bowing among the Titians;
By Madame de Tornquist, in the dark room
Shifting the candles; Fräulein von Kulp
Who turned in the hall, one hand on the door.
        Vacant shuttles   30
Weave the wind. I have no ghosts,
An old man in a draughty house
Under a windy knob.

After such knowledge, what forgiveness? Think now
History has many cunning passages, contrived corridors   35
And issues, deceives with whispering ambitions,

Guides us by vanities. Think now
She gives when our attention is distracted
And what she gives, gives with such supple confusions
That the giving famishes the craving. Gives too late   40
What's not believed in, or is still believed,
In memory only, reconsidered passion. Gives too soon
Into weak hands, what's thought can be dispensed with
Till the refusal propagates a fear. Think
Neither fear nor courage saves us. Unnatural vices   45
Are fathered by our heroism. Virtues
Are forced upon us by our impudent crimes.
These tears are shaken from the wrath-bearing tree.

The tiger springs in the new year. Us he devours. Think at last
We have not reached conclusion, when I   50
Stiffen in a rented house. Think at last
I have not made this show purposelessly
And it is not by any concitation
Of the backward devils.
I would meet you upon this honestly.   55
I that was near your heart was removed therefrom
To lose beauty in terror, terror in inquisition.
I have lost my passion: why should I need to keep it
Since what is kept must be adulterated?
I have lost my sight, smell, hearing, taste and touch: 60
How should I use them for your closer contact?

These with a thousand small deliberations
Protract the profit of their chilled delirium,
Excite the membrane, when the sense has cooled,
With pungent sauces, multiply variety   65
In a wilderness of mirrors. What will the spider do,
Suspend its operations, will the weevil
Delay? De Bailhache, Fresca, Mrs. Cammel, whirled
Beyond the circuit of the shuddering Bear
In fractured atoms. Gull against the wind, in the windy straits   70
Of Belle Isle, or running on the Horn.
White feathers in the snow, the Gulf claims,
And an old man driven by the Trades
To a sleepy corner.

                     Tenants of the house,   75
Thoughts of a dry brain in a dry season.

                                        T. S. Eliot

A first reading of the poem reveals that it does not tell a chronolog-
ical story, nor does it follow some other "logical" order of presentation.[1]
There is a quality of reverie—thoughts, memories, and fears flowing
into one another. This initial impression is confirmed by *I an old man,
/ A dull head among windy spaces* (15–16) and the final line, *Thoughts of
a dry brain in a dry season.*

But what exactly is going on in the *dull head*, the *dry brain* of Ger-
ontion? (His name is Greek for "little old man.")

The ebb and flow of his consciousness is partly indicated by the
sections of the poem. Lines 1–16 show him at the present, in his *decayed
house*, observing his own withered-up state of life, and thinking about
the heroic experiences that were never his. In lines 16–20 the Christ
theme is introduced, suggesting the most passionate intrusion of life
into human affairs, and contrasting with the actual condition of Ger-
ontion. Somehow (21–33) the intrusion of Christ—a fearsome event,
like a tiger's leap—is related to the new life of Spring, but the new life
has a sinister quality about it—*depraved May . . . , flowering judas.* The
sacrament of Holy Communion, supposed to be a sharing of the divine
life, is perverted into something *To be eaten, to be divided, to be drunk
/ Among whispers,* followed by a strange list of participants—Mr. Silvero,
Hakagawa, Madame de Tornquist, Fräulein von Kulp, all of whom are
doing uneasy things. By this time the Christ theme has been compro-
mised, so that a cluster of unhealthy associations surrounds it.

Lines 34–48 seem to be a philosophical meditation, in which Geron-
tion (as increasingly allegorical personage) speaks as much for his age
as for himself. In the next section (49–61) the tiger reappears, now a
symbol of destruction. The nature imagery that earlier surrounded the
tiger (*dogwood and chestnut, flowering judas*) is stripped away; what re-
mains is a power of life that brings nothing but death for such as Geron-
tion. The latter now returns to thoughts of his present condition, the
loss of all vitality and passion, his inability to make human contact.

In lines 62–74 there is the suggestion of frantic efforts made by
Geronition (perhaps by his whole society) to achieve a temporary,
make-believe vitality—*Excite the membrane, when the sense has cooled,
/ With pungent sauces, multiply variety / In a wilderness of mirrors* (64–66).
Then images of desolation and decay flood into his mind—spider, weevil—

---

[1]Some of the insights in this discussion are derived from Elizabeth Drew,
T. S. Eliot: The Design of His Poetry (New York: Charles Scribner's Sons, 1953).

and the meditation moves toward a vision of future dissolution—
fractured atoms, White feathers in the snow. And finally, the poem ends
on the same note with which it began:

> And an old man driven by the Trades
> To a sleepy corner.
> Tenants of the house,
> Thoughts of a dry brain in a dry season.

He is back with his memories, thoughts, fears of the future.

Thus a brief examination of the poem shows that it is based on
free association, and that one must not expect a formal conclusion;
there is nowhere an explicit "message" that could be singled out as the
meaning of the poem. If anything the poem seems to go in a circle,
leaving the reader where he began, but with a richer insight into Geron-
tion's consciousness.

All this is very far from a complete explication of the poem; it
is only the essential first step. The poem is much more opaque to under-
standing than most of those in this book. But even a first reading sug-
gests some glimmers of the theme: modern man's condition of diminished
natural and spiritual vitality, the sense of drying up, withering away
in a world drained of meaning.

To penetrate the poem further demands attention to the numerous
literary and historical allusions. A partial list is given below. See whether
they clarify the poem in any way:

*Thou hast nor youth nor age | But as it were an after dinner sleep | Dream-
ing of both.* This epigraph is from Shakespeare's *Measure for Measure*
(Act III, Scene i). Claudio, under sentence of death, is visited in prison by
the Duke in the role of a spiritual adviser. The Duke is speaking here.

Hot gates (3). The literal meaning of Thermopylae.

Signs are taken for wonders. "We would see a sign!" (17). Compare
Matthew 12:38.

The word within a word, unable to speak a word, | Swaddled with darkness
(18–19). Compare passage from a Nativity sermon preached by Bishop
Lancelot Andrewes in 1618: "Signs are taken for wonders. 'Master,
we would fain see a sign,' that is, a miracle . . . . the Word without a
word; the eternal Word not able to speak a word; a wonder sure.
And . . . swaddled, a wonder too. He that takes the sea 'and rolls it
about with the swaddling bands of darkness';—He to come thus into
clouts, Himself!"

Christ the tiger (20). Compare Blake's Poem, "The Tiger" (p. 181).

Flowering judas (21). The Judas tree, often called redbud in the United States. Traditionally, the tree on which Judas Iscariot hanged himself.

D.   *Reread the poem, and see whether there are any specific ways you can now bring your understanding of it into sharper focus.*

E.   *Do all the allusions serve clear-cut functions, or is there ambiguity about some of them—or perhaps a cluster of implications?*

F.   *One scholar*[2] *has suggested that depraved May, dogwood and chestnut, flowering judas (21) refer not only to pre-Christian paganism but also to the Renaissance, a brilliant period of human history, but one also bequeathing new divisions in the human soul. If this theory makes sense, perhaps the poem is about the twentieth century as the final stage of the Renaissance. Does this idea make sense to you on the basis of a careful reading of the poem? (Be on the look-out for passages that confirm or contradict the theory.)*

G.   *In any case, the poem seems to involve a contrast between vitality and creativity (symbolized by Christ) and a dessicated world. Read Yeats' "The Second Coming" (p. 233). Does it have the same theme? If so, show parallels. If you find the themes different, demonstrate specifically what the differences are.*

For several decades a civil war has raged among literary critics. Should a poem be studied by itself, or is it better to look at it in relation to the poet's life, the other poems he has written, the spirit of his age?

Each approach has its dangers. The first may lead to misunderstandings that could be cleared up by taking background information into account. The second may turn the study of poetry into biography, sociology, and history, and the individual poem becomes nothing more than a document, rather than a work of art.

In this brief and incomplete examination of "Gerontion," we have concentrated on the poem itself. But with some poets—and Eliot is one of them—it is possible to trace the gradual evolution of particular themes. "The Love Song of J. Alfred Prufrock" (p. 000) is in many ways an earlier, and somewhat clearer, version of "Gerontion." Its protagonist, as futile as Gerontion but funnier, lives in the same wasteland of spiritual

---

[2] Ruth Bailey, *A Dialogue on Modern Poetry* (New York: Oxford University Press, 1939).

aridity. It is interesting to read the "Love Song" and observe how it points toward "Gerontion."

H. (*1*) *Read the "Love Song" and look for the particular problems discussed in this chapter. List several types that you encounter. If you were doing a thorough study of the poem, how would you go about solving them? (2) On the basis of your initial understanding of the "Love Song," compare the themes of the two poems, indicating differences as well as similarities. (3) Do you find a difference of tone? If so, what brings it about?*

So far this book has been rather like a medical text that examines each part of the human anatomy in turn, while deferring for a later chapter any discussion of the way that arms, legs, eyes, stomach, and brain all work together in a functioning body. It is time now to put the scattered parts together and see that a poem—like a human being—is more than the arithmetical sum of its parts.

To compare a poem to a living organism is not far fetched or far out. In a really successful poem the reader is always confronted with an irreducible mystery. He can dutifully observe and analyze all the individual features: the way language is used, the patterns of sound, symbolism, poetic form, and all the rest. But when he has finished this analytic task he is in danger of having a dismembered corpse displayed in front of him, not a living poem. What he must do is make the final leap of imagination and intuition by which he senses and knows inside of himself what the poem is, what it is doing in and for him.

It is rather like the meeting of two people. If they look each other up in reference works and learn about childhood background, achievements, and special interests, it provides an initial basis of acquaintance. But only by being together for a sufficient length of time does real knowledge come— the almost wordless communion of the relation that Martin Buber calls "I and Thou."

In poetry, a careful study of all

Poems

9

the separate features that go to make up a poem does not guarantee this final leap of insight. But it does mean that if and when the leap occurs, the insight will be deeper and richer than if the reader had by-passed careful consideration of details.

When you come on a poem that somehow appeals to you, a three stage process is likely to ensue. Stage one is the first spontaneous reaction, one of surprised delight. You like the sound of it, the feeling the poem somehow evokes, the thing the poem seems to be saying. Stage two is when you begin to suspect that the poem is richer than a first reading suggested. You now read it more slowly, and become aware of all the devices used by the poet to make the poem "work." This can become so fascinating an activity that before you know it, your original total response to the poem fades out, and it begins to seem a complex mecha-nism rather than a living organism. If you stop at this point, you may have turned the poem into a kind of fossil—a dead thing but showing the shape of the life it once had.

Stage three is when you put aside the detailed analysis and again look at the *whole poem*. The delight returns, the sense of the living *Thou* with which you have an unspoken communion. But this is not a simple return to a paradise of unanalyzed sensation. Rather, it is a recovery of the original response, but now enriched by all you have learned about the poem during stage two. If all has gone well, the delight is greater than at the beginning, because it is better informed.

This chapter will focus on three very different poems. In each case, all three stages will be involved, though numbers one and three will be mostly up to you. There is little a book can do to evoke a spontaneous response when you first read a poem, and almost equally little to inspire the synthesizing leap of insight after you have gone through the middle stage of analysis. Most of the discussions and experiments, therefore, are confined to stage two, the analytical.

Certainly it takes no more than a quick reading to sense that each poem is a totally different experience. Robinson's quiet understatement, the almost prosaic quality of his language, is in sharp contrast to the tight stanzas of Donne's poem, and the latter's movement of thought, so organized as to function like a series of syllogisms. And Stevens' poem at first glance seems as much the score for a musical performance as a poem.

After reading each poem and experiencing it in an unanalyzed way, you can next think about it in relation to the different aspects of poetry which earlier chapters have dealt with. The questions are included for whatever help they can give; it is better for you to be on your own as much as possible, simply asking yourself, "How does this poem work? What is it doing?" And you will be entirely on your own at stage three, when you use your imagination and insight to recapture the poem as a *living whole*.

The first poem, E. A. Robinson's "Mr. Flood's Party," is the least obviously "poetic" of the three. It has about it something of the direct speech and understated conversational tone traditionally attributed to New Englanders. It is not a poem that hits the reader in the face; rather, one that grows on him slowly as he becomes aware of the nuances and implications:

MR. FLOOD'S PARTY

Old Eben Flood, climbing alone one night
Over the hill between the town below
And the forsaken upland hermitage
That held as much as he should ever know
On earth again of home, paused warily. 5
The road was his with not a native near;
And Eben, having leisure, said aloud,
For no man else in Tilbury Town to hear:

"Well, Mr. Flood, we have the harvest moon
Again, and we may not have many more; 10
The bird is on the wing, the poet says,
And you and I have said it here before.
Drink to the bird." He raised up to the light
The jug that he had gone so far to fill,
And answered huskily: "Well, Mr. Flood, 15
Since you propose it, I believe I will."

Alone, as if enduring to the end
A valiant armor of scarred hopes outworn,
He stood there in the middle of the road
Like Roland's ghost winding a silent horn. 20
Below him, in the town among the trees,
Where friends of other days had honored him,
A phantom salutation of the dead
Rang thinly till old Eben's eyes were dim.

Then, as a mother lays her sleeping child 25
Down tenderly, fearing it may awake,
He set the jug down slowly at his feet
With trembling care, knowing that most things break;

And only when assured that on firm earth
It stood, as the uncertain lives of men   30
Assuredly did not, he paced away,
And with his hand extended paused again:

"Well, Mr. Flood, we have not met like this
In a long time; and many a change has come
To both of us, I fear, since last it was   35
We had a drop together. Welcome home!"
Convivially returning with himself,
Again he raised the jug up to the light;
And with an acquiescent quaver said:
"Well, Mr. Flood, if you insist, I might.   40

"Only a very little, Mr. Flood—
For auld lang syne. No more, sir; that will do."
So, for the time, apparently it did,
And Eben evidently thought so too;
For soon amid the silver loneliness   45
Of night he lifted up his voice and sang,
Secure, with only two moons listening,
Until the whole harmonious landscape rang—

"For auld lang syne." The weary throat gave out,
The last word wavered, and the song was done.   50
He raised again the jug regretfully
And shook his head, and was again alone.
There was not much that was ahead of him,
And there was nothing in the town below—
Where strangers would have shut the many doors   55
That many friends had opened long ago.

E. A. Robinson

Each stanza has eight lines, rhyming *xaxaxbxb*. The rhyme consti-
tutes a regular, pleasant, but not blatant pattern. The rhyme is pure
except for two cases of orthographical rhyme. The same plain regu-
larity characterizes the rhythm, which is iambic pentameter with very
few variations.

"Mr. Flood's Party" is obviously about an old man, alone in the
world. The *forsaken upland hermitage* contrasts with the *town below*.
The loneliness is accentuated in other ways: lines like *The road was his
with not a native near*, and *He stood there in the middle of the road | Like
Roland's ghost winding a silent horn*. Most of all it is emphasized by Eben's
drinking habits—there is a strong, implied contrast (brought out by

his conversation with himself) between the usual sociability of drinking and Mr. Flood's one-man "party."

The reader gradually becomes aware of *the town below* in relation to Eben Flood. A deliberate veil of vagueness blurs over the exact connection between Eben and the townspeople. We get the impression that he can drink most happily not in town but on the lonely road *with not a native near.* There are hints that this was not always so. Perhaps he lived in town at one time, though this is not stated. At any rate, his upland hermitage now holds *as much as he should ever know | On earth again of home,* and after he has drained the jug dry, *There was not much that was ahead of him, | And there was nothing in the town below—| Where strangers would have shut the many doors | That many friends had opened long ago.* A studied ambiguity marks the word, *strangers.* It could be taken literally. Perhaps his friends are all dead, and he doesn't know the people now living in town. Or perhaps—for unspecified reasons—his friends have turned against him and are now "strangers" to him. The reader finds himself speculating. Has Eben quarreled with all his friends? Has he suffered some kind of disgrace? Drink, perhaps? We are not told. The obscurity of his relation with the *town below* focuses attention more sharply on the essential fact—he is a lonely old man, driven to the ultimate humiliation of holding a party at which he is both host and guest.

At this point, it might seem that the poem is slipping into outright bathos. But the poet expertly controls the mood and tone. Though his attitude is basically one of compassion for Eben, a quiet undercurrent of humor and irony prevents the poem from sliding into sentimentality. For one thing, Eben himself has a tough-minded sense of humor that repels too cheap a sympathy. He can quote verse, he parodies the manners of good society (*"Well, Mr. Flood, | Since you propose it, I believe I will."*), and he can say to himself with conscious irony, *"Welcome home!"* The poem is sometimes mock-heroic, as in the allusion to Roland. And there is a simile that marvelously combines sympathy and a wry sense of incongruity: *Then, as a mother lays her sleeping child | Down tenderly, fearing it may awake, | He set the jug down slowly at his feet | With trembling care, knowing that most things break; . . .* The ironic tone reaches a climax in: *For soon amid the silver loneliness | Of night he lifted up his voice and sang. | Secure, with only two moons listening, | Until the whole harmonious landscape rang—| "For auld lang syne."* . . . The understatement *only two moons listening* epitomizes the tone of the whole poem. Mr. Flood is to be pitied, but he is also funny.

The organization of the poem presents no problems. It is night;

Eben is walking home from the town. When he is far enough away, he pauses to have a drink; when the poem ends, the jug is empty. Presumably, though this is not stated, he continues on to his solitary home.

Anyone accustomed to poetry in the Eliot-Pound tradition may at first find "Mr. Flood's Party" too direct, more like a prose essay than a richly-textured poem. But the complex tone of the poem has already been made apparent, and some of its other intricacies come out on a further examination:

A.   *Underline all the words actually spoken by Eben Flood. Is there any kind of progression in what he says?*

B.   *Underline all the phrases that indicate anything he does in regard to the jug. In what ways does the jug become a symbol? Does the jug provide a key to the deeper meaning of the poem?*

C.   *Does Eben Flood, the man, serve any symbolic function? Is there any indication in the poem itself that this is more than a poem about a lonely old man?*

D.   *Look up the reference to Roland's horn (near the end of the French epic,* The Song of Roland). *Does the context there throw any light on "Mr. Flood's Party"? Why does the poem refer to Roland's ghost?*

E.   *Make a list of instances of verbal irony. What purpose does each serve?*

F.   *In line 47, what would be the difference in effect if* two moons *were changed to* one moon? *to* three moons?

G.   *The last stanza is written in a particularly flat, prosaic style. Is this a weak ending, or does it serve some purpose?*

The next poem is much more compressed, and on first reading poses formidable difficulties of several kinds:

A VALEDICTION: FORBIDDING MOURNING

As virtuous men pass mildly away
   And whisper to their souls to go,
Whilst some of their sad friends do say,
   "The breath goes now," and some say, "No":

So let us melt, and make no noise,   5
   No tear-floods, nor sigh-tempests move;
'Twere profanation of our joys
   To tell the laity our love.

Moving of th' earth brings harms and fears,
    Men reckon what it did and meant,   10
But trepidation of the spheres,
    Though greater far, is innocent.

Dull sublunary lovers' love
    (Whose soul is sense) cannot admit
Absence, because it doth remove   15
    Those things which elemented it.

But we by a love, so much refined,
    That our selves know not what it is,
Inter-assured of the mind,
    Care less, eyes, lips, and hands to miss.   20

Our two souls, therefore, which are one,
    Though I must go, endure not yet
A breach, but an expansion,
    Like gold to airy thinness beat.

If they be two, they are two so   25
    As stiff twin compasses are two;
Thy soul, the fixed foot, makes no show
    To move, but doth if the other do.

And though it in the center sit,
    Yet when the other far doth roam,   30
It leans and harkens after it,
    And grows erect, as that comes home.

Such wilt thou be to me, who must,
    Like th' other foot, obliquely run;
Thy firmness draws my circle just,   35
    And makes me end where I begun.

John Donne

    The initial problem in this poem is the language. Donne was a younger contemporary of Shakespeare's. The meaning of words has in many cases altered over the years. Certain words make little sense if given their modern value. For instance, *trepidation* (line 11) now means "tremulous alarm or agitation." But it has an additional meaning in the Ptolemaic astronomy which Donne uses for poetic purposes: it refers to the motion of the concentric hollow spheres supposed to surround the earth. These were thought to move silently and carry the planets and stars with them in their courses. Thus the poet is contrasting the quiet nature of far-reaching astronomical events, as compared to the chaos and panic associated with small-scale things like an earthquake.

Look up in the Oxford Dictionary any puzzling words, and make a list of the most likely meanings. Among the words that need attention are: *valediction, profanation, laity, trepidation, spheres, innocent, sense, elemented, refined, just.* Be sure to jot down the earliest and latest dates given for each meaning of a word. This will help you judge whether the word might have been used in the poem with a particular meaning.

Glance through your list and think about each word in the context of the total poem. Underline the meaning that seems most appropriate. (In some cases, there may be two or three possible meanings. Underline all of them in that case.) As you continue with your study of the poem, you will perhaps find that Donne is deliberately using some words in double or triple senses. For example, *refined* might mean "free of coarseness" or it might also refer to the process by which metals are purified.

After this preliminary work on difficult words, read the poem again and determine whether it has any emotional or intellectual structure. Sometimes the very form of a poem will provide clues. This one is written in very precise quatrains, each of which (with the exception of the first) constitutes a complete sentence. The form thus emphasizes the separation between stanzas. (Number them so you can refer to them easily.)

The first two stanzas constitute one syntactic unit, and you might tentatively decide that the general theme of the poem is stated here, with the rest of the poem as a development of the theme. But what is the theme? The title suggests a leave-taking. The first stanza confirms this by its description of a deathbed scene. The second stanza carries on the tone of valedictory serenity but has a change of setting. It is no longer a death-bed, but perhaps the marriage bed. The word *So* at the beginning of stanza 2 implies that the two beds have something in common. The similarity becomes clearer as the poem progresses. But what about the word *laity* in the second stanza? It stands out oddly. It suggests those who do not belong to a priesthood. Does this mean that the poet and the woman he is addressing constitute a kind of priesthood? If so, how does their love differ from that of the "laity."

Stanza 3 develops a contrast between crude occurrences on earth (such as an earthquake) which spread damage and fear, and those events in the heavens that involve much greater movements but are harmless. Is it possible that there is an analogy here with the two kinds of lovers? Do the earthquakes correspond to the storms and upheavals of ordinary lovers (the "laity") and the vast but silent motions of the heavenly bodies to the experiences of a "priesthood" or circle of insiders?

Stanza 4 seems to confirm this conjecture. *Sublunary* literally means "under the moon," but is easily extended to mean commonplace or "earthly." This meaning is reinforced by *dull* and the parenthetical phrase *Whose soul is sense*. The laity are the dull sublunary lovers, and their love is a physical, sensual thing (unlike the love of the "priesthood"). Therefore—the poem continues with rigorous logic—they cannot endure separation, inasmuch as it deprives them of the one thing that gives their love any reality. This stanza also reintroduces the theme of parting, which was implied in the title and stated in the first stanza. The poem, then, is about a forthcoming separation. The speaker is discussing the effect that separation has on two types of lovers: those whose love is only physical, and those who have a spiritual basis to their love.

The nature of the laity's love has been plainly stated in stanza 4. The poet is now ready, in stanza 5, to contrast it sharply with the other kind of love—a love spiritualized to the point where physical contact is less essential. "Our kind" of love, he is saying, can endure separation and not be destroyed.

The spiritual nature of this love is further emphasized in stanza 6. The two souls are so complete a unity that when they are separated by absence, they will not break in two, but will expand to fill all the intervening distance. The simile here is a striking one—gold can be beaten until it becomes very thin gold leaf, and a small quantity can thus cover an enormous area. Gold also suggests other things: purity, splendor, great riches. A golden radiance, so to speak, is imparted to the relationship between the two.

Stanza 7 begins another figure of speech, which continues to the end of the poem. It reexpresses the idea of stanza 6, but this time with an image taken from geometry. In a sense, the poet grants, the two souls are really two (he had previously spoken of them as one). But after making the concession, he introduces a basic simile which emphasizes that each soul is accurately responsive to the other. The idea of oneness is paradoxically reasserted: the oneness of their two souls is that which comes of a reciprocating relationship.

The rigorously logical structure of the poem is developed not in abstract language but vivid imagery. The initial assumption—that the poem is about the contrast between spiritualized lovers who constitute a kind of priesthood, and the "laity" who have nothing but physical passion—is borne out. The unity of the lovers, however, is not a simple merging of two souls, but a state of being in which each soul is exquisitely attuned and responsive to the other.

So much for a general grasp of the poem. But its intricacy and precision of statement deserve more attention. Perhaps the following questions will suggest something of the compact complexity of the poem:

H.   Donne wrote this poem when he had to be absent from his wife. Does this information add anything to an understanding and appreciation of the poem?

I.   Which words in the poem are used with a double or triple meaning? Explain how each is used, and what it contributes to the accurate complexity of the poem.

J.   What words carry out the "religious" tone of the poem? What words emphasize the "secular" nature of the love of the "laity"?

K.   What would be the effect of the poem if it ended with stanza 6? What would be the effect if the image of gold and gold leaf were omitted, and the image of the compass retained? What does the combination of the two images accomplish that could not be achieved by one alone?

The next poem is divided into four sections, and has much greater variety of rhythm and stanza form than the two others:

PETER QUINCE AT THE CLAVIER

I

Just as my fingers on these keys
Make music, so the self-same sounds
On my spirit make a music, too.

Music is feeling, then, not sound;
And thus it is that what I feel,   5
Here in this room, desiring you,

Thinking of your blue-shadowed silk
Is music. It is like the strain
Waked in the elders by Susanna:

Of a green evening, clear and warm,   10
She bathed in her still garden, while
The red-eyed elders, watching, felt

The basses of their beings throb
In witching chords, and their thin blood
Pulse pizzicati of Hosanna.   15

II

In the green water, clear and warm
Susanna lay,
She searched
The touch of springs,
And found   20
Concealed imaginings.
She sighed,
For so much melody.

Upon the bank, she stood
In the cool   25
Of spent emotions.
She felt, among the leaves,
The dew
Of old devotions.

She walked upon the grass,   30
Still quavering.
The winds were like her maids
On timid feet,
Fetching her woven scarves,
Yet wavering.   35

A breath upon her hand
Muted the night.
She turned—
A cymbal crashed,
And roaring horns.   40

III

Soon, with a noise like tambourines,
Came her attendant Byzantines.

They wondered why Susanna cried
Against the elders by her side;

And as they whispered the refrain   45
Was like a willow swept by rain.

Anon, their lamps' uplifted flame
Revealed Susanna and her shame.

And then, the simpering Byzantines
Fled, with a noise like tambourines.   50

IV

Beauty is momentary in the mind—
The fitful tracing of a portal;
But in the flesh it is immortal.

The body dies; the body's beauty lives.
So evenings die, in their green going,   55
A wave, interminably flowing.
So gardens die, their meek breath scenting
The cowl of winter, done repenting.
So maidens die, to the auroral
Celebration of a maiden's choral.   60

Susanna's music touched the bawdy strings
Of those white elders; but escaping,
Lift only Death's ironic scraping.
Now, in its immortality, it plays
On the clear viol of her memory,   65
And makes a constant sacrament of praise.

Wallace Stevens

The poem will not make much sense to any reader who does not
know the story of this particular Susanna. It is found in "The History
of Susanna," a book in the Apocrypha, the portion of the Bible that
comes between the Old and New Testaments. (It is an official part of
the Roman Catholic Bible, but is usually omitted in Protestant edi-
tions.) The best background for understanding the poem is to read this
brief book in its entirety. The story can be summarized as follows:
Susanna is a very beautiful and virtuous woman, the wife of Joachim.
One hot afternoon she decides to take a bath in her enclosed garden.
While her two maids are away getting the equipment for the bath
ready, two prominent elders, who lust for her, hide in the garden. They
seize the opportunity and run toward her as she stands there naked.
"Behold, the garden doors are shut," they say, "that no man can see
us, and we are in love with thee; therefore consent unto us, and lie
with us." They add the threat, no empty one in view of their influence,
"If thou wilt not, we will bear witness against thee, that a young man was
with thee: and therefore thou didst send away thy maids from thee."

Under Hebraic law, the testimony of two witnesses was sufficient to convict her and condemn her to death by stoning, the penalty for adultery. But Susanna decides to trust in the Lord and refuse the demand of the elders. She shouts for help, and the two elders raise an outcry of accusation. The servants rush into the garden from the house and are horrified to hear the charges brought by the elders. The next day her trial is held, the elders testifying they had seen her sleeping with a young man who escaped. Their testimony convinces the assembly, which condemns Susanna to death. She protests her innocence and prays. The Lord hears her prayer and inspires Daniel to come to her defense. Daniel urges the people not to be precipitate. He then questions each of the elders separately, in the presence of the people, and leads them into giving contradictory testimony. One says she had been under a "mastick tree," the other asserts it was a "holm tree." They are thus proved to be perjurers. The assembled people cry out in indignation and praise God "who saveth them that trust in him." The two elders are now promptly convicted of perjury, and receive the punishment originally destined for Susanna.

The moral of the story, from the Biblical viewpoint, is that those who wholly trust in the Lord will not come to grief. Does the story have the same purpose in the poem or has the poet used it to another end? A careful reading indicates that Susanna is not a symbol of religious faith in "Peter Quince at the Clavier." Rather, the poem seems to be concerned with a number of other things: love, lust, music, beauty, immortality. With its use of Susanna as a symbol, the poem combines these themes into a complex whole.

The poem begins with the speaker sitting at the clavier, playing. His fingers make music, and *the self-same sounds | On my spirit make a music too.* A four-fold relation is set up: *fingers—keys—music—music of the spirit.*

Thus what starts as the physical action of fingers on keys, producing audible music, ends as a silent, *inner music.* Or as the poet puts it: *Music is feeling, then, not sound.* This prepares the way for the next statement: *And thus it is that what I feel, | Here in this room, desiring you, | Thinking of your blue-shadowed silk, | Is Music . . .* the same kind of "inner music" that he experiences when he plays the clavier. By this time two ideas have been firmly and vividly established; that music is an inner thing of the spirit and feelings, and that a beautiful woman can arouse this kind of silent music.

The poet is now ready to apply the foregoing to the case of Susanna.

In the remainder of section I he pictures the elders as they inwardly respond to the beauty of Susanna. The musical symbolism is further developed by using the language of music to suggest the love (or lust) of the old men: *The red-eyed elders, watching, felt | The basses of their being throb | In witching chords, and their thin blood | Pulse pizzicati of Hosanna.*

Section II focuses attention directly on Susanna, as she reclines in the garden, waiting for her maids to return. She has no idea that the elders are watching. An inner music—innocent though richly sensuous —stirs her. Suddenly her dream-like responsiveness to memories and the languorous afternoon is shattered. The elders reveal themselves: *A breath upon her hand | Muted the night. | She turned—| A cymbal crashed, | And roaring horns.* The delicate, inner music is destroyed and replaced by the crude *cymbal* and *roaring horns* of the intrusion.

Section III pictures the servants pouring into the garden, Susanna's panic, the suspicions of the servants, the humiliation of Susanna, and the flight of the servants, leaving Susanna to her shame. The section is dominated by another instrument not noted for soft melody, the tambourine.

The poet does not carry the narrative further. This in itself is evidence that he is not trying to make the same point as the Biblical story. Susanna *in this poem* is not a symbol of trust in the Lord. Rather, she symbolizes the eternal power of beauty to inspire deathless inner music.

Section IV brings together the themes of love, lust, music, beauty, immortality. Though *Beauty is momentary in the mind*—yet . . . *in the flesh it is immortal*, the poem paradoxically states. By a series of illustrations, the poem wins the reader to at least momentary acquiescence in the assertion that *The body dies; the body's beauty lives.* After this flat statement he gives three examples of apparently transient beauty: an evening, gardens, maidens. Susanna, too, is no more, but the memory of the "music" she inspired lives on. *Now in its immortality, it* [Susanna's "music"] *plays | On the clear viol of her memory, | And makes a constant sacrament of praise.* These last lines, clear enough as they stand, are especially rich in implication. The *viol* is a melodious instrument, contrasting with cymbals, roaring horns, and tambourines. The word *sacrament* is also carefully chosen. Its primary meaning is a ritual act conferring grace upon those who participate. The memory of Susanna, in arousing the inner music, makes *a constant sacrament of praise.*

A poem like this, with its elaborate interweaving of themes, and its delicate but powerful blend of sensuality and spirituality, suffers badly from any attempt to dissect it. The danger is that "music" will be lost, and nothing but a series of debatable philosophic propositions remain.

At this point, it is a good idea to read the poem aloud several times, to regain a sense of its wholeness. Once this is reestablished, the reader can safely examine some of its details:

    L.   Underline all the references to musical instruments and musical terms. Study the function of each reference, in terms of the immediate context and the total poem. Arrange the references in several lists according to the mood or emotion engendered by each.

    M.   Study the use of rhyme patterns, rhythm, and line length in the four sections. Why did the poet choose the particular form for each section?

    N.   Sometimes a reader needs to practice a "willing suspension of disbelief" in order to respond to a poem (e.g., a stockbroker reading an ode to Lenin). Was any suspension of disbelief involved in reading this poem?

    O.   How do the references to colors tie in with the musical references?

    P.   Compare the concept of love in this poem and that in "A Valediction: Forbidding Mourning." Are the two poems praising the same kind of love?

And now an admonition, based on personal experience. When you first read a poem (stage one) you may respond to it so strongly that your initial interpretation becomes fixed in your mind, and no subsequent study can dislodge it. As you move to stage two you unconsciously look for evidence to support your off-the-cuff interpretation; you seize on anything that does, and twist or disregard anything that doesn't. Your interpretation, in fact, has become a part of your own ego and you don't want to part with it or modify it. Thus you can end by doing violence to the author's intention.

The moral is that the first spontaneous reaction, and whatever interpretation goes with it, should be regarded as a hypothesis and not an established theory. Stage two is when you test it, and perhaps modify it or replace it entirely.

The touchstone is *consistency*. As you study a poem in detail, see whether everything in it is compatible with your interpretation. If not, test modifications of the interpretation or alternatives, and try to reach consistency.

I can illustrate these perils by a poem that I had occasion to discuss in a book review. I read it with great enthusiasm, was sure I knew what the author was doing, and in consequence failed to perform stage two with proper skepticism and care:

THE EXAMINATION

Under the thick beams of that swirly smoking light,
  The black robes are clustering, huddled in together.
Hunching their shoulders, they spread short, broad sleeves like
      night-
  Black grackles' wings; then they reach bone-yellow
      leather-

y fingers, each to each. And are prepared. Each turns   5
  His single eye—or since one can't discern their eyes,
That reflective, single, moon-pale disc which burns
  Over each brow—to watch this uncouth shape that lies

Strapped to their table. One probes with his ragged nails
  The slate-sharp calf, explores the thigh and the lean thews   10
Of the groin. Others raise, red as piratic sails,
  His wing, stretching, trying the pectoral sinews.

One runs his finger down the whet of that cruel
  Golden beak, lifts back the horny lids from the eyes,
Peers down in one bright eye malign as a jewel,   15
  And steps back suddenly. "He is anaesthetized?"

"He is. He is. Yes. Yes." The tallest of them, bent
  Down by the head, rises: "This drug possesses powers
Sufficient to still all gods in this firmament.
  This is Garuda who was fierce. He's yours for hours.   20

"We shall continue, please." Now, once again, he bends
  To the skull, and its clamped tissues. Into the cran-
ial cavity, he plunges both of his hands
  Like obstetric forceps and lifts out the great brain,

Holds it aloft, then gives it to the next who stands   25
  Beside him. Each, in turn, accepts it, although loath,
Turns it this way, that way, feels it between his hands
  Like a wasp's nest or some sickening outsized growth.

They must decide what thoughts each part of it must think;
  They tap at, then listen beside, each suspect lobe;   30
Next, with a crows' quill dipped into India ink,
  Mark on its surface, as if on a map or globe,

Those dangerous areas which need to be excised.
  They rinse it, then apply antiseptics to it.
Now silver saws appear which, inch by inch, slice   35
  Through its ancient folds and ridges, like thick suet.

It's rinsed, dried, and daubed with thick salves. The smoky
      saws
Are scrubbed, resterilized, and polished till they gleam.
The brain is repacked in its case. Pinched in their claws,
      Glimmering needles stitch it up, that leave no seam.   40

Meantime, one of them has set blinders to the eyes,
      Inserted light packing beneath each of the ears
And calked the nostrils in. One, with thin twine, ties
      The genitals off. With long wooden-handled shears,

Another chops pinions out of the scarlet wings.   45
      It's hoped that with disuse he will forget the sky
Or, at least, in time, learn, among other things,
      To fly no higher than his superiors fly.

Well; that's a beginning. The next time, they can split
      His tongue and teach him to talk correctly, can give   50
Him memory of fine books and choose clothing fit
      For the integrated area where he'll live.

Their candidate may live to give them thanks one day.
      He will recover and may hope for such success
He might return to join their ranks. Bowing away,   55
      They nod, whispering, "One of ours; one of ours.
      Yes. Yes."

W. D. Snodgrass

My eye leaped to the phrase, "integrated area," in the next to the
last stanza. "This is the key to the poem," I happily told myself, and
proceeded to say in my review:[1]

Most of all, in a few poems he makes as powerful a commentary on the times
and their public problems as I have seen anywhere. For instance, "The Examina-
tion" deals apparently with a Negro undergoing a kind of collective brain-
washing so that he will become acceptable to the WASP world.

The mailman soon put me right. Among the gentler letters of correction
was this free-verse communication:[2]

      "The Examination" is
      W. D. Snodgrass

---

[1] Quoted by permission of *Book World*.
[2] Quoted by permission of Mary-Ellen Jacobs.

sardonically satirizing the
Phi Beta Kappa Academic Community
(whose ranks he could never join   5
because of inbred indolence).
the poem was written
to be read
at an annual conclave
of these stern, key-carrying scholars   10
robed in billowy, blackling black.

but

your WASPish interpretation
is uncomfortably valid
in today's fierce heat of   15
jungle madness.

I reread the poem and quickly discovered that I had not done my homework adequately at stage two. I should have paid more careful attention to the very first stanza:

Under the thick beams of that swirly smoking light,
  The black robes are clustering, huddled in together.
Hunching their shoulders, *they spread short, broad sleeves like
    night-*
  Black grackles' wings; then they reach bone-yellow
    leather-

This certainly sounds more like a conclave of professors, complete with academic attire, than the reception committee of a suburban country club. The academic flavor recurs more subtly in the diction of the dialogue—"*He is. He is. Yes. Yes.*" (line 17), "*We shall continue, please.*" (line 21), and especially "*One of ours; one of ours. Yes. Yes.*" (line 56).
  The final stanza provided the conclusive evidence:

Their *candidate* may live to give them thanks one day.
  He will recover and *may hope for such success*
He might return to join their ranks. Bowing away,
  They nod, whispering, "*One of ours; one of ours. Yes. Yes.*"

Clearly, this is a bright young student being initiated into Phi Beta Kappa and sent forth into the world (hopefully graduate school), from which he may return as a *candidate* for an academic position—*one of ours.*

Thus in my mind I recanted and decided that this was a Phi Beta Kappa poem and only that.

And yet . . . sometimes a poet says more than he consciously intends. Granted that Snodgrass wrote the poem for a Phi Beta Kappa initiation and assume that he had nothing else on his mind—is it possible that nonetheless the poem is actually about any situation in which a free soul is undergoing a mutilation of the spirit in order to join some dominant and privileged group? Could the poem apply to the middle-class Black who moves into an integrated suburb, the writer who comes to terms with Madison Avenue, the student rebel who is appointed to a college committee and soon finds himself speaking of his fellow students as *they?*

And there still remains the line (52)—*For the integrated area where he'll live.* This *could* suggest the ideal of an academic community, where teachers and students are closely associated. Or perhaps it implies that the student undergoing surgery *does* have something in common with a Negro moving to a predominantly white area. Thus the question comes full circle.

Q.   *Study the poem carefully. Apply the test of consistency to any interpretation you attempt. Do you conclude that the poem is focused entirely on the academic scene, or would you argue that its scope is broader? If so, define (if you can) the limits of your interpretation.*

The subject matter of poetry is anything and everything—all items of human experience, observation, and imagination are fair game. Nor does the subject of a poem have to be something novel and unexpected for the poem to seem new and fresh. Much more important than the ostensible subject is what the poet does with it: his angle of vision, his way of getting inside the subject, and what he reveals from the inside.

Below are five pairs of poems. In each pair, two poets have dealt with what (at least on the surface) is the same subject. Study the poems one pair at a time, taking into account all that you have learned about the craft and devices of poetry. Try to determine why the two poems in a given pair are totally different experiences, even though they are "about" the same thing. A few questions, but not many, are included. They are intended *only as starters*: otherwise be on your own.

Pairs of Poems

10

Marriage

THE DINNER

It wasn't so much
That she regretted
Slicing off pieces of her own flesh
To cook for them
But when John sent his plate   5
Back to the kitchen
With loud complaints,
When all of them said that the meat
                was just too tough,

Then
She cried . . .   10
A little.

Elva McAllaster

126

THE ACCOMPLICES

Must now accomplish the division of remains,
assassins, they must now be scrupulous, take pains
to be exact in the division of each part.
(Let not the question of the genitals impede
them in the disposition of their Singular Dead)   5
Each must be left with half a hand and half a heart.
A hand for him. A hand for her. A lung apiece
and an iambic foot for each, and then surcease.

As to disposal of the parts his portion will rot
up in the attic, carried there and then forgot,   10
his half the heart plopped into an Etruscan jar
they bought in Tuscany. The rest of his share he will lock
in a trunk. Her half of heart she will pound in a mortar
and eat. The rest of her share will be burned until charred
                    black.

His odds and ends of her, dispensed with casually, will stink.   15
To be consumed by gut and fire is cleaner, I should think.

Isabella Gardner

*A.   Does the difference in length of the two poems make any important
difference in the experience they create for the reader?*
*B.   Both poems use the symbol of mutilation. Does the symbol have
the same significance and force in each case?*
*C.   Which poem expresses the more bitter mood? Give reasons for
your answer.*

A Legend

THE FALL OF ICARUS
(FROM BRUEGHEL'S PAINTING)

The bulging sails by a riotous wind caught
pull the ships and their rigging nets toward shore
to be emptied. The sailors quickly will calm their floors
and their houses in the evening light will melt into the moun-
                    tains.

And on the hill with one foot planted in the earth   5
his plowing almost done; his eyes cast down and fully shielded
from the sun which now is growing shadow, the farmer
turns in soil and toil the final circles of the day.

Below him a quiet pastoral: on lichen bearing rocks
the feeding sheep, the quiet watching dog, the silent shepherd   10
so stalking with his eyes the homing flights of birds
that neither he nor the intent fisherman closer to the shore,

none has seen the silent fall of Icarus
through the riotous wind and the shadows of the coming
                                    evening light,
nor do they hear his sigh, both of pity and delight   15
of his remembered waxed and winged flight.

                                              Charles F. Madden

MUSÉE DES BEAUX ARTS

About suffering they were never wrong,
The Old Masters: how well they understood
Its human position; how it takes place
While someone else is eating or opening a window or just
                              walking dully along;
How, when the aged are reverently, passionately waiting   5
For the miraculous birth, there always must be
Children who did not specially want it to happen, skating
On a pond at the edge of the wood:
They never forgot
That even the dreadful martyrdom must run its course   10
Anyhow, in a corner, some untidy spot
Where the dogs go on with their doggy life and the torturer's
                              horse
Scratches its innocent behind on a tree.

In Brueghel's *Icarus*, for instance: how everything turns away
Quite leisurely from the disaster; the ploughman may   15
Have heard the splash, the forsaken cry,
But for him it was not an important failure; the sun shone
As it had to on the white legs disappearing into the green
Water; and the expensive delicate ship that must have seen
Something amazing, a boy falling out of the sky,   20
Had somewhere to get to and sailed calmly on.

                                                   W. H. Auden

D.   The poems appear to have been inspired by the same painting, and they have a similar tone: irony. In both poems study the choice of words that build up and accentuate the sense of irony. In which poem is it strongest?

E.   Madden confines himself to the Brueghel painting; Auden uses it merely as his most detailed example. How does this affect the experience that the two poems create?

Death

HOLY SONNET 10

Death, be not proud, though some have called thee
Mighty and dreadful, for thou art not so;
For those whom thou think'st thou dost overthrow
Die not, poor death, nor yet canst thou kill me.
From rest and sleep, which but thy pictures be,   5
Much pleasure, then from thee, much more must flow
And soonest our best men with thee do go—
Rest of their bones and souls' delivery.
Thou art slave to Fate, Chance, kings and desperate men,
And dost with poison, war, and sickness dwell;   10
And poppy or charms can make us sleep as well,
And better than thy stroke. Why swell'st thou then?
One short sleep past, we wake eternally,
And death shall be no more. Death, thou shalt die.

John Donne

SONNET 146

Poor soul, the center of my sinful earth,
Thrall to these rebel powers that thee array,
Why dost thou pine within and suffer dearth,
Painting thy outward walls so costly gay?
Why so large cost, having so short a lease,   5
Dost thou upon thy fading mansion spend?
Shall worms, inheritors of this excess,
Eat up thy charge? Is this thy body's end?
Then, soul, live thou upon thy servant's loss,
And let that pine to aggravate thy store;   10
Buy terms divine in selling hours of dross;
Within be fed, without be rich no more.
So shalt thou feed on Death, that feeds on men,
And Death once dead, there's no more dying then.

William Shakespeare

*F.   In Donne's poem, Death is addressed; in Shakespeare's, the soul.
How does this affect the choice of imagery throughout the two poems? Does
it lead to a different tone at the end?*

*G.   Examine the rhyme scheme of the two poems and see whether this
corresponds to the flow of thought and feeling.*

*H.   Which is the more introspective poem? the more dramatic? Show
how the imagery of each poem contributes to this.*

A Train

I LIKE TO SEE IT LAP THE MILES

I like to see it lap the miles,
And lick the valleys up,
And stop to feed itself at tanks;
And then, prodigious, step

Around a pile of mountains,   5
And, supercilious, peer
In shanties by the sides of roads;
And then a quarry pare

To fit its ribs, and crawl between,
Complaining all the while   10
In horrid, hooting stanza;
Then chase itself down hill

And neigh like Boanerges,
Then, punctual as a star,
Stop—docile and omnipotent—   15
At its own stable door.

Emily Dickinson

TO A LOCOMOTIVE IN WINTER

Thee for my recitative
Thee in the driving storm even as now, the snow, the winter-
          day declining,
Thee in thy panoply, thy measur'd dual throbbing and thy
          beat convulsive,

Thy black cylindric body, golden brass and silvery steel,
Thy ponderous side-bars, parallel and connecting rods,
          gyrating, shuttling at thy sides,   5

Thy metrical, now swelling pant and roar, now tapering in
the distance,
Thy great protruding head-light fix'd in front,
Thy long, pale, floating vapor-pennants, tinged with delicate
purple,
The dense and murky clouds out-belching from thy smoke
stack,
Thy knitted frame, thy springs and valves, the tremulous
twinkle of thy wheels,   10
Thy train of cars behind, obedient, merrily following,
Through gale or calm, now swift, now slack, yet steadily
careening;
Type of the modern—emblem of motion and power—pulse
of the continent,
For once come serve the Muse and merge in verse, even as
here I see thee,
With storm and buffeting gusts of wind and falling snow,   15
By day thy warning ringing bell to sound its notes,
By night thy silent signal lamps to swing.

Fierce-throated beauty!
Roll through my chant with all thy lawless music, thy swing-
ing lamps at night,
Thy madly-whistled laughter, echoing, rumbling like an
earthquake, rousing all,   20
Law of thyself complete, thine own track firmly holding,
(No sweetness debonair of tearful harp or glib piano thine,)
Thy trills of shrieks by rocks and hills return'd,
Launch'd o'er the prairies wide, across the lakes,
To the free skies unpent and glad and strong.   25

Walt Whitman

I.   In Dickinson's poem the train is implicitly compared to a horse.
*Try rewriting the poem to make the comparison a mule, tiger, or elephant.
What changes have you made in the words? Does the use of a different animal
change the poem basically?*

J.   *Is Whitman's locomotive symbolic of anything? What? Pick out
words and phrases that develop the symbolism.*

K.   *Analyze the rhythm of the two poems, and see whether the rhythm
in each case is appropriate to what the poem is expressing.*

L.   *When these poems were written, trains were thought of as the
ultimate in modern progress. Today one associates them with irksome delays,*

delapidated stations, and abandoned routes. Does this affect the way you respond to the two poems? Is there any way you can recapture within yourself the spirit of the first persons who read the poems? Can you think of any other poems, written in the past, that pose a similar problem—how to respond to an attitude that no longer prevails?

War

BASE DETAILS

If I were fierce, and bald, and short of breath,
    I'd live with scarlet Majors at the Base,
And speed glum heroes up the line to death.
    You'd see me with my puffy petulant face,
Guzzling and gulping in the best hotel,   5
    Reading the Roll of Honor. "Poor young chap,"
I'd say—"I used to know his father well;
    Yes, we've lost heavily in this last scrap."
And when the war is done and youth stone dead,
I'd toddle safely home and die—in bed.

                 Siegfried Sassoon

LIFE AT WAR

The disasters numb within us
caught in the chest, rolling
in the brain like pebbles. The feeling
resembles lumps of raw dough

weighing down a child's stomach on baking day.   5
Or Rilke said it, "My heart . . .
Could I say of it, it overflows
with bitterness . . . but no, as though

its contents were simply balled into
formless lumps, thus   10
do I carry it about."
The same war

continues.
We have breathed the grits of it in, all our lives,
our lungs are pocked with it,   15

the mucous membrane of our dreams
coated with it, the imagination
filmed over with the gray filth of it:

the knowledge that humankind,

delicate Man, whose flesh   20
responds to a caress, whose eyes
are flowers that perceive the stars,

whose music excels the music of birds,
whose laughter matches the laughter of dogs,
whose understanding manifests designs   25
fairer than the spider's most intricate web,
still turns without surprise, with mere regret
to the scheduled breaking open of breasts whose milk
runs out over the entrails of still-alive babies,
transformation of witnessing eyes to pulp-fragments,   30
implosion of skinned penises into carcass-gulleys.

We are the humans, men who can make;
whose language imagines *mercy*,
lovingkindness; we have believed one another
mirrored forms of a God we felt as good—   35

who do these acts, who convince ourselves
it is necessary; these acts are done
to our own flesh; burned human flesh
is smelling in Viet Nam as I write.

Yes, this is the knowledge that jostles for space   40
in our bodies along with all we
go on knowing of joy, of love;

our nerve filaments twitch with its presence
day and night,
nothing we say has not the husky phlegm of it in the
    saying,   45
nothing we do has the quickness, the sureness,
the deep intelligence living at peace would have.

Denise Levertov

    M.   Historians sometimes turn to the poetry of the past in an effort to get the "feel" of earlier periods. Here are two poems expressing an antiwar spirit—one (Sassoon) from World War I, the other (Levertov) from the Viet Nam war. Just on the basis of these two poems (an inadequate basis, of course),

would you say that the feeling is the same, or has it changed in some way?
Support your conclusions by reference to specific lines in the two poems.

Little has been said in this book about the comparative evaluation of poems. We have gone on the assumption that it is better to understand and enjoy each poem for whatever it has to offer, rather than viewing them as horses in a race and trying to pick the winner. Still, some poems are better than others. You might glance back at the five pairs of poems and see if there is one pair where you "know in your heart" or "feel in your bones" that the two poems are of unequal poetic quality. In that case—

N. Analyze as rigorously as you can why you consider one poem better than the other. Jot down a short list of qualities that seem to make it superior. Think about this list and see whether it can provide a few touchstones for evaluating other poems. Then write an essay (based primarily on the two poems but referring to others in the book if you wish) on the subject, "What Makes a Good Poem Good."

So far the missing man in this whole book has been the poet himself, sitting with pencil in hand or pecking at a typewriter. This neglect has been quite deliberate. It is easy to become fascinated with the life of a poet, particularly if it was picturesque or scandalous, and to begin reading his poems as autobiographical documents rather than as works of art. A good poem is good even if nothing is known about the author, or his name has vanished completely. A good poem enters upon an independent life of its own once it has been released to the public.

At the same time, it does no harm to realize that flesh-and-blood human beings have produced every last poem in this book. Furthermore, a poet's particular experiences, his temperament, his psychological makeup, his convictions—all these influence and color his work. They help determine *what* he will write about, and the *tone* he will employ in a given poem.

The question of temperament and angle of vision can be crucial. Two poets may have experiences which, to an outsider, appear identical, but create two quite different poems, for the simple reason that they are two quite different men. To illustrate this, we shall take a pair of poems inspired by the same occasion.

The setting is Finland. Two American poets, assigned overseas as Fulbright lecturers, were being taken with a group of other Americans to Hietaniemi Heroes' Cemetery in Helsinki. It was late August, and the

Poets

at

Work

11

graves of the Finnish soldiers who had fallen in battle against the Russians were covered with roses in full blossom. Around the cemetery was a stone wall with the names of other soldiers who were buried in different parts of the country. The two men stood there, deeply moved as they realized the heavy cost to Finland of the struggle to maintain her independence. On an impulse, they agreed that each would write a poem to capture what he felt; they would not confer together until both poems were finished.

The two poems follow, each prefaced with a short statement by the poet explaining what he was trying to do, and the problems he encountered along the way.

Statement by first poet

How does one write a poem about "heroes" anyway? The poem had to be written; that much was certain. Yet in a generation which has demanded "irony" in poetry, which has distrusted the expression in prose of the traditional abstractions like *honor*, and *heroism*, and *patriotism*—a distrust explicitly stated by Ernest Hemingway following an earlier war—there is naturally, and perhaps inevitably, a lurking fear which may almost become a conviction on the part of the poet that the tone hit upon in a poem about heroes may ring falsely. The poet wishes to be honest with himself, to treat his subject honestly, without sentimentality. At the same time he hopes to avoid naivete. If he does not desire to fool, neither does he wish to be fooled.

This poem about a war cemetery in Helsinki, Finland, is an attempt to face these problems of tone, to write honestly about an abstraction like *heroism*, without fooling or being fooled. It is difficult when one has lived through an age in which such concepts have been regarded almost exclusively with disillusionment and cynical reservations.

The circumstances under which this poem was conceived, written, and rewritten are rather unusual. I had gone to Finland for a year with other American teachers and students to accept a Fulbright lectureship at Helsinki University. My colleagues and I were shown the greatest kindness by our Finnish hosts who showed us proudly Finnish homes and farms, hospitals and schools, factories and museums, churches and cemeteries. I think all the visitors shared a mounting admiration for the four and one-half million people of this nation, so few in numbers as compared with our homeland, yet so steadfast, so free from panic in a world where peace is daily threatened, so unhysterical, and, yes, so courageous and heroic. I found myself constantly reexamining attitudes that I had long held. I found my cynicism slipping. I discovered that here was a nation that felt like a nation, that had a sense of community, that possessed a unity and a pride in nationhood which had been forged in the furnace of its wars for survival itself. It was a community in which the dead had their honored place with the living.

On the day that we first visited this beautiful national cemetery, with its gravelled paths, its row upon row of flat stones marking the graves of the fallen, a small rose bush bloomed above each grave. There was this color to soften the restrained, almost classical severity, the formality of the gardens, the walks, and the great central tomb of Finland's Marshal Mannerheim, her leader in war and peace. I remember the simple, unaffected words of my Finnish companion on that occasion: "Some of my best friends are here." And I remember a night of bitter December cold upon which thousands of students led the torchlight parade to pay their annual tribute on the day of Finnish Independence, a small candle winking through the night on each grave.

There was something awesome about the place. I remember feeling resentful and expressing annoyance about the levity and banter which I overheard being expressed by other foreign visitors. In the course of our visit I spoke with my American friend and learned that he too had been moved by the spirit of this place. From that exchange grew the agreement that we should each write a poem which, after completion, we might compare to discover the nature of our respective responses. "Hietaniemi" represents my part of that agreement.

The poem had to be simple; it had to be as direct as possible; it had to have the restraint, the almost classical severity of the place itself. Most important, it had to express honestly and with restrained emotion the Finnish conviction that the death of "heroes" is not in vain. The poem was written and rewritten, changed and changed again. Generally, the changes were always in the interest of greater simplicity, removing ambiguities. In this poem the general had to be more important than the particular. Additional stanzas were written and then excised entirely. I had written something about that banter I had heard, which had *blown on the alien winds indifferently* and *chilling the grieving heart with mockery*. I saw that it was not right. I chose rather to stress the fact that the "insensitive stranger" might learn from this place something of the quality of the men the nation bred. I wanted, in short, to show the link between the living and the dead. I hoped that the music might be muted as is all beauty in Finland. But I hoped above all else to write with the same honesty of *courage* and *glory* and *heroism* that one feels in the hearts of the Finnish people when they visit in their thousands this final resting place of their fallen sons. One never knows for sure, in such circumstances, how well, or ill, he has succeeded.

HIETANIEMI
(HEROES' CEMETERY—HELSINKI)

Upon this marbled memory of their fame
Appears a brother's and a father's name.
Laments of women, the stricken mother's tear
Interpret wordlessly those buried here.

Grave ends for these have tokened mute repose   5
Beneath the petalled bloom upon the rose
That flowered to fall above them in its season,
As they fell reaped and ravaged by Death's treason.

But still if beauty blooms upon these paths,
And grave decorum dignifies these deaths,   10
Can living men who trod these walks remain
Unsepulchred in greatness with these slain?

The stranger on these grounds, insensitive
To Finland's furrowed flesh, the empty sleeve
Of living heroes, brothers to these dead,   15
May fail to know what men this nation bred.

If decorous stones, the very walls pronounce
The name for glory, if the solemn rows
Proclaim a changeless faith through winter snows,
Through rains of spring and warming suns, one counts   20

The bitter cost and stands again renewed,
Again with courage, heart, and faith imbued.
Accord these honor who for Finland bled
That future sons might walk with lifted head.

                                                    John Gross

Statement by second poet

When I went home and tried to make a poem from my experience at Hie-taniemi I quickly discovered that emotion alone, however deeply felt, is not enough to create a poem. Emotion is a raw, chaotic thing. I had to give it focus and form. Suddenly the solution came to me: my friend and I had said something in passing about Finland's reminding us of ancient Greece—the same combination of patriotism, courage, and a highly developed esthetic sense; each country also standing alone against a much larger eastern country (ancient Persia and the Soviet Union) as the defender of what the West represents. This gave me the basic metaphor that made the poem possible. I did some reading to refresh my memory of the war between the Greeks and Persians, and deliberately developed the parallel all through the poem. In doing this, I of course used history in an oversimplified way. I treated the "West" as the symbol of freedom and the worth of the individual, and the "East" as representing despotism and a monstrous, blind threat. The facts of history lack this schematic neatness, but at least, in a relative way, Greece and Finland in their climactic moments of heroism have embodied a free and humane tradition as compared with Persia and the USSR.

Once I had my basic metaphor, the poem was rather easy to write. The metaphor determined the tone. If my parallel was between ancient Greece and modern Finland, I wanted the tone to be appropriate to the outlook of the Hellenes who stopped the Persians. The emphasis had to be on the plainest virtues, such as courage, fortitude, love of country, self-sacrifice. I wanted no touch of irony, no oblique sniping at these virtues. In fact, I aimed at a rather archaic thing: to make platitudes resume the nobility they once had, and to celebrate patriotism in a way not dissimilar from Pericles' Funeral Oration. (I could have written a very different poem, questioning the value of any war and the supposed virtues of military courage, but my mood was another, and my basic metaphor conformed to my mood.)

As for form, I decided early on iambic pentameter as my normal line. It has a steady dignified march, and is flexible enough not to be a straitjacket. I knew I wanted the visible and auditory sense of form that rhyme can give, but I didn't want it to be too blatant. So I experimented in the first stanza until I had a rhyme scheme that was obviously there, but didn't clang and rattle. Once I had written the first stanza, I decided to keep the form for the rest of the poem, so as to emphasize *what* the poem was saying, rather than *how* it was being said.

One other thing calls for comment. The images representing the "West" are taken from nature (roses, birch trees, etc.) and from ordinary human activities. For the "East," I wished imagery that would suggest menacing power and an ominous blindness. Several images combine to create this impression: idolaters, stone icons, hierophants, beast, wooden puppets. These are deliberately vague, and intended to invoke, perhaps, memories of Assyrian stone lions, carved images of ancient kings from the Near East, formal, priestly, and cultic figures, as well as the ritual of Communistic ceremonies. The fourth stanza, which some of my friends feel is out of tone with the rest of the poem, was written to provide "a dash of bitters" by highlighting the "East"—its dehumanized quality—in contrast with the "West." It marks the point of farthest departure from the images that symbolize the West, and prepares the reader for the sharp swing-back to the glorification of the plain, humane virtues in the last stanza.

ODE TO THE FINNISH DEAD

In the soft Finnish summer they become
Briefly acres of roses. One hardly sees
The standard stones with name and date and rank;
Nor would a slow addition make the sum
Of all who have their rights here. The very walls   5
Are eloquent with names that other trees
And flowers hold in trust, who stood and sank
To earth as the gold of a birch tree falls.

There were no roses blooming when they flowered
In winter beauty. Their garden was a dim   10

Disorder of the frozen lakes, and firs
Lifting with snow. And some the night devoured
And some the darkness of the crouching east,
Folded petals at the west's utter rim,
Faithful in death against the idolaters   15
And the stone icons of their blinded beast.

In their far Northern tongue, they had a name
For Marathon: they held Thermopylae;
No traitor could be bought to sell the way.
Suomussalmi, Tolvajärvi became   20
The rolling syllables Pheidippides
Spoke dying to the Athens that was free.
Thou stranger, pause, and in Helsinki say,
We kept her laws amid these witness trees.

"Remember the Finns," intoned the hierophants   25
In triple invocation to the beast,
And to the west it turned its sightless eyes.
From reddened squares the univocal chants
Of nameless choirs came to its ears with words
Of antiphon. And when their voices ceased   30
It rose by jerks, as wooden puppets rise,
And twittered like a tree of maddened birds.

Walk here amid the superficial beauty
Of roses sprung from loveliness beneath.
Here is renewal of our tattered speech.   35
Dulce et decorum and honest *duty*
Shine innocent in silver, gold, and red;
A goodness brightens in the word of *death*.
Bloom in the beauty of your giving, each
By each, in mankind's heart, brave Finnish dead.   40

Chad Walsh

    *A.   The first poem remains focused on the cemetery; the other begins
and ends with the cemetery, but moves away from it during the middle part of
the poem. Why do you think each poet chose the particular focus that is reflected
in his poem?*

    *B.   Study the description of the cemetery in the two poems. What
visual details are used by both poets? Does the use of the same detail create
the same poetic effect? If not, what is the reason for the difference? Be as specific
as possible, remembering that each detail of a poem must be experienced and
analyzed in the context of the total poem.*

The Fountain
(Sheepfold Hill)

In the evening

~~behind~~ me I heard the leaves,   *dead*
~~dead~~ leaves skittering along blue asphalt,
~~in the little cold wind of evening;~~
the ~~lost breathings of the trees,~~
                ~~the trees now falling asleep.~~

saw
In the morning,I ~~had seen~~ a sequin of sunlight
bright ~~yellow~~ on the woodshed floor   *gold*
        gold slotted through a crack betwe n shingles;
but no,it did not waver,~~it~~ was only
the wet ~~bright~~ leaf of the locust.

And look now— *—thro*
~~In the evening~~ the golden tree-toad   *beneath*
skips ~~into the~~ drift of ~~them~~ *shadow*
        thrush   ~~and~~ bre the~~s~~ under ~~the~~ bird's nest;
~~while~~ the goldfinch ~~peps under the~~ eaves   *Sheepfold*
for the last time,and ~~the Hill~~
draws closely about it ~~its~~ Joseph's Coat of colors,
~~and~~ geese honk by the tide-line.

while-under-it
Voices of death and creation:
for the blond rondure of the moon;
~~and~~ the ~~lone~~ bat's sky-skatings.   *crazy*
Now ~~While we~~ light the ~~late~~ candle,   *first*
~~and~~ shelter~~it~~ between palms of tenderness,
for an instant of self.

O phrase,be praise!and praise,be phrase!
from the brook with stones in its mouth,
and the man with no thought in his mind,
and the girl with no love in her heart,
~~a~~ the falling star lost in a vapor,
~~or~~ the wind stilled at sunset!   *is motionless*

Let ~~be~~ framed with these for a moment of silence,
~~all~~ in one instant of the forever-together.
~~The~~ fountain of god-speech ~~frozen~~ in falling,
action~~,~~ entranced in the moment of meaning,
stars and words still enough,to be counted,
if there ~~was~~ someone to count them,
        was only
                    —at last—

WORKSHEET I
"*The Fountain*," by Conrad Aiken

#2

(Sheepfold Hill)

In the evening I hear the dead leaves
skittering ~~upon the~~ cold asphalt:
in the morning,saw a sequin of sunlight,
bright,~~bright~~,on the woodshed floor,
slotted through a crack betwe n shingles.
But no,it did not waver,was only
the wet yellow leaf of the locust.

away

fold

And look,now,the golden-eyed tree-toad
skips through a ~~drift~~ of shadows
to breathe ~~beneath~~ a bird's-nest!
the goldfinch taps ~~under~~ eaves
for the last time,Sheepfold Hill
draws ~~gaily~~ about it a Joseph's Coat of colors;
~~and~~ far off,at the tide-line,the wild geese.

Thicket

in the fallen

in "noose" of light.

Voices of death,voices of creation, ——— *great*
for the ~~blown~~ rondure of the ~~full~~ moon,
~~and~~ the bat's intricate sky-skatings:
now we light the first candle
and shelter it between tender-bright palms
for a secret instant of self.

Light now.

O phrase be praise, *and* praise be phrase,
for the brook with a stone in its mouth
for the man·with ~~no~~ thought in his mind
for the girl with ~~no~~ love in her heart
and the shooting star lost in a vapor
and the wind stilled at sunset.

Framed with these ~~for~~ a moment of silence
we are one instant of the forever-together:
The fountain of god-speech is motionless in falling,
action is entranced at the moment of meaning;
words and worlds all still enough,at last,to be counted,
if there was only someone to count them.

WORKSHEET 2
"The Fountain," by Conrad Aiken

C.   *Examine the stanza form in the two poems. In what ways does the difference contribute to a difference in the total impact of the poems?*

D.   *Read Allen Tate's "Ode to the Confederate Dead" (p. 268). How does it differ in tone and attitude from the two poems about Hietaniemi? What formal elements of the poem contribute to the difference?*

One interesting way of peering over the poet's shoulder is to examine the successive worksheets of a poem and trace it from the first vague or chaotic beginning to the published poem. The Lockwood Memorial Library at the University of Buffalo has assembled a vast collection of such material from contemporary poets. A few of these worksheets are reproduced in this chapter, for comparison with the final version of the poem as it appeared in print.

In Conrad Aiken's "The Fountain" the poet seems to have had from the beginning an over-all idea of what he was attempting; his successive revisions are concentrated on matters of language—the effort to choose the right words and to avoid excess verbiage.

THE FOUNTAIN

In the evening we heard the dead leaves
skittering away over asphalt
in the morning saw a sequin of sunlight
slotted through a crack in the wall
bright gold on the woodshed floor   5
but no it did not tremble it was only
the pale yellow leaf of the locust.

And look now the golden-eyed tree-toad
flips through a thicket of shadow
to breathe by the sodden bird's nest   10
the goldfinch caught in a ring of light
taps at the eaves and Sheepfold Hill
once more wears its Joseph's coat colors
while wild geese honk at the tideline.

Voices of death voices of creation   15
for the blonde rondure of the full moon
and the bat's dizzy sky-skatings
we light now the first candle
sheltered between tender-bright palms
for a secret instant of self.   20

Now phrase be praise and praise be phrase
for the brook with a stone in its path
the man with no thought in his mind
the girl with no love in her heart
the shooting star lost in a vapor   25
and the wind stilled at sunset.

Caught with these in a moment of silence
we become one instant of the forever-together
the fountain of god-speech motionless in falling
action spellbound in the moment of meaning   30
words and worlds still enough at last to be counted
if only there was someone to count them.

Conrad Aiken

E.   *Go through the worksheets and the final version and make a list
of changes in choice of words, showing how the poet strove for greater precision
or vividness* (e.g., golden tree-toad *becomes the more interesting* golden-
eyed tree-toad).

F.   *Note how the poet kept changing the first line:* Behind me I heard
the leaves—In the evening I hear the dead leaves—In the evening we
heard the dead leaves. *In the light of the finished poem, why do you think
he decided to use* we *in place of* I *and the past tense instead of the present?*

G.   *Note how the poet vacillated in the fourth stanza between* no thought
and no love *and the omission of the negative* no. *Again in the light of the
final poem, why do you think he reverted to the negative?*

When you are reading a poem for the first time there is often a sense
of interesting but unfocused chaos. Something is going on in the poem,
and your imagination responds now and then, but not in any clear-cut
way that you can describe. Only gradually, as you reread the poem, does
it begin to take on a total shape and convey a unified experience. At
this point the separate impressions come into focus, and you respond
to the poem as a whole.

Frequently the poet goes through a parallel process. *Something*
comes to him or arises in him: a strong but nameless feeling, a phrase,
a memory. It can be anything. *Something* sets him going, and he finds
himself doing a kind of poetic doodling, writing words and phrases down
with no clear understanding of how they all relate together. Then gra-

THE PYLONS.

They break the tall perspective of the future
Where after the cloud shall lean its swanwhite neck.

They stand ~~alone~~ among our little hills

They stand ~~off~~ with weeping hands and with strange piety
above our small chalk downs
like girls of a tall ~~slender~~ race, ~~noticed~~ unused to country,
~~Rather awkward & strangers.~~
~~with~~ are Graceful, deprecating, ~~ask~~
and delirious from towns

~~Uneasy for the ~~~~ valley ~~~~ border ~~~~
~~ or for dolls~~
Uneasing for the valley and the truth.
Between the hills

Above our small chalk ~~hills~~ downs, where ~~they great~~ winding road
Meet hidden villages, and loads
of stones, the scent of these hills, lie on the paths
The pylons ~~erects to~~   (wrath)
~~that trail of raw wire~~
The tall and strange perspectives of the future
With ~~trail of raw wire~~ mourning lines of wire.
The concrete pillars

WORKSHEET I
"The Pylons," by Stephen Spender

144

like the huge   compass arm
That swings to its prodigious North

The secret of these hillside stone   and villages cottages
From that stone made
And crumbling roads
That turn on sudden hidden villages

Now over they
But above our small slate flint stone down, they have built the pylon
Tall concrete pillars
That trail black wire

The brief look of a frog   The brief look

like the dried pancge of a brook

The secret of these hills was stone, and cottages
Of that stone made,
And crumbling roads
That turn on sudden hidden villages.

Now over these small hills they have built the concrete
Pylons, ~~those pillars~~ That ~~with~~ ~~slack wire~~:
~~mmmmmmmmm~~ Pylons, those pillars
~~mmmmmmmm~~ ~~gis~~ ~~have~~ ~~no secret.~~
Made like a ~~pion~~ race of girls that have no secret.

The valley with its gilded, evening loom
                    green
And the ~~careful~~ ~~the~~ chestnut
~~the~~ If comfortable rot
Are withered like the parched bed of a broom.

          But
~~Now~~ far above, and far as sight endures,
                            little whispers
~~mmmmmmmm~~ ~~mmmmmm~~ ~~on~~ Thunder
                sued
And with its danger.
          move   still swift
There ~~trees~~, the ~~strange~~ perspective of the future,
        This
~~to reach~~, dwarfing the hills and valleys with its ~~in~~ trek

And after the cloud shall lean its swan-white neck.

THE PYLONS.

The secret of those hills was stone, and cottages
Of that stone made,
And crumbling roads
That turned on sudden hidden villages -

Now over these small hills they have built the concrete
That trails black wire :
Pylons, those pillars
Bare like nude, giant girls that have no secret.

The valley with its gilt and evening look
And the green chestnut
Of custom, root
Are blocked try like the parched bed of a brook.

But far above and far ~~wider~~ as sight endures
Like whips of anger ~~lightning~~ lightnings
With ~~thunders~~ danger
There ~~moves~~ runs the swift perspective of the future ,

This dwarfs our emerald ~~custom~~ country, by with its trek
So tall ~~assurance~~ ~~its~~ with prophecy :
Dreaming of cities
Where after ~~the~~ clouds shall ~~nod its~~ lean their swanwhite neck.

148

dually, by trial and error and in the very process of setting words down, he begins to sense the whole thing coming into focus; he discovers what it is that he (or the poem) wishes to express. At this point he is ready to go back to the start and begin rewriting the poem on the basis of his clearer understanding of it.

This apparently haphazard but actually meaningful process seems to be illustrated by the evolution of Stephen Spender's "The Pylons."

THE PYLONS

The secret of these hills was stone, and cottages
Of that stone made,
And crumbling roads
That turned on sudden hidden villages.

Now over these small hills they have built the concrete   5
That trails black wire:
Pylons, those pillars
Bare like nude, giant girls that have no secret.
The valley with its gilt and evening look
And the green chestnut   10
Of customary root
Are mocked dry like the parched bed of a brook.

But far above and far as sight endures
Like whips of anger
With lightning's danger   15
There runs the quick perspective of the future.
This dwarfs our emerald country by its trek
So tall with prophecy:
Dreaming of cities
Where often clouds shall lean their swan-white neck.   20

Stephen Spender

The evidence of the worksheets suggests that two lines came to the poet (*They trek the tall perspective of the future* / *Where often the cloud shall lean its swan white neck*) and that his task was to discover, by trial and error, the as yet unwritten poem toward which they pointed. Before he was done, he had composed three stanzas leading up to the final one in which the original pair of lines, now somewhat revised, could find a place.

"The Florist Rose," by Robert Graves

The Florist's Rose

This wax-mannequin-nude, the florist's rose,

She of the long stem and too glossy leaf,
Is dead to ~~honest~~
~~The scorned of busy~~ greenfly and leaf-cutter,
Behind plate-glass watches the yellow toss
Is bride of the robust male aeroplane ~~in~~
Who has no legend, as she fails
(~~Undergoing, as she decays~~ from legend ~~life~~ —
~~from fellowship~~ ~~also~~   and sail o crown).
~~Compensation~~ with pearl ~~and~~ sword ~~and crown and ship/sea~~);

Whom ~~the~~ eagles hate   and all surviving truth;
~~to~~ Posterity's (scentless ~~doug~~ [flowers]   ~~as~~ she its ~~to~~ ~~was bird~~)
futurity's

Is ectogenetic of the garden ~~bush~~;

Is dewed by the spray-gun; is ~~tending~~ ~~thorn~~,   of Thorn

~~Is by cheque feed by messenger escorted;~~
                       between
~~Pouts venereal, steals~~ ~~seems need~~ neither bud ~~nor~~ ~~was and~~ blooms;
                                                    and falls sick
Exhales no scent, ~~droops within the day~~
       Escorted elsewhere, droops within the day
~~By messenger escorted   droops~~

The Florists Rose.

This wax-mannequin nude, the florists rose,
She of the long stem and ~~the~~ roof-glossy leaf ~~once glossy~~
Is dead to honest greenfly and leaf-cutter:
Behind plate-glass watches the yellow fogs.

Is bride of the robust male aeroplane
Whom eagles hate and all surviving truth,
Who has no legend, as she fails from legend —
From fellowship with sword and sail and crown.

Futurity's flower, scentless (he its bird);
Is dewed with the spray-gun; is tender-thorned;
Ponts venereal, between bud and bloom;
Escorted elsewhere, droops within the day.

H. Pick out certain phrases that undergo successive changes, and try to figure out why the poet made the changes (e.g., Like girls of a tall race, unused to country—Nude like a race of girls that have no secret—Bare like nude, giant girls that have no secret.).

I.   The chapter on "The Architecture of Poetry" discussed the relation of form to content, and the trial-and-error methods the poet often uses to arrive at form. Study Spender's poem from that angle. Trace the evolution of the stanza forms and the use of rhyme and half-rhyme. Do you see any point at which the poet began to give conscious attention to these matters?

Finally, for the benefit of anyone further interested in tracing the creative process, here are the worksheets of a short poem, "The Florist Rose," by Robert Graves. See what you can deduce from them.

THE FLORIST ROSE

This wax-mannequin nude, the florist rose,
She of the long stem and too glossy leaf,
Is dead to honest greenfly and leaf-cutter:
Behind plate-glass watches the yellow fogs.

Claims kin with the robust male aeroplane   5
Whom eagles hate and phantoms of the air,
Who has no legend, as she breaks from legend—
From fellowship with sword and sail and crown.

Experiment's flower, scentless (he its bird);
Is dewed by the spray-gun; is tender-thorned;   10
Pouts, false-virginal, between bud and bloom;
Bought as a love-gift, droops within the day.

Robert Graves

Postscript

Having read through this book and performed a number of the experiments, you probably know by now whether poetry is for you. Though infinitely rewarding to those who love it, poetry is not essential to salvation, and no state in the Union requires an *explication* of "The Love Song of J. Alfred Prufrock" as a prerequisite for a driver's license. Everybody has the potentiality to understand and enjoy a large part of the world's great poetry, but perhaps some other art, such as painting or music, touches you more deeply. Or you may find in the sciences an austere beauty that moves you as poetry moves another. Should this be your conclusion, you will at least have learned something about one art that is profoundly meaningful to many of your fellows.

But assuming you want to go farther in the understanding and enjoyment of poetry, there are several things you can do. For one, if you find any pleasure at all in writing poetry, keep at it. However doubtful the merits of your verse, you acquire through writing it a sensitivity and sober appreciation for the craft that is difficult to gain in any other way.

Certainly, read poetry aloud a great deal. The ability to read it with some skill is within the reach of almost everyone. Listen to good phonograph recordings by those poets who read well (such as Dylan Thomas) or by good professional poetry-readers. You may find, as many people have, that reading poetry aloud is an acceptable and enjoyable way to spend part of an evening with a small group of friends, particularly if the program is varied and several passable readers take turns.

Beyond this, what? Simply read widely, among the old poets and the new. Don't be hypnotized by critical fashions: they change. John Donne sank almost out of sight; now he is enthroned among the immortals. Milton was under an Eliotesque cloud for several decades; then Eliot blew the cloud away with a puff of breath. If you discover some poorly esteemed poet rewarding, read him. You may eventually exhaust him and come to agree with the critics—but meanwhile he will have spoken to your condition, and your appreciation of poetry will have grown. By the same token, if you find that some highly touted poet baffles or irritates you, feel under no obligation to admire and understand him. Perhaps he is the right poet for you ten years from now, but not now.

If particular poems haunt you, read and reread them. They are the right poems for you. But don't stagnate. If you like only the Moderns, or only the Romantics, or only the Cavaliers, explore other periods once in a while—not grimly, but in an inquisitive spirit.

In any case, if poetry has become a delight to you, none of this advice is needed. You have already found your own way.

Sir Thomas Wyatt (*1503?–1542*)

THEY FLEE FROM ME

They flee from me, that sometime
      did me seek,
With naked foot stalking in my
      chamber.
I have seen them gentle, tame, and
      meek,
That now are wild, and do not
      remember
That sometime they put themselves
      in danger   5
To take bread at my hand; and now
      they range
Busily seeking with a continual
      change.

Thankèd be fortune it hath been
      otherwise
Twenty times better; but once,
      in special,
In thin array, after a pleasant guise,   10
When her loose gown from her
      shoulders did fall,
And she me caught in her arms
      long and small,
Therewithal sweetly did me kiss,
And softly said, Dear heart, how
      like you this?

It was no dream; I lay broad waking: 15
But all is turnèd thorough my
      gentleness
Into a strange fashion of forsaking;
And I have leave to go of her
      goodness,
And she also to use newfangleness.
But since that I so kindely am servèd,   20
How like you this, what hath she
      now deservèd?

Additional

Poems

George Gascoigne (*1542–1577*)

THE LULLABY OF A LOVER

Sing lullaby, as women do,
Wherewith they bring their babes to rest,
And lullaby can I sing too,
As womanly as can the best.
With lullaby they still the child,   5
And if I be not much beguiled,
Full many wanton babes have I,
Which must be stilled with lullaby.

First lullaby my youthful years,
It is now time to go to bed,   10
For crooked age and hoary hairs
Have won the haven within my head:
With lullaby then youth be still,
With lullaby content thy will,
Since courage quails and comes behind,   15
Go sleep, and so beguile thy mind.

Next lullaby my gazing eyes,
Which wonted were to glance apace.
For every glass may now suffice
To show the furrows in my face: 20
With lullaby then wink awhile,
With lullaby your looks beguile:
Let no fair face, nor beauty bright,
Entice you eft with vain delight.

And lullaby my wanton will,   25
Let reason rule, now rein thy thought
Since all too late I find by skill
How dear I have my fancies bought:
With lullaby now take thine ease,
With lullaby thy doubts appease: 30
For trust to this, if thou be still,
My body shall obey thy will.

Eke lullaby my loving boy,
My little Robin take thy rest,
Since age is cold and nothing coy,   35
Keep close thy coign, for so is best:
With lullaby be thou content,

With lullaby thy lusts relent,
Let others pay which hath more pence,
Thou art too poor for such expense.   40

Thus lullaby my youth, mine eyes,
My will, my ware, and all that was,
I can no more delays devise,
But welcome pain, let pleasure pass:
With lullaby now take your leave,   45
With lullaby your dream deceive,
And when you rise with waking eye,
Remember then this lullaby.

Edmund Spenser (*1552?–1599*)

MOST GLORIOUS LORD OF LIFE, THAT ON THIS DAY

Most glorious Lord of life, that on this day,
Didst make Thy triumph over death and sin:
And having harrowed hell, didst bring away
Captivity thence captive us to win:
This joyous day, dear Lord, with joy begin,   5
And grant that we for whom thou diddest die
Being with thy dear blood clean washed from sin,
May live forever in felicity.
And that thy love we weighing worthily,
May likewise love Thee for the same again: 10
And for Thy sake that all like dear didst buy,
With love may one another entertain.
So let us love, dear love, like as we ought,
Love is the lesson which the Lord us taught.

Michael Drayton (*1563–1631*)

SINCE THERE'S NO HELP, COME LET US KISS AND PART

Since there's no help, come let us kiss and part.
Nay, I have done; you get no more of me.

And I am glad, yea glad with all my heart
That thus so cleanly I myself can free.
Shake hands forever, cancel all our vows,   5
And when we meet at any time again
Be it not seen in either of our brows
That we one jot of former love retain;
Now at the last gasp of Love's latest breath,
When his pulse failing, Passion speechless lies, 10
When Faith is kneeling by his bed of Death,
And Innocence is closing up his eyes,
Now if thou would'st, when all have given him over,
From Death to Life, thou might'st him recover.

William Shakespeare (1564–1616)

SONNET 129

The expense of spirit in a waste of shame
Is lust in action, and till action, lust
Is perjured, murderous, bloody, full of blame,
Savage, extreme, rude, cruel, not to trust,
Enjoyed no sooner but despisèd straight,   5
Past reason hunted, and no sooner had,
Past reason hated, as a swallowed bait,
On purpose laid to make the taker mad.
Mad in pursuit, and in possession so,
Had, having, and in quest to have, extreme,   10
A bliss in proof, and proved, a very woe.
Before, a joy proposed, behind, a dream.
All this the world well knows, yet none knows well
To shun the Heaven that leads men to this Hell.

SONNET 130

My mistress' eyes are nothing like the sun,
Coral is far more red than her lips' red.
If snow be white, why then her breasts are dun,
If hairs be wires, black wires grow on her head.
I have seen roses damasked, red and white,   5
But no such roses see I in her cheeks.
And in some perfumes is there more delight

Than in the breath that from my mistress reeks.
I love to hear her speak, yet well I know
That music hath a far more pleasing sound.   10
I grant I never saw a goddess go,
My mistress, when she walks, treads on the ground.
And yet, by Heaven, I think my love as rare
As any she belied with false compare.

SONNET 143

Lo, as a careful housewife runs to catch
One of her feathered creatures broke away,
Sets down her babe, and makes all swift dispatch
In pursuit of the thing she would have stay;
Whilst her neglected child holds her in chase,   5
Cries to catch her whose busy care is bent
To follow that which flies before her face,
Not prizing her poor infant's discontent—
So runn'st thou after that which flies from thee,
Whilst I, thy babe, chase thee afar behind;   10
But if thou catch thy hope, turn back to me
And play the mother's part, kiss me, be kind.
So will I pray that thou mayst have thy Will,
If thou turn back and my loud crying still.

Thomas Campion (*1567–1620*)

CHERRY-RIPE

There is a garden in her face
    Where roses and white lilies grow;
A heavenly paradise is that place,
    Wherein all pleasant fruits do flow.
        There cherries grow which none may buy
        Till "Cherry-ripe" themselves do cry.   5

Those cherries fairly do inclose
    Of orient pearl a double row,
Which when her lovely laughter shows,
    They look like rosebuds filled with snow;   10
        Yet them nor peer nor prince can buy
        Till "Cherry-ripe" themselves do cry.

Her eyes like angels watch them still;
　　　Her brows like bended bows do stand,
Threatening with piercing frowns to kill　　　　　　　　15
　　　　All that attempt with eye or hand
　　　　　　Those sacred cherries to come nigh,
　　　　　　Till "Cherry-ripe" themselves do cry.

John Donne (1572–1631)

HOLY SONNET 7

At the round earth's imagined corners, blow
Your trumpets, angels, and arise, arise
From death, you numberless infinities
Of souls, and to your scattered bodies go;
All whom the flood did, and fire shall o'erthrow;　　　　　5
All whom war, dearth, age, agues, tyrannies,
Despair, law, chance, hath slain, and you whose eyes
Shall behold God, and never taste death's woe.
But let them sleep, Lord, and me mourn a space,
For, if above all these, my sins abound,　　　　　　　　10
'Tis late to ask abundance of Thy grace,
When we are there; here on this lowly ground,
Teach me how to repent; for that's as good
As if Thou hadst sealed my pardon, with Thy blood.

HOLY SONNET 18

Show me, dear Christ, thy spouse so bright and clear.
What! is it she which on the other shore
Goes richly painted? or which, robb'd and tore,
Laments and mourns in Germany and here?
Sleeps she a thousand, then peeps up one year?　　　　　5
Is she self-truth and errs? now new, now outwore?
Doth she, and did she, and shall she evermore
On one, on seven, or on no hill appear?
Dwells she with us, or, like adventuring knights,
First travel we to seek, and then make love?　　　　　　10
Betray, kind husband, thy spouse to our sights,
And let mine amorous soul court thy mild dove,
Who is most true and pleasing to thee then,
When she's embrac'd and open to most men.

A HYMN TO GOD THE FATHER

Wilt Thou forgive that sin where I begun,
    Which was my sin, though it were done before?
Wilt Thou forgive that sin, through which I run,
    And do run still, though still I do deplore?
        When Thou hast done, Thou hast not done,   5
        For I have more.

Wilt Thou forgive that sin which I have won
    Others to sin, and made my sin their door?
Wilt Thou forgive that sin which I did shun
    A year, or two: but wallowed in, a score?   10
        When Thou hast done, Thou hast not done,
        For I have more.

I have a sin of fear, that when I have spun
    My last thread, I shall perish on the shore;
But swear by Thy self, that at my death Thy Son   15
    Shall shine as he shines now, and heretofore;
        And, having done that, Thou hast done;
        I fear no more.

ON HIS MISTRESS

By our first strange and fatal interview,
By all desires which thereof did ensue,
By our long starving hopes, by that remorse
Which my words' masculine persuasive force
Begot in thee, and by the memory   5
Of hurts, which spies and rivals threatened me,
I calmly beg. But by thy father's wrath,
By all pains, which want and divorcement hath,
I conjure thee, and all the oaths which I
And thou have sworn to seal joint constancy,   10
Here I unswear, and overswear them thus:
Thou shalt not love by ways so dangerous.
Temper, O fair love, love's impetuous rage;
Be my true mistress still, not my feigned page.
I'll go, and, by thy kind leave, leave behind   15
Thee, only worthy to nurse in my mind,
Thirst to come back; O! if thou die before,
My soul from other lands to thee shall soar.
Thy (else almighty) beauty cannot move
Rage from the seas, nor thy love teach them love,   20

Nor tame wild Boreas' harshness; thou hast read
How roughly he in pieces shiverèd
Fair Orithea, whom he swore he loved.
Fall ill or good, 'tis madness to have proved
Dangers unurged; feed on this flattery,   25
That absent lovers one in th' other be.
Dissemble nothing, not a boy, nor change
Thy body's habit, nor mind; be not strange
To thyself only. All will spy in thy face
A blushing womanly discovering grace;   30
Richly clothed apes are callèd apes, and as soon
Eclipsed as bright, we call the moon the moon.
Men of France, changeable cameleons,
Spitals of diseases, shops of fashions,
Love's fuellers, and the rightest company   35
Of players, which upon the world's stage be,
Will quickly know thee, and no less, alas!
Th' indifferent Italian, as we pass
His warm land, well content to think thee page,
Will hunt thee with such lust, and hideous rage,   40
As Lot's fair guests were vexed. But none of these,
Nor spongy hydroptic Dutch shall thee displease,
If thou stay here. O stay here, for, for thee,
England is only a worthy gallery,
To walk in expectation, till from thence   45
Our greatest king call thee to his presence.
When I am gone, dream me some happiness;
Nor let thy looks our long-hid love confess;
Nor praise, nor dispraise me, nor bless nor curse
Openly love's force, nor in bed fright thy nurse   50
With midnight's startings, crying out, O! O!
Nurse, O! my love is slain; I saw him go
O'er the white Alps alone; I saw him, I,
Assailed, fight, taken, stabbed, bleed, fall, and die.
Augur me better chance, except dread Jove   55
Think it enough for me to have had thy love.

THE RELIC

When my grave is broke up again
Some second guest to entertain
(For graves have learned that womanhead

To be to more than one a bed)
And he that digs it, spies   5
A bracelet of bright hair about the bone,
Will he not let us alone,
And think that there a loving couple lies,
Who thought that this device might be some way
To make their souls, at the last busy day,   10
Meet at this grave, and make a little stay?

If this fall in a time, or land,
Where misdevotion doth command,
Then he that digs us up will bring
Us to the Bishop and the King,   15
To make us relics; then
Thou shalt be a Mary Magdalen, and I
A something else thereby;
All women shall adore us, and some men;
And since at such time, miracles are sought,   20
I would have that age by this paper taught
What miracles we harmless lovers wrought.

First, we loved well and faithfully,
Yet knew not what we loved, nor why;
Difference of sex no more we knew   25
Than our guardian angels do;
Coming and going, we
Perchance might kiss, but not between those meals;
Our hands ne'er touched the seals
Which nature, injured by late law, sets free: 30
These miracles we did; but now alas,
All measure, and all language, I should pass
Should I tell what a miracle she was.

THE SUN RISING

Busy old fool, unruly Sun,
Why dost thou thus,
Through windows, and through curtains, call on us?
Must to thy motions lovers' seasons run?
Saucy pedantic wretch, go chide   5
Late school-boys and sour prentices,
Go tell court-huntsmen that the King will ride,
Call country ants to harvest offices;

Love, all alike, no season knows nor clime,
Nor hours, days, months, which are the rags of time.   10

Thy beams so reverend and strong
Why shouldst thou think?
I could eclipse and cloud them with a wink,
But that I would not lose her sight so long.
If her eyes have not blinded thine,   15
Look, and tomorrow late tell me,
Whether both th' Indias of spice and mine
Be where thou left'st them, or lie here with me.
Ask for those Kings whom thou saw'st yesterday,
And thou shalt hear, all here in one bed lay.   20

She's all States, and all Princes I;
Nothing else is;
Princes do but play us; compared to this,
All honor's mimic, all wealth alchemy.
Thou, Sun, art half as happy as we,   25
In that the world's contracted thus;
Thine age asks ease, and since thy duties be
To warm the world, that's done in warming us.
Shine here to us, and thou art everywhere;
This bed thy center is, these walls thy sphere.   30

William Browne (1591–1643)

ON THE COUNTESS DOWAGER OF PEMBROKE

Underneath this sable hearse
Lies the subject of all verse:
Sidney's sister, Pembroke's mother;
Death, ere thou hast slain another,
Fair, and learn'd, and good as she,   5
Time shall throw a dart at thee.
Marble piles let no man raise
To her name for after days;
Some kind woman born as she,
Reading this, like Niobe   10
Shall turn marble, and become
Both her mourner and her tomb.

George Herbert (*1593–1633*)

LOVE

Love bade me welcome; yet my soul drew back,
    Guilty of dust and sin.
But quick-eyed Love, observing me grow slack
    From my first entrance in,
Drew nearer to me, sweetly questioning   5
    If I lacked anything.

A guest, I answered, worthy to be here.
    Love said, You shall be he.
I, the unkind, ungrateful? Ah, my dear,
    I cannot look on Thee.   10
Love took my hand, and smiling, did reply,
    Who made the eyes but I?

Truth, Lord, but I have marred them: let my shame
    Go where it doth deserve.
And know you not, says Love, who bore the blame?   15
    My dear, then I will serve.
You must sit down, says Love, and taste my meat:
    So I did sit and eat.

Edmund Waller (*1606–1687*)

OF A FAIR LADY PLAYING WITH A SNAKE

Strange that such horror and such grace
Should dwell together in one place,
A fury's arm, an angel's face.

'Tis innocence and youth which makes
In *Chloris's* fancy such mistakes,   5
To start at love, and play with snakes.

By this and by her coldness barred,
Her servants have a task too hard,
The tyrant has a double guard.

Thrice happy snake, that in her sleeve   10

May boldly creep, we dare not give
Our thoughts so unconfined a leave:

Contented in that nest of snow
He lies, as he his bliss did know,
And to the wood no more would go.   15

Take heed, fair *Eve*, you do not make
Another tempter of this snake,
A marble one so warmed would speak.

John Milton (*1608–1674*)

LYCIDAS

In this Monody the Author bewails a learned
Friend, unfortunately drown'd in his Passage
from *Chester* on the *Irish* Seas, 1637. And by
occasion foretells the ruin of our corrupted
Clergy then in their height.

Yet once more, O ye Laurels, and once more
Ye Myrtles brown, with Ivy never sere,
I come to pluck your Berries harsh and crude,
And with forc'd fingers rude,
Shatter your leaves before the mellowing year.   5
Bitter constraint, and sad occasion dear,
Compels me to disturb your season due:
For *Lycidas* is dead, dead ere his prime,
Young *Lycidas*, and hath not left his peer:
Who would not sing for *Lycidas*? he knew   10
Himself to sing, and build the lofty rhyme.
He must not float upon his wat'ry bier
Unwept, and welter to the parching wind,
Without the meed of some melodious tear.
    Begin then, Sisters of the sacred well,   15
That from beneath the seat of *Jove* doth spring,
Begin, and somewhat loudly sweep the string.
Hence with denial vain, and coy excuse,
So may some gentle Muse
With lucky words favour my destin'd Urn,   20

And as he passes turn,
And bid fair peace be to my sable shroud.
For we were nurst upon the self-same hill,
Fed the same flock, by fountain, shade, and rill.
    Together both, ere the high Lawns appear'd   25
Under the opening eye-lids of the morn,
We drove afield, and both together heard
What time the Gray-fly winds her sultry horn,
Batt'ning our flocks with the fresh dews of night,
Oft till the Star that rose, at Ev'ning, bright   30
Toward Heav'n's descent had slop'd his westering wheel.
Meanwhile the Rural ditties were not mute,
Temper'd to th'Oaten Flute;
Rough *Satyrs* danc'd, and *Fauns* with clov'n heel,
From the glad sound would not be absent long,   35
And old *Damaetas* lov'd to hear our song.
    But O the heavy change, now thou art gone,
Now thou art gone, and never must return!
Thee Shepherd, thee the Woods, and desert Caves,
With wild Thyme and the gadding Vine o'ergrown,   40
And all their echoes mourn.
The Willows and the Hazel Copses green
Shall now no more be seen,
Fanning their joyous Leaves to thy soft lays.
As killing as the Canker to the Rose,   45
Or Taint-worm to the weanling Herds that graze,
Or Frost to Flowers, that their gay wardrobe wear,
When first the White-thorn blows,
Such, *Lycidas*, thy loss to Shepherd's ear.
    Where were ye Nymphs when the remorseless deep   50
Clos'd o'er the head of your lov'd *Lycidas?*
For neither were ye playing on the steep,
Where your old *Bards*, the famous *Druids*, lie,
Nor on the shaggy top of *Mona* high,
Nor yet where *Deva* spreads her wizard stream: 55
Ay me, I fondly dream!
Had ye been there—for what could that have done?
What could the Muse herself that *Orpheus* bore,
The Muse herself, for her enchanting son
Whom Universal nature did lament,   60
When by the rout that made the hideous roar,
His gory visage down the stream was sent,
Down the swift *Hebrus* to the *Lesbian* shore?

Alas! What boots it with uncessant care
To tend the homely slighted Shepherd's trade,   65
And strictly meditate the thankless Muse?
Were it not better done as others use,
To sport with *Amaryllis* in the shade,
Or with the tangles of *Neaera's* hair?
Fame is the spur that the clear spirit doth raise   70
(That last infirmity of Noble mind)
To scorn delights, and live laborious days;
But the fair Guerdon when we hope to find,
And think to burst out into sudden blaze,
Comes the blind *Fury* with th'abhorred shears,   75
And slits the thin-spun life. But not the praise,
Phoebus repli'd, and touch'd my trembling ears;
Fame is no plant that grows on mortal soil,
Nor in the glistering foil
Set off to th'world, nor in broad rumour lies,   80
But lives and spreads aloft by those pure eyes
And perfect witness of all judging *Jove;*
As he pronounces lastly on each deed,
Of so much fame in Heav'n expect thy meed.
        O Fountain *Arethuse,* and thou honour'd flood,   85
Smooth-sliding *Mincius,* crown'd with vocal reeds,
That strain I heard was of a higher mood:
But now my Oat proceeds,
And listens to the Herald of the Sea
That came in *Neptune's* plea.   90
He ask'd the Waves, and ask'd the Felon winds,
What hard mishap hath doom'd this gentle swain?
And question'd every gust of rugged wings
That blows from off each beaked Promontory.
They knew not of his story,   95
And sage *Hippotades* their answer brings,
That not a blast was from his dungeon stray'd,
The Air was calm, and on the level brine,
Sleek *Panope* with all her sisters play'd.
It was that fatal and perfidious Bark   100
Built in th'eclipse, and rigg'd with curses dark,
That sunk so low that sacred head of thine.
        Next *Camus,* reverend Sire, went footing slow,
His Mantle hairy, and his Bonnet sedge,
Inwrought with figures dim, and on the edge   105
Like to that sanguine flower inscrib'd with woe.

Ah! Who hath reft (quoth he) my dearest pledge?
Last came, and last did go,
The Pilot of the *Galilean* lake.
Two massy Keys he bore of metals twain,   110
(The Golden opes, the Iron shuts amain).
He shook his Mitred locks, and stern bespake:
How well could I have spar'd for thee, young swain,
Enough of such as for their bellies' sake,
Creep and intrude and climb into the fold?   115
Of other care they little reck'ning make,
Than how to scramble at the shearers' feast,
And shove away the worthy bidden guest.
Blind mouths! that scarce themselves know how to hold
A Sheep-hook, or have learn'd aught else the least   120
That to the faithful Herdman's art belongs!
What recks it them? What need they? They are sped;
And when they list, their lean and flashy songs
Grate on their scrannel Pipes of wretched straw.
The hungry Sheep look up, and are not fed,   125
But swoln with wind, and the rank mist they draw,
Rot inwardly, and foul contagion spread:
Besides what the grim Wolf with privy paw
Daily devours apace, and nothing said;
But that two-handed engine at the door   130
Stands ready to smite once, and smite no more.
      Return *Alpheus*, the dread voice is past,
That shrunk thy streams; Return *Sicilian* Muse,
And call the Vales, and bid term hither cast
Their Bells and Flourets of a thousand hues.   135
Ye valleys low where the mild whispers use
Of shades and wanton winds and gushing brooks,
On whose fresh lap the swart Star sparely looks,
Throw hither all your quaint enamell'd eyes,
That on the green turf suck the honied showers,   140
And purple all the ground with vernal flowers.
Bring the rather Primrose that forsaken dies,
The tufted Crow-toe, and pale Jessamine,
The white Pink, and the Pansy freakt with jet,
The glowing Violet,   145
The Musk-rose, and the well attir'd Woodbine,
With Cowslips wan that hang the pensive head,
And every flower that sad embroidery wears:
Bid *Amaranthus* all his beauty shed,

And Daffadillies fill their cups with tears,   150
To strew the Laureate Hearse where *Lycid* lies.
For so to interpose a little ease,
Let our frail thoughts dally with false surmise.
Ay me! Whilst thee the shores, and sounding Seas
Wash far away, where'er thy bones are hurl'd,   155
Whether beyond the stormy *Hebrides*,
Where thou perhaps under the whelming tide
Visit'st the bottom of the monstrous world;
Or whether thou to our moist vows denied,
Sleep'st by the fable of *Bellerus* old,   160
Where the great vision of the guarded Mount
Looks toward *Namancos* and *Bayona's* hold;
Look homeward Angel now, and melt with ruth:
And, O ye *Dolphins*, waft the hapless youth.
    Weep no more, woeful Shepherds weep no more,   165
For *Lycidas* your sorrow is not dead,
Sunk though he be beneath the wat'ry floor,
So sinks the day-star in the Ocean bed,
And yet anon repairs his drooping head,
And tricks his beams, and with new spangled Ore,   170
Flames in the forehead of the morning sky:
So *Lycidas*, sunk low, but mounted high,
Through the dear might of him that walk'd the waves,
Where other groves, and other streams along,
With *Nectar* pure his oozy Locks he laves,   175
And hears the unexpressive nuptial Song,
In the blest Kingdoms meek of joy and love.
There entertain him all the Saints above,
In solemn troops, and sweet Societies
That sing, and singing in their glory move,   180
And wipe the tears for ever from his eyes.
Now *Lycidas* the Shepherds weep no more;
Henceforth thou art the Genius of the shore,
In thy large recompense, and shalt be good
To all that wander in that perilous flood.   185
    Thus sang the uncouth Swain to th'Oaks and rills,
While the still morn went out with Sandals gray.
He touch't the tender stops of various Quills,
With eager thought warbling his *Doric* lay:
And now the Sun had stretch't out all the hills,   190
And now was dropt into the Western bay;
At last he rose, and twitch't his Mantle blue:
Tomorrow to fresh Woods, and Pastures new.

William Cartwright (*1611–1643*)

NO PLATONIC LOVE

Tell me no more of minds embracing minds,
    And hearts exchanged for hearts;
That spirits spirits meet, as winds do winds,
    And mix their subtlest parts;
That two unbodied essences may kiss,   5
And then like angels, twist and feel one bliss.

I was that silly thing that once was wrought
    To practice this thin love;
I climbed from sex to soul, from soul to thought;
    But thinking there to move,   10
Headlong I rolled from thought to soul, and then
From soul I lighted at the sex again.

As some strict down-looked men pretend to fast,
    Who yet in closets eat;
So lovers who profess they spirits taste,   15
    Feed yet on grosser meat;
I know they boast they souls to souls convey,
Howe'er they meet, the body is the way.

Come, I will undeceive thee, they that tread
    Those vain aërial ways   20
Are like young heirs and alchemists misled
    To waste their wealth and days,
For searching thus to be forever rich
They only find a medicine for the itch.

Andrew Marvell (*1621–1678*)

TO HIS COY MISTRESS

Had we but world enough, and time,
This coyness, lady, were no crime.
We would sit down, and think which way
To walk, and pass our long love's day.

Thou by the Indian Ganges' side   5
Should'st rubies find: I by the tide
Of Humber would complain. I would
Love you ten years before the Flood,
And you should, if you please, refuse
Till the conversion of the Jews.   10
My vegetable love should grow
Vaster than empires, and more slow.
An hundred years should go to praise
Thine eyes, and on thy forehead gaze:
Two hundred to adore each breast: 15
But thirty thousand to the rest;
An age at least to every part,
And the last age should show your heart.
For, lady, you deserve this state,
Nor would I love at lower rate.   20
     But at my back I always hear
Time's wingèd chariot hurrying near:
And yonder all before us lie
Deserts of vast eternity.
Thy beauty shall no more be found;   25
Nor, in thy marble vault, shall sound
My echoing song: then worms shall try
That long-preserved virginity,
And your quaint honor turn to dust,
And into ashes all my lust.   30
The grave's a fine and private place,
But none, I think, do there embrace.
     Now, therefore, while the youthful hue
Sits on thy skin like morning dew,
And while thy willing soul transpires   35
At every pore with instant fires,
Now let us sport us while we may;
And now, like amorous birds of prey,
Rather at once our Time devour,
Than languish in his slow-chapt power.   40
Let us roll all our strength and all
Our sweetness up into one ball,
And tear our pleasures with rough strife
Through the iron gates of life.
Thus, though we cannot make our sun   45
Stand still, yet we will make him run.

Henry Vaughan (*1622–1695*)

THE WORLD

I saw eternity the other night
Like a great ring of pure and endless light,
    All calm as it was bright;
And round beneath it, time in hours, days, years,
      Driv'n by the spheres,   5
Like a vast shadow moved, in which the world
    And all her train were hurled:
The doting lover in his quaintest strain
      Did there complain;
Near him his lute, his fancy, and his flights,   10
      Wit's sour delights,
With gloves and knots, the silly snares of pleasure,
      Yet his dear treasure,
All scattered lay, while he his eyes did pore
      Upon a flower.   15

The darksome statesman, hung with weights and woe,
Like a thick midnight fog moved there so slow
    He did not stay, nor go;
Condemning thoughts, like sad eclipses, scowl
      Upon his soul,   20
And clouds of crying witnesses without
    Pursued him with one shout;
Yet digged the mole, and lest his ways be found
      Worked underground,
Where he did clutch his prey, but One did see   25
      That policy;
Churches and altars fed him; perjuries
      Were gnats and flies;
It rained about him blood and tears, but he
      Drank them as free.   30

The fearful miser on a heap of rust
Sat pining all his life there, did scarce trust
    His own hands with the dust,
Yet would not place one piece above, but lives
      In fear of thieves.   35
Thousands there were as frantic as himself,

And hugged each one his pelf:
The downright epicure placed heav'n in sense,
    And scorned pretense;
While others, slipped into a wide excess,   40
    Said little less;
The weaker sort slight trivial wares enslave,
    Who think them brave;
And poor despisèd truth sat counting by
    Their victory.   45

Yet some, who all this while did weep and sing,
And sing and weep, soared up into the ring;
    But most would use no wing.
O fools, said I, thus to prefer dark night
    Before true light,   50
To live in grots and caves, and hate the day
    Because it shows the way,
The way which from this dead and dark abode
    Leads up to God,
A way where you might tread the sun, and be   55
    More bright than he.
But as I did their madness so discuss,
    One whispered thus:
This ring the bridegroom did for none provide
    But for his bride.   60

John Dryden (1631–1700)

A SONG FOR SAINT CECILIA'S DAY
NOVEMBER 22, 1687

From harmony, from heavenly harmony
    This universal frame began;
    When Nature underneath a heap
      Of jarring atoms lay,
    And could not heave her head,   5
The tuneful voice was heard from high,
    Arise, ye more than dead.
Then cold and hot and moist and dry
    In order to their stations leap,
    And Music's power obey.   10

From harmony, from heavenly harmony
  This universal frame began;
  From harmony to harmony
Through all the compass of the notes it ran,
The diapason closing full in Man.   15

What passion cannot Music raise and quell?
  When Jubal struck the corded shell,
 His listening brethren stood around,
  And, wondering, on their faces fell
 To worship that celestial sound.   20
Less than a god they thought there could not dwell
 Within the hollow of that shell,
 That spoke so sweetly, and so well.
What passion cannot Music raise and quell?

  The trumpet's loud clangor   25
   Excites us to arms
  With shrill notes of anger
   And mortal alarms.
  The double, double, double beat
   Of the thundering drum   30
   Cries, "Hark! the foes come;
Charge, charge, 'tis too late to retreat!"

  The soft complaining flute
  In dying notes discovers
  The woes of hopeless lovers,   35
Whose dirge is whispered by the warbling lute.

  Sharp violins proclaim
Their jealous pangs and desperation,
Fury, frantic indignation,
Depth of pains and height of passion,   40
  For the fair, disdainful dame.

 But, oh! what art can teach,
 What human voice can reach
  The sacred organ's praise?
 Notes inspiring holy love,   45
Notes that wing their heavenly ways
 To mend the choirs above.

Orpheus could lead the savage race,
And trees unrooted left their place,
  Sequacious of the lyre;   50
But bright Cecilia raised the wonder higher;

When to her organ vocal breath was given,
An angel heard, and straight appeared,
    Mistaking earth for heaven.

As from the power of sacred lays   55
    The spheres began to move,
And sung the great Creator's praise
    To all the blest above;
So when the last and dreadful hour
This crumbling pageant shall devour,   60
The trumpet shall be heard on high,
The dead shall live, the living die,
And Music shall untune the sky.

John Wilmot, Earl of Rochester (1647–1680)

THE MAIMED DEBAUCHEE

As some brave Admiral, in former war
    Deprived of force, but pressed with courage still,
Two rival fleets appearing from afar,
    Crawls to the top of an adjacent hill;

From whence (with thoughts full of concern) he views   5
    The wise and daring conduct of the fight:
And each bold action to his mind renews
    His present glory, and his past delight.

From his fierce eyes flashes of rage he throws,
    As from black clouds when lightning breaks away,   10
Transported thinks himself amidst his foes,
    And absent, yet enjoys the bloody day.

So when my days of impotence approach,
    And I'm by love and wine's unlucky chance
Driven from the pleasing billows of debauch,   15
    On the dull shore of lazy temperance;

My pains at last some respite shall afford,
    While I behold the battles you maintain:
When fleets of glasses sail around the board,
    From whose broadsides volleys of wit shall rain.   20

Nor shall the sight of honorable scars,
    Which my too forward valor did procure,
Frighten new-listed soldiers from the wars;
    Past joys have more than paid what I endure.

Should some brave youth (worth being drunk) prove nice   25
    And from his fair inviter meanly shrink,
'Twould please the ghost of my departed vice,
    If, at my counsel, he repent and drink.

Or should some cold-complexioned sot forbid,
    With his dull morals, our night's brisk alarms,   30
I'll fire his blood, by telling what I did
    When I was strong, and able to bear arms.

I'll tell of whores attacked, their lords at home,
    Bawd's quarters beaten up, and fortress won,
Windows demolished, watches overcome,   35
    And handsome ills by my contrivance done.

With tales like these I will such heat inspire
    As to important mischief shall incline;
I'll make him long some ancient church to fire,
    And fear no lewdness they're called to by wine.   40

Thus statesmanlike I'll saucily impose,
    And safe from danger, valiantly advise;
Sheltered in impotence, urge you to blows,
    And being good for nothing else, be wise.

Alexander Pope (*1688–1744*)

ODE ON SOLITUDE

Happy the man, whose wish and care
    A few paternal acres bound,
Content to breathe his native air,
        In his own ground.

Whose herds with milk, whose fields with bread,   5
    Whose flocks supply him with attire,
Whose trees in summer yield him shade,
        In winter fire.

Blest, who can unconcernedly find
    Hours, days, and years slide soft away,   10
In health of body, peace of mind,
        Quiet by day,

Sound sleep by night; study and ease,
    Together mixed; sweet recreation;
And innocence, which most does please   15
        With meditation.

Thus let me live, unseen, unknown,
    Thus unlamented let me die,
Steal from the world, and not a stone
        Tell where I lie.   20

Thomas Gray (1716–1771)

ODE ON THE DEATH OF A FAVOURITE CAT
DROWNED IN A TUB OF GOLD FISHES

'Twas on a lofty vase's side,
Where China's gayest art had dy'd
    The azure flowers, that blow;
Demurest of the tabby kind,
The pensive Selima, reclin'd,   5
    Gaz'd on the lake below.

Her conscious tail her joy declar'd;
The fair round face, the snowy beard,
    The velvet of her paws,
Her coat, that with the tortoise vies,   10
Her ears of jet, and emerald eyes,
    She saw; and purr'd applause.

Still had she gaz'd; but 'midst the tide
Two angel forms were seen to glide,
    The Genii of the stream: 15
Their scaly armour's Tyrian hue
Through richest purple to the view
    Betray'd a golden gleam.

The hapless nymph with wonder saw:
A whisker first, and then a claw,   20

With many an ardent wish,
She stretch'd, in vain, to reach the prize.
What female heart can gold despise?
    What Cat's averse to fish?

Presumptuous maid! with looks intent   25
Again she stretch'd, again she bent,
    Nor knew the gulf between.
(Malignant Fate sat by, and smil'd)
The slipp'ry verge her feet beguil'd,
    She tumbled headlong in.   30

Eight times emerging from the flood
She mew'd to ev'ry wat'ry God,
    Some speedy aid to send.
No Dolphin came, no Nereid stirr'd:
Nor cruel Tom, nor Susan heard.   35
    A fav'rite has no friend!

From hence, ye beauties, undeceiv'd,
Know, one false step is ne'er retriev'd,
    And be with caution bold.
Not all that tempts your wand'ring eyes   40
And heedless hearts is lawful prize,
    Nor all, that glisters, gold.

William Cowper (*1731–1800*)

LINES WRITTEN UNDER THE INFLUENCE
OF DELIRIUM

Hatred and vengeance, my eternal portion,
Scarce can endure delay of execution,
Wait with impatient readiness to seize my
    Soul in a moment.

Damned below Judas; more abhorred that he was,   5
Who for a few pence sold his holy Master!
Twice-betrayed Jesus me, the last delinquent,
    Deems the profanest.

Man disavows, and Deity disowns me,
Hell might afford my miseries a shelter;   10

Therefore Hell keeps her ever-hungry mouths all
    Bolted against me.

Hard lot! encompassed with a thousand dangers;
Weary, faint, trembling with a thousand terrors,
I'm called, if vanquished, to receive a sentence   15
    Worse than Abiram's.

Him the vindictive rod of angry justice
Sent quick and howling to the centre headlong;
I, fed with judgment, in a fleshy tomb, am
    Buried above ground.   20

William Blake (*1757–1827*)

THE ECHOING GREEN

The Sun does arise,
And make happy the skies;
The merry bells ring
To welcome the Spring;
The skylark and thrush,   5
The birds of the bush,
Sing louder around
To the bells' cheerful sound,
While our sports shall be seen
On the Echoing Green.   10

Old John, with white hair,
Does laugh away care,
Sitting under the oak,
Among the old folk.
They laugh at our play,   15
And soon they all say:
"Such, such were the joys
When we all, girls and boys,
In our youth time were seen
On the Echoing Green."   20

Till the little ones, weary,
No more can be merry;
The sun does descend,
And our sports have an end.
Round the laps of their mothers   25

Many sisters and brothers,
Like birds in their nest,
Are ready for rest,
And sport no more seen
On the darkening Green.   30

THE TIGER

Tiger! Tiger! burning bright
In the forests of the night,
What immortal hand or eye
Could frame thy fearful symmetry?

In what distant deeps or skies   5
Burnt the fire of thine eyes?
On what wings dare he aspire?
What the hand dare seize the fire?

And what shoulder, and what art,
Could twist the sinews of thy heart?   10
And when thy heart began to beat,
What dread hand? and what dread feet?

What the hammer? what the chain?
In what furnace was thy brain?
What the anvil? what dread grasp   15
Dare its deadly terrors clasp?

When the stars threw down their spears,
And watered heaven with their tears,
Did he smile his work to see?
Did he who made the Lamb make thee?   20

Tiger! Tiger! burning bright
In the forests of the night,
What immortal hand or eye,
Dare frame thy fearful symmetry?

Robert Burns (*1759–1796*)

SONG From THE JOLLY BEGGARS
[TUNE: *Sodger Laddie*]

I once was a maid, though I cannot tell when,
And still my delight is in proper young men;

Some one of a troop of dragoons was my daddie,
No wonder I'm fond of a sodger laddie.
     Sing, Lal de dal, &c.   5

The first of my loves was a swaggering blade,
To rattle the thundering drum was his trade;
His leg was so tight, and his cheek was so ruddy,
Transported I was with my sodger laddie.

But the godly old chaplain left him in the lurch;   10
The sword I forsook for the sake of the church;
He ventured the soul, and I risked the body,—
'Twas then I proved false to my sodger laddie.

Full soon I grew sick of my sanctified sot,
The regiment at large for a husband I got;   15
From the gilded spontoon to the fife I was ready,
I asked no more but a sodger laddie.

But the peace it reduced me to beg in despair,
Till I met my old boy at a Cunningham fair;
His rags regimental they fluttered so gaudy: 20
My heart it rejoiced at a sodger laddie.

And now I have lived—I know not how long,
And still I can join in a cup or a song;
But whilst with both hands I can hold the glass steady,
Here's to thee, my hero, my sodger laddie!   25

William Wordsworth (1770–1850)

ANDREW JONES

I hate that Andrew Jones: he'll breed
His children up to waste and pillage:
I wish the press-gang or the drum
Would, with its rattling music, come—
And sweep him from the village.   5

I said not this, because he loves
Through the long day to swear and tipple;
But for the poor dear sake of one
To whom a foul deed he had done,
A friendless man, a travelling Cripple.   10

For this poor crawling helpless wretch
Some Horseman, who was passing by,
A penny on the ground had thrown;
But the poor Cripple was alone
And could not stoop—no help was nigh.   15

Inch-thick the dust lay on the ground
For it had long been droughty weather:
So with his staff the Cripple wrought
Among the dust till he had brought
The halfpennies together.   20

It chanced that Andrew passed that way
Just at the time; and there he found
The Cripple in the mid-day heat
Standing alone, and at his feet
He saw the penny on the ground.   25

He stooped and took the penny up:
And when the Cripple nearer drew,
Quoth Andrew, "*Under half-a-crown,*
What a man finds is all his own;
And so, my Friend, good day to you."   30

And *hence* I say, that Andrew's boys
Will all be trained to waste and pillage;
And wished the press-gang, or the drum
Would, with its rattling music, come—
And sweep him from the village.   35

THE SOLITARY REAPER

Behold her, single in the field,
Yon solitary highland lass!
Reaping and singing by herself;
Stop here, or gently pass!
Alone she cuts and binds the grain,   5
And sings a melancholy strain;
O listen! for the vale profound
Is overflowing with the sound.

No nightingale did ever chaunt
More welcome notes to weary bands   10
Of travelers in some shady haunt,
Among Arabian sands:
A voice so thrilling ne'er was heard

In spring-time from the cuckoo-bird,
Breaking the silence of the seas   15
Among the farthest Hebrides.

Will no one tell me what she sings?—
Perhaps the plaintive numbers flow
For old, unhappy, far-off things,
And battles long ago: 20
Or is it some more humble lay,
Familiar matter of today?
Some natural sorrow, loss, or pain,
That has been, and may be again?

Whate'er the theme, the maiden sang   25
As if her song could have no ending;
I saw her singing at her work,
And o'er the sickle bending;—
I listened, motionless and still;
And, as I mounted up the hill   30
The music in my heart I bore,
Long after it was heard no more.

Samuel Taylor Coleridge (*1772–1834*)

KUBLA KHAN

In Xanadu did Kubla Khan
A stately pleasure-dome decree:
Where Alph, the sacred river, ran
Through caverns measureless to man
    Down to a sunless sea.   5
So twice five miles of fertile ground
With walls and towers were girdled round:
And there were gardens bright with sinuous rills,
Where blossomed many an incense-bearing tree;
And here were forests ancient as the hills,   10
Enfolding sunny spots of greenery.

But oh! that deep romantic chasm which slanted
Down the green hill athwart a cedarn cover!

A savage place! as holy and enchanted
As e'er beneath a waning moon was haunted   15
By woman wailing for her demon-lover!
And from this chasm, with ceaseless turmoil seething,
As if this earth in fast thick pants were breathing,
A mighty fountain momently was forced:
Amid whose swift half-intermitted burst   20
Huge fragments vaulted like rebounding hail,
Or chaffy grain beneath the thresher's flail:
And 'mid these dancing rocks at once and ever
It flung up momently the sacred river.
Five miles meandering with a mazy motion   25
Through wood and dale the sacred river ran,
Then reached the caverns measureless to man,
And sank in tumult to a lifeless ocean:
And 'mid this tumult Kubla heard from far
Ancestral voices prophesying war!   30
    The shadow of the dome of pleasure
        Floated midway on the waves;
    Where was heard the mingled measure
        From the fountain and the caves.
It was a miracle of rare device,   35
A sunny pleasure-dome with caves of ice!

    A damsel with a dulcimer
    In a vision once I saw:
    It was an Abyssinian maid,
    And on her dulcimer she played,   40
    Singing of Mount Abora.
    Could I revive within me
        Her symphony and song,
        To such a deep delight 'twould win me,
That with music loud and long,   45
I would build that dome in air,
That sunny dome! those caves of ice!
And all who heard should see them there,
And all should cry, Beware! Beware!
His flashing eyes, his floating hair!   50
Weave a circle round him thrice,
And close your eyes with holy dread,
For he on honey-dew hath fed,
And drunk the milk of Paradise.

George Gordon, Lord Byron (*1788–1824*)

THE DESTRUCTION OF SENNACHERIB

The Assyrian came down like the wolf on the fold,
And his cohorts were gleaming in purple and gold;
And the sheen of their spears was like stars on the sea,
When the blue wave rolls nightly on deep Galilee.

Like the leaves of the forest when Summer is green,   5
That host with their banners at sunset were seen:
Like the leaves of the forest when Autumn hath blown,
That host on the morrow lay withered and strown.

For the Angel of Death spread his wings on the blast,
And breathed in the face of the foe as he passed;   10
And the eyes of the sleepers waxed deadly and chill,
And their hearts but once heaved—and for ever grew still!

And there lay the steed with his nostril all wide,
But through it there rolled not the breath of his pride;
And the foam of his gasping lay white on the turf,   15
And cold as the spray of the rock-beating surf.

And there lay the rider distorted and pale,
With the dew on his brow, and the rust on his mail:
And the tents were all silent—the banners alone—
The lances unlifted—the trumpet unblown.   20

And the widows of Ashur are loud in their wail,
And the idols are broke in the temple of Baal;
And the might of the Gentile, unsmote by the sword,
Hath melted like snow in the glance of the Lord!

WHEN A MAN HATH NO FREEDOM
TO FIGHT FOR AT HOME

When a man hath no freedom to fight for at home,
    Let him combat for that of his neighbors;
Let him think of the glories of Greece and of Rome,
    And get knocked on the head for his labors.

To do good to Mankind is the chivalrous plan,   5
    And is always as nobly requited;
Then battle for Freedom wherever you can,
    And, if not shot or hanged, you'll get knighted.

Percy Bysshe Shelley (*1792–1822*)

ODE TO THE WEST WIND

I

O wild West Wind, thou breath of Autumn's being,
Thou, from whose unseen presence the leaves dead
Are driven, like ghosts from an enchanter fleeing,

Yellow, and black, and pale, and hectic red,
Pestilence-stricken multitudes: O thou,   5
Who chariotest to their dark wintry bed

The wingèd seeds, where they lie cold and low,
Each like a corpse within its grave, until
Thine azure sister of the spring shall blow

Her clarion o'er the dreaming earth, and fill   10
(Driving sweet buds like flocks to feed in air)
With living hues and odours plain and hill;

Wild Spirit, which art moving everywhere;
Destroyer and preserver; hear, Oh hear!

II

Thou on whose stream, 'mid the steep sky's commotion,   15
Loose clouds like earth's decaying leaves are shed,
Shook from the tangled boughs of heaven and ocean,

Angels of rain and lightning: there are spread
On the blue surface of thine airy surge,
Like the bright hair uplifted from the head   20

Of some fierce Mænad, even from the dim verge
Of the horizon to the zenith's height,
The locks of the approaching storm. Thou dirge

Of the dying year, to which this closing night
Will be the dome of a vast sepulchre,   25
Vaulted with all thy congregated might

Of vapours, from whose solid atmosphere
Black rain, and fire, and hail will burst: Oh hear!

III

Thou who didst waken from his summer dreams
The blue Mediterranean, where he lay,   30
Lulled by the coil of his crystalline streams,

188

Beside a pumice isle in Baiæ's bay,
And saw in sleep old palaces and towers
Quivering within the wave's intenser day,

All overgrown with azure moss and flowers   35
So sweet, the sense faints picturing them! Thou
For whose path the Atlantic's level powers

Cleave themselves into chasms, while far below
The sea-blooms and the oozy woods which wear
The sapless foliage of the ocean, know   40

Thy voice, and suddenly grow gray with fear,
And tremble and despoil themselves: Oh hear!

IV

If I were a dead leaf thou mightest bear;
If I were a swift cloud to fly with thee;
A wave to pant beneath thy power, and share   45

The impulse of thy strength, only less free
Than thou, O uncontrollable! If even
I were as in my boyhood, and could be

The comrade of thy wanderings over heaven,
As then, when to outstrip thy skiey speed   50
Scarce seemed a vision; I would ne'er have striven

As thus with thee in prayer in my sore need.
Oh! lift me as a wave, a leaf, a cloud!
I fall upon the thorns of life! I bleed!

A heavy weight of hours has chained and bowed   55
One too like thee; tameless, and swift, and proud.

V

Make me thy lyre, even as the forest is:
What if my leaves are falling like its own!
The tumult of thy mighty harmonies

Will take from both a deep, autumnal tone,   60
Sweet though in sadness. Be thou, spirit fierce,
My spirit! Be thou me, impetuous one!

Drive my dead thoughts over the universe
Like withered leaves to quicken a new birth!
And, by the incantation of this verse,   65

Scatter, as from an unextinguished hearth
Ashes and sparks, my words among mankind!
Be through my lips to unawakened earth

The trumpet of a prophecy! O, wind,
If Winter comes, can Spring be far behind?   70

John Keats (*1795–1821*)

ODE ON A GRECIAN URN

Thou still unravished bride of quietness,
          Thou foster-child of silence and slow time,
Sylvan historian, who canst thus express
          A flowery tale more sweetly than our rhyme:
What leaf-fringed legend haunts about thy shape   5
          Of deities or mortals, or of both,
                    In Tempe or the dales of Arcady?
          What men or gods are these? What maidens loth?
          What mad pursuit? What struggle to escape?
                    What pipes and timbrels? What wild ecstasy?   10

Heard melodies are sweet, but those unheard
          Are sweeter; therefore, ye soft pipes, play on;
Not to the sensual ear, but, more endeared,
          Pipe to the spirit ditties of no tone:
Fair youth, beneath the trees, thou canst not leave   15
          Thy song, nor ever can those trees be bare;
                    Bold Lover, never, never canst thou kiss,
Though winning near the goal—yet, do not grieve;
          She cannot fade, though thou hast not thy bliss,
                    For ever wilt thou love, and she be fair!   20

Ah, happy, happy boughs! that cannot shed
          Your leaves, nor ever bid the Spring adieu;
And, happy melodist, unwearièd,
          For ever piping songs for ever new;
More happy love! more happy, happy love!   25
          For ever warm and still to be enjoyed,
                    For ever panting, and for ever young;
All breathing human passion far above,

That leaves a heart high-sorrowful and cloyed,
    A burning forehead, and a parching tongue.   30

Who are these coming to the sacrifice?
    To what green altar, O mysterious priest,
Lead'st thou that heifer lowing at the skies,
    And all her silken flanks with garlands drest?
What little town by river or sea shore,   35
    Or mountain-built with peaceful citadel,
        Is emptied of this folk, this pious morn?
And, little town, thy streets for evermore
    Will silent be; and not a soul to tell
        Why thou art desolate, can e'er return.   40

O Attic shape! Fair attitude! with brede
    Of marble men and maidens overwrought,
With forest branches and the trodden weed;
    Thou, silent form, dost tease us out of thought
As doth eternity: Cold Pastoral!   45
    When old age shall this generation waste,
        Thou shalt remain, in midst of other woe
Than ours, a friend to man, to whom thou say'st,
    "Beauty is truth, truth beauty,"—that is all
        Ye know on earth, and all ye need to know.   50

Ralph Waldo Emerson (*1803–1882*)

THE TITMOUSE

You shall not be overbold
When you deal with arctic cold,
As late I found my lukewarm blood
Chilled wading in the snow-choked wood.
How should I fight? my foeman fine   5
Has million arms to one of mine:
East, west, for aid I looked in vain,
East, west, north, south, are his domain.
Miles off, three dangerous miles, is home;
Must borrow his winds who there would come.   10
Up and away for life! be fleet!—
The frost-king ties my fumbling feet,

Sings in my ears, my hands are stones,
Curdles the blood to the marble bones,
Tugs at the heart-strings, numbs the sense,   15
And hems in life with narrowing fence.
Well, in this broad bed lie and sleep,—
The punctual stars will vigil keep,—
Embalmed by purifying cold;
The winds shall sing their dead-march old,   20
The snow is no ignoble shroud,
The moon thy mourner, and the cloud.

    Softly,—but this way fate was pointing,
'T was coming fast to such anointing,
When piped a tiny voice hard by,   25
Gay and polite, a cheerful cry,
Chic-chic-a-dee-dee! saucy note
Out of sound heart and merry throat,
As if it said, "Good day, good sir!
Fine afternoon, old passenger!   30
Happy to meet you in these places,
Where January brings few faces."

    This poet, though he live apart,
Moved by his hospitable heart,
Sped, when I passed his sylvan fort,   35
To do the honors of his court,
As fits a feathered lord of land;
Flew near, with soft wing grazed my hand,
Hopped on the bough, then, darting low,
Prints his small impress on the snow,   40
Shows feats of his gymnastic play,
Head downward, clinging to the spray.

    Here was this atom in full breath,
Hurling defiance at vast death;
This scrap of valor just for play   45
Fronts the north-wind in waistcoat gray,
As if to shame my weak behavior;
I greeted loud my little savior,
"You pet! what dost here? and what for?
In these woods, thy small Labrador,   50
At this pinch, wee San Salvador!
What fire burns in that little chest
So frolic, stout and self-possest?
Henceforth I wear no stripe but thine;
Ashes and jet all hues outshine.   55

Why are not diamonds black and gray,
To ape thy dare-devil array?
And I affirm, the spacious North
Exists to draw thy virtue forth.
I think no virtue goes with size;   60
The reason of all cowardice
Is, that men are overgrown,
And, to be valiant, must come down
To the titmouse dimension."

 'T is good will makes intelligence, 65
And I began to catch the sense
Of my bird's song: "Live out of doors
In the great woods, on prairie floors.
I dine in the sun; when he sinks in the sea,
I too have a hole in a hollow tree;   70
And I like less when Summer beats
With stifling beams on these retreats,
Than noontide twilights which snow makes
With tempest of the blinding flakes.
For well the soul, if stout within,   75
Can arm impregnably the skin;
And polar frost my frame defied,
Made of the air that blows outside."

 With glad remembrance of my debt,
I homeward turn; farewell, my pet! 80
When here again thy pilgrim comes,
He shall bring store of seeds and crumbs.
Doubt not, so long as earth has bread,
Thou first and foremost shalt be fed;
The Providence that is most large 85
Takes hearts like thine in special charge,
Helps who for their own need are strong,
And the sky doats on cheerful song.
Henceforth I prize thy wiry chant
O'er all that mass and minster vaunt; 90
For men mis-hear thy call in Spring,
As 't would accost some frivolous wing,
Crying out of the hazel copse, *Phe-be!*
And, in winter, *Chic-a-dee-dee!*
I think old Cæsar must have heard 95
In northern Gaul my dauntless bird,
And, echoed in some frosty wold,
Borrowed thy battle-numbers bold.

And I will write our annals new,
And thank thee for a better clew,   100
I, who dreamed not when I came here
To find the antidote of fear,
Now hear thee say in Roman key,
Pæan! Veni, vidi, vici.

Henry Wadsworth Longfellow (*1807–1882*)

THE GALAXY

Torrent of light and river of the air,
Along whose bed the glimmering stars are seen
Like gold and silver sands in some ravine
Where mountain streams have left their channels bare!
The Spaniard sees in thee the pathway, where   5
His patron saint descended in the sheen
Of his celestial armor, on serene
And quiet nights, when all the heavens were fair.
Not this I see, nor yet the ancient fable
Of Phaeton's wild course, that scorched the skies   10
Where'er the hoofs of his hot coursers trod;
But the white drift of worlds o'er chasms of sable,
The star-dust, this is whirled aloft and flies
From the invisible chariot-wheels of God.

Alfred, Lord Tennyson (*1809–1892*)

ULYSSES

It little profits that an idle king,
By this still hearth, among these barren crags,
Match'd with an aged wife, I mete and dole
Unequal laws unto a savage race,
That hoard, and sleep, and feed, and know not me.   5
I cannot rest from travel: I will drink
Life to the lees: all times I have enjoy'd

Greatly, have suffer'd greatly, both with those
That loved me, and alone; on shore, and when
Thro' scudding drifts the rainy Hyades   10
Vext the dim sea: I am become a name;
For always roaming with a hungry heart
Much have I seen and known: cities of men,
And manners, climates, councils, governments,
Myself not least, but honour'd of them all;   15
And drunk delight of battle with my peers,
Far on the ringing plains of windy Troy.
I am a part of all that I have met;
Yet all experience is an arch wherethro'
Gleams that untravell'd world, whose margin fades   20
For ever and for ever when I move.
How dull it is to pause, to make an end,
To rust unburnish'd, not to shine in use!
As tho' to breathe were life. Life piled on life
Were all too little, and of one to me   25
Little remains: but every hour is saved
From that eternal silence, something more,
A bringer of new things; and vile it were
For some three suns to store and hoard myself,
And this gray spirit yearning in desire   30
To follow knowledge like a sinking star,
Beyond the utmost bound of human thought.
      This is my son, mine own Telemachus,
To whom I leave the sceptre and the isle—
Well-loved of me, discerning to fulfil   35
This labour, by slow prudence to make mild
A rugged people, and thro' soft degrees
Subdue them to the useful and the good.
Most blameless is he, centred in the sphere
Of common duties, decent not to fail   40
In offices of tenderness, and pay
Meet adoration to my household gods,
When I am gone. He works his work, I mine.
      There lies the port; the vessel puffs her sail:
There gloom the dark broad seas. My mariners,   45
Souls that have toil'd, and wrought, and thought with me—
That ever with a frolic welcome took
The thunder and the sunshine, and opposed
Free hearts, free foreheads—you and I are old;
Old age hath yet his honour and his toil;   50
Death closes all: but something ere the end,

Some work of noble note, may yet be done,
Not unbecoming men that strove with Gods.
The lights begin to twinkle from the rocks:
The long day wanes: the slow moon climbs: the deep   55
Moans round with many voices. Come, my friends,
'Tis not too late to seek a newer world.
Push off, and sitting well in order smite
The sounding furrows; for my purpose holds
To sail beyond the sunset, and the baths   60
Of all the western stars, until I die.
It may be that the gulfs will wash us down:
It may be we shall touch the Happy Isles,
And see the great Achilles, whom we knew.
Tho' much is taken, much abides; and tho'   65
We are not now that strength which in old days
Moved earth and heaven; that which we are, we are;
One equal temper of heroic hearts,
Made weak by time and fate, but strong in will
To strive, to seek, to find, and not to yield.   70

Robert Browning (*1812–1889*)

ANDREA DEL SARTO
(CALLED "THE FAULTLESS PAINTER")

But do not let us quarrel any more,
No, my Lucrezia; bear with me for once:
Sit down and all shall happen as you wish.
You turn your face, but does it bring your heart?
I'll work then for your friend's friend, never fear,   5
Treat his own subject after his own way,
Fix his own time, accept too his own price,
And shut the money into this small hand
When next it takes mine. Will it? tenderly?
Oh, I'll content him,—but to-morrow, Love!   10
I often am much wearier than you think,
This evening more than usual, and it seems
As if—forgive now—should you let me sit
Here by the window with your hand in mine
And look a half-hour forth on Fiesole,   15

Both of one mind, as married people use,
Quietly, quietly the evening through,
I might get up to-morrow to my work
Cheerful and fresh as ever. Let us try.
To-morrow, how you shall be glad for this!   20
Your soft hand is a woman of itself,
And mine the man's bared breast she curls inside.
Don't count the time lost, neither; you must serve
For each of the five pictures we require:
It saves a model. So! keep looking so—   25
My serpentining beauty, rounds on rounds!
—How could you ever prick those perfect ears,
Even to put the pearl there! oh, so sweet—
My face, my moon, my everybody's moon,
Which everybody looks on and calls his,   30
And, I suppose, is looked on by in turn,
While she looks—no one's: very dear, no less.
You smile? why, there's my picture ready made,
There's what we painters call our harmony!
A common greyness silvers everything,—   35
All in a twilight, you and I alike
—You, at the point of your first pride in me
(That's gone you know),—but I, at every point;
My youth, my hope, my art, being all toned down
To yonder sober pleasant Fiesole.   40
There's the bell clinking from the chapel-top;
That length of convent-wall across the way
Holds the trees safer, huddled more inside;
The last monk leaves the garden; days decrease,
And autumn grows, autumn in everything.   45
Eh? the whole seems to fall into a shape
As if I saw alike my work and self
And all that I was born to be and do,
A twilight-piece. Love, we are in God's hand.
How strange now, looks the life he makes us lead;   50
So free we seem, so fettered fast we are!
I feel he laid the fetter: let it lie!
This chamber for example—turn your head—
All that's behind us! You don't understand
Nor care to understand about my art,   55
But you can hear at least when people speak:
And that cartoon, the second from the door
—It is the thing, Love! so such things should be—
Behold Madonna!—I am bold to say.

I can do with my pencil what I know,   60
What I see, what at bottom of my heart
I wish for, if I ever wish so deep—
Do easily, too—what I say, perfectly,
I do not boast, perhaps: yourself are judge,
Who listened to the Legate's talk last week,   65
And just as much they used to say in France.
At any rate 't is easy, all of it!
No sketches first, no studies, that's long past:
I do what many dream of, all their lives,
—Dream? strive to do, and agonize to do,   70
And fail in doing. I could count twenty such
On twice your fingers, and not leave this town,
Who strive—you don't know how the others strive
To paint a little thing like that you smeared
Carelessly passing with your robes afloat,—   75
Yet do much less, so much less, Someone says,
(I know his name, no matter)—so much less!
Well, less is more, Lucrezia: I am judged.
There burns a truer light of God in them,
In their vexed beating stuffed and stopped-up brain,   80
Heart, or whate'er else, than goes on to prompt
This low-pulsed forthright craftsman's hand of mine.
Their works drop groundward, but themselves, I know,
Reach many a time a heaven that's shut to me,
Enter and take their place there sure enough,   85
Though they come back and cannot tell the world.
My works are nearer heaven, but I sit here.
The sudden blood of these men! at a word—
Praise them, it boils, or blame them, it boils too.
I, painting from myself and to myself,   90
Know what I do, am unmoved by men's blame
Or their praise either. Somebody remarks
Morello's outline there is wrongly traced,
His hue mistaken; what of that? or else,
Rightly traced and well ordered; what of that?   95
Speak as they please, what does the mountain care?
Ah, but a man's reach should exceed his grasp,
Or what's a heaven for? All is silver-grey
Placid and perfect with my art: the worse!
I know both what I want and what might gain,   100
And yet how profitless to know, to sigh
"Had I been two, another and myself,
"Our head would have o'erlooked the world!" No doubt.

Yonder's a work now, of that famous youth
The Urbinate who died five years ago. 105
('T is copied, George Vasari sent it me.)
Well, I can fancy how he did it all,
Pouring his soul, with kings and popes to see,
Reaching, that heaven might so replenish him,
Above and through his art—for it gives way; 110
That arm is wrongly put—and there again—
A fault to pardon in the drawing's lines,
Its body, so to speak: its soul is right,
He means right—that, a child may understand.
Still, what an arm! and I could alter it: 115
But all the play, the insight and the stretch—
Out of me, out of me! And wherefore out?
Had you enjoined them on me, given me soul,
We might have risen to Rafael, I and you!
Nay, Love, you did give all I asked, I think— 120
More than I merit, yes, by many times.
But had you—oh, with the same perfect brow,
And perfect eyes, and more than perfect mouth,
And the low voice my soul hears, as a bird
The fowler's pipe, and follows to the snare— 125
Had you, with these the same, but brought a mind!
Some women do so. Had the mouth there urged
"God and the glory! never care for gain.
"The present by the future, what is that?
"Live for fame, side by side with Agnolo! 130
"Rafael is waiting: up to God, all three!"
I might have done it for you. So it seems:
Perhaps not. All is as God over-rules.
Beside, incentives come from the soul's self;
The rest avail not. Why do I need you? 135
What wife had Rafael, or has Agnolo?
In this world, who can do a thing, will not;
And who would do it, cannot, I perceive:
Yet the will's somewhat—somewhat, too, the power—
And thus we half-men struggle. At the end, 140
God, I conclude, compensates, punishes.
'T is safer for me, if the award be strict,
That I am something underrated here,
Poor this long while, despised, to speak the truth.
I dared not, do you know, leave home all day, 145
For fear of chancing on the Paris lords.
The best is when they pass and look aside;
But they speak sometimes; I must bear it all.

Well may they speak! That Francis, that first time,
And that long festal year at Fontainebleau!   150
I surely then could sometimes leave the ground,
Put on the glory, Rafael's daily wear,
In that humane great monarch's golden look,—
One finger in his beard or twisted curl
Over his mouth's good mark that made the smile,   155
One arm about my shoulder, round my neck,
The jingle of his gold chain in my ear,
I painting proudly with his breath on me,
All his court round him, seeing with his eyes,
Such frank French eyes, and such a fire of souls   160
Profuse, my hand kept plying by those hearts,—
And, best of all, this, this, this face beyond,
This in the background, waiting on my work,
To crown the issue with a last reward!
A good time, was it not, my kingly days?   165
And had you not grown restless . . . but I know—
'T is done and past; 't was right, my instinct said;
Too live the life grew, golden and not grey,
And I'm the weak-eyed bat no sun should tempt
Out of the grange whose four walls make his world.   170
How could it end in any other way?
You called me, and I came home to your heart.
The triumph was—to reach and stay there; since
I reached it ere the triumph, what is lost?
Let my hands frame your face in your hair's gold,   175
You beautiful Lucrezia that are mine!
"Rafael did this, Andrea painted that;
"The Roman's is the better when you pray,
"But still the other's Virgin was his wife—"
Men will excuse me. I am glad to judge   180
Both pictures in your presence; clearer grows
My better fortune, I resolve to think.
For, do you know, Lucrezia, as God lives,
Said one day Agnolo, his very self,
To Rafael . . . I have known it all these years . . .   185
(When the young man was flaming out his thoughts
Upon a palace-wall for Rome to see,
Too lifted up in heart because of it)
"Friend, there's a certain sorry little scrub
"Goes up and down our Florence, none cares how,   190
"Who, were he set to plan and execute
"As you are, pricked on by your popes and kings,
"Would bring the sweat into that brow of yours!"

To Rafael's!—And indeed the arm is wrong.
I hardly dare . . . yet, only you to see,   195
Give the chalk here—quick, thus the line should go!
Ay, but the soul! he's Rafael! rub it out!
Still, all I care for, if he spoke the truth,
(What he? why, who but Michel Agnolo?
Do you forget already words like those?)   200
If really there was such a chance, so lost,—
Is, whether you're—not grateful—but more pleased.
Well, let me think so. And you smile indeed!
This hour has been an hour! Another smile?
If you would sit thus by me every night   205
I should work better, do you comprehend?
I mean that I should earn more, give you more.
See, it is settled dusk now; there's a star;
Morello's gone, the watch-lights show the wall,
The cue-owls speak the name we call them by.   210
Come from the window, love,—come in, at last,
Inside the melancholy little house
We built to be so gay with. God is just.
King Francis may forgive me: oft at nights
When I look up from painting, eyes tired out,   215
The walls become illumined, brick from brick
Distinct, instead of mortar, fierce bright gold,
That gold of his I did cement them with!
Let us but love each other. Must you go?
That Cousin here again? he waits outside?   220
Must see you—you, and not with me? Those loans?
More gaming debts to pay? you smiled for that?
Well, let smiles buy me! have you more to spend?
While hand and eye and something of a heart
Are left me, work's my ware, and what's it worth?   225
I'll pay my fancy. Only let me sit
The grey remainder of the evening out,
Idle, you call it, and muse perfectly
How I could paint, were I but back in France,
One picture, just one more—the Virgin's face,   230
Not yours this time!. I want you at my side
To hear them—that is, Michel Agnolo—
Judge all I do and tell you of its worth.
Will you? To-morrow, satisfy your friend.
I take the subjects for his corridor,   235
Finish the portrait out of hand—there, there,
And throw him in another thing or two
If he demurs; the whole should prove enough

To pay for this same Cousin's freak. Beside,
What's better and what's all I care about,   240
Get you the thirteen scudi for the ruff!
Love, does that please you? Ah, but what does he,
The Cousin! what does he to please you more?
    I am grown peaceful as old age to-night.
I regret little, I would change still less.   245
Since there my past life lies, why alter it?
The very wrong to Francis!—it is true
I took his coin, was tempted and complied,
And built this house and sinned, and all is said.
My father and my mother died of want.   250
Well, had I riches of my own? you see
How one gets rich! Let each one bear his lot.
They were born poor, lived poor, and poor they died:
And I have laboured somewhat in my time
And not been paid profusely. Some good son   255
Paint my two hundred pictures—let him try!
No doubt, there's something strikes a balance. Yes,
You loved me quite enough, it seems to-night.
This must suffice me here. What would one have?
In heaven, perhaps, new chances, one more chance—   260
Four great walls in the New Jerusalem,
Meted on each side by the angel's reed,
For Leonard, Rafael, Agnolo and me
To cover—the three first without a wife,
While I have mine! So—still they overcome   265
Because there's still Lucrezia,—as I choose.

Again the Cousin's whistle! Go, my Love.

MEETING AT NIGHT

    The gray sea and the long black land;
    And the yellow half-moon large and low;
    And the startled little waves that leap
    In fiery ringlets from their sleep,
    As I gain the cove with pushing prow,   5
    And quench its speed i' the slushy sand.

    Then a mile of warm sea-scented beach;
    Three fields to cross till a farm appears;
    A tap at the pane, the quick sharp scratch
    And blue spurt of a lighted match,   10
    And a voice less loud, through its joys and fears,
    Than the two hearts beating each to each!

Walt Whitman *(1819–1892)*

O CAPTAIN! MY CAPTAIN!

O Captain! my Captain! our fearful trip is done,
The ship has weather'd every rack, the prize we sought is won,
The port is near, the bells I hear, the people all exulting,
While follow eyes the steady keel, the vessel grim and daring;
    But O heart! heart! heart!   5
      O the bleeding drops of red,
         Where on the deck my Captain lies,
         Fallen cold and dead.

O Captain! my Captain! rise up and hear the bells;
Rise up—for you the flag is flung—for you the bugle trills,   10
For you bouquets and ribbon'd wreaths—for you the shores
         a-crowding,
For you they call, the swaying mass, their eager faces
         turning;
    Here Captain! dear father!
      The arm beneath your head!
         It is some dream that on the deck,   15
         You've fallen cold and dead.

My Captain does not answer, his lips are pale and still,
My father does not feel my arm, he has no pulse nor will,
The ship is anchor'd safe and sound, its voyage closed and
         done,
From fearful trip the victor ship comes in with object won: 20
    Exult O shores, and ring O bells!
      But I with mournful tread,
         Walk the deck my Captain lies,
         Fallen cold and dead.

WHEN LILACS LAST IN THE DOORYARD BLOOM'D

I

When lilacs last in the dooryard bloom'd,
And the great star early droop'd in the western sky in the
         night,
I mourn'd, and yet shall mourn with ever-returning spring.
Ever-returning spring, trinity sure to me you bring,

Lilac blooming perennial and drooping star in the west,   5
And thought of him I love.

2

O powerful western fallen star!
O shades of night—O moody, tearful night!
O great star disappear'd—O the black murk that hides the
                        star!
O cruel hands that hold me powerless—O helpless soul of
                        me!   10
O harsh surrounding cloud that will not free my soul.

3

In the dooryard fronting an old farm-house near the white-
                        wash'd palings,
Stands the lilac-bush tall-growing with heart-shaped leaves
                        of rich green,
With many a pointed blossom rising delicate, with the
                        perfume strong I love,
With every leaf a miracle—and from this bush in the door-   15
                        yard,
With delicate-color'd blossoms and heart-shaped leaves of
                        rich green,
A sprig with its flower I break.

4

In the swamp in secluded recesses,
A shy and hidden bird is warbling a song.

Solitary the thrush,   20
The hermit withdrawn to himself, avoiding the settlements,
Sings by himself a song.

Song of the bleeding throat,
Death's outlet song of life, (for well dear brother I know,
If thou wast not granted to sing thou would'st surely die.)   25

5

Over the breast of the spring, the land, amid cities,
Amid lanes and through old woods, where lately the violets
                        peep'd from the ground, spotting the
                        gray debris,
Amid the grass in the fields each side of the lanes, passing the
                        endless grass,
Passing the yellow-spear'd wheat, every grain from its shroud
                        in the dark-brown fields uprisen,

Passing the apple-tree blows of white and pink in the orchards,   30
Carrying a corpse to where it shall rest in the grave,
Night and day journeys a coffin.

6

Coffin that passes through lanes and streets,
Through day and night with the great cloud darkening the
        land,
With the pomp of the inloop'd flags with the cities draped
        in black,   35
With the show of the States themselves as of crape-veil'd
        women standing,
With processions long and winding and the flambeaus of
        the night,
With the countless torches lit, with the silent sea of faces and
        the unbared heads,
With the waiting depot, the arriving coffin, and the somber
        faces,
With dirges through the night, with the thousand voices
        rising strong and solemn,   40
With all the mournful voices of the dirges pour'd around
        the coffin,
The dim-lit churches and the shuddering organs—where amid
        these you journey,
With the tolling tolling bells' perpetual clang,
Here, coffin that slowly passes,
I give you my sprig of lilac.   45

7

(Nor for you, for one alone,
Blossoms and branches green to coffins all I bring,
For fresh as the morning, thus would I chant a song for you
        O sane and sacred death.

All over bouquets of roses,
O death, I cover you over with roses and early lilies,   50
But mostly and now the lilac that blooms the first,
Copious I break, I break the sprigs from the bushes,
With loaded arms I come, pouring for you,
For you and the coffins all of you O death.)

8

O western orb sailing the heaven,   55
Now I know what you must have meant as a month since I
        walk'd,

As I walk'd in silence the transparent shadowy night,
As I saw you had something to tell as you bent to me night
        after night,
As you droop'd from the sky low down as if to my side, (while
        the other stars all look'd on,)
As we wander'd together the solemn night, (for something I
        know not what kept me from sleep,)   60
As the night advanced, and I saw on the rim of the west how
        full you were of woe,
As I stood on the rising ground in the breeze in the cool
        transparent night,
As I watch'd where you pass'd and was lost in the netherward
        black of the night,
As my soul in its trouble dissatisfied sank, as where you sad
        orb,
Concluded, dropt in the night, and was gone.   65

9

Sing on there in the swamp,
O singer bashful and tender, I hear your notes, I hear your
        call,
I hear, I come presently, I understand you,
But a moment I linger, for the lustrous star has detain'd me.
The star my departing comrade holds and detains me.   70

10

O how shall I warble myself for the dead one there I loved?
And how shall I deck my song for the large sweet soul that
        has gone?
And what shall my perfume be for the grave of him I love?

Sea-winds blown from east and west,
Blown from the Eastern sea and blown from the Western sea,   75
        till there on the prairies meeting,
These and with these and the breath of my chant,
I'll perfume the grave of him I love.

11

O what shall I hang on the chamber walls?
And what shall the pictures be that I hang on the walls,
To adorn the burial-house of him I love?   80
Pictures of growing spring and farms and homes,

With the Fourth-month eve at sundown, and the gray smoke
      lucid and bright,
With floods of the yellow gold of the gorgeous, indolent,
      sinking sun, burning, expanding the air,
With the fresh sweet herbage under foot, and the pale green
      leaves of the trees prolific,
In the distance the flowing glaze, the breast of the river, with
      a wind-dapple here and there,   85
With ranging hills on the banks, with many a line against the
      sky, and shadows,
And the city at hand, with dwellings so dense, and stacks of
      chimneys,
And all the scenes of life and the workshops, and the workmen
      homeward returning.

12

Lo, body and soul—this land,
My own Manhattan with spires, and the sparkling and hur-
      rying tides, and the ships,   90
The varied and ample land, the South and the North in the
      light, Ohio's shores and flashing Missouri,
And ever the far-spreading prairies cover'd with grass and
      corn.

Lo, the most excellent sun so calm and haughty,
The violet and purple morn with just-felt breezes,
The gentle soft-born measureless light,   95
The miracle spreading bathing all, the fulfill'd noon,
The coming eve delicious, the welcome night and the stars,
Over my cities shining all, enveloping man and land.

13

Sing on, sing on you gray-brown bird,
Sing from the swamps, the recesses, pour your chant from the
      bushes,   100
Limitless out of the dusk, out of the cedars and pines.

Sing on dearest brother, warble your reedy song,
Loud human song, with voice of uttermost woe.

O liquid and free and tender!
O wild and loose to my soul—O wondrous singer!   105
You only I hear—yet the star holds me, (but will soon depart,)
Yet the lilac with mastering odor holds me.

14

Now while I sat in the day and look'd forth,
In the close of the day with its light and the fields of spring,
                    and the farmers preparing their crops,
In the large unconscious scenery of my land with its lakes and
                    forests,   110
In the heavenly aerial beauty, (after the perturb'd winds and
                    the storms,)
Under the arching heavens of the afternoon swift passing, and
                    the voices of children and women,
The many-moving sea-tides, and I saw the ships how they
                    sail'd,
And the summer approaching with richness, and the fields
                    all busy with labor,
And the infinite separate houses, how they all went on, each
                    with its meals and minutia of daily usages,   115
And the streets how their throbbings throbb'd, and the cities
                    pent—lo, then and there,
Falling upon them all and among them all, enveloping me
                    with the rest,
Appear'd the cloud, appear'd the long black trail,
And I knew death, its thought, and the sacred knowledge of
                    death.

Then with the knowledge of death as walking one side of me,   120
And the thought of death close-walking the other side of me,
And I in the middle as with companions, and as holding the
                    hands of companions,
I fled forth to the hiding receiving night that talks not,
Down to the shores of the water, the path by the swamp in the
                    dimness,
To the solemn shadowy cedars and ghostly pines so still.   125

And the singer so shy to the rest receiv'd me,
The gray-brown bird I know receiv'd us comrades three,
And he sang the carol of death, and a verse for him I love.

From deep secluded recesses,
From the fragrant cedars and the ghostly pines so still,   130
Came the carol of the bird.

And the charm of the carol rapt me
As I held as if by their hands my comrades in the night,
And the voice of my spirit tallied the song of the bird.

Come lovely and soothing death,   135
Undulate round the world, serenely arriving, arriving.

In the day, in the night, to all, to each,
Sooner or later delicate death.

Prais'd be the fathomless universe,
For life and joy, and for objects and knowledge curious,   140
And for love, sweet love—but praise! praise! praise!
For the sure-enwinding arms of cool-enfolding death.

Dark mother always gliding near with soft feet,
Have none chanted for thee a chant of fullest welcome?
Then I chant it for thee, I glorify thee above all,   145
I bring thee a song that when thou must indeed come, come unfal-
            teringly.

Approach strong deliveress,
When it is so, when thou hast taken them I joyously sing the dead,
Lost in the loving floating ocean of thee,
Laved in the flood of thy bliss O death.   150

From me to thee glad serenades,
Dances for thee I propose saluting thee, adornments and feastings
            for thee,
And the sights of the open landscape and the high-spread sky are
            fitting,
And life and the fields, and the huge and thoughtful night.

The night in silence under many a star,   155
The ocean shore and the husky whispering wave whose voice I
            know,
And the soul turning to thee O vast and well-veil'd death,
And the body gratefully nestling close to thee.

Over the tree-tops I float thee a song,
Over the rising and sinking waves, over the myriad fields and the
            prairies wide   160
Over the dense-pack'd cities all and the teeming wharves and ways,
I float this carol with joy, with joy to thee O death.

15

To the tally of my soul,
Loud and strong kept up the gray-brown bird,
With pure deliberate notes spreading filling the night.   165

Loud in the pines and cedars dim,
Clear in the freshness moist and the swamp-perfume,
And I with my comrades there in the night.

While my sight that was bound in my eyes unclosed,
As to long panoramas of visions.   170

And I saw askant the armies,
I saw as in noiseless dreams hundreds of battle-flags,
Borne through the smoke of the battles and pierc'd with
      missiles I saw them,
And carried hither and yon through the smoke, and torn and
      bloody,
And at last but a few shreds left on the staffs, (and all in
      silence,)   175
And the staffs all splinter'd and broken.

I saw battle-corpses, myriads of them,
And the white skeletons of young men, I saw them,
I saw the debris and debris of all the slain soldiers of the war,
But I saw they were not as was thought,   180
They themselves were fully at rest, they suffer'd not,
The living remain'd and suffer'd, the mother suffer'd,
And the wife and the child and the musing comrade suffer'd,
And the armies that remain'd suffer'd.

16

Passing the visions, passing the night,   185
Passing, unloosing the hold of my comrades' hands,
Passing the song of the hermit bird and the tallying song of my
      soul,
Victorious song, death's outlet song, yet varying ever-altering
      song,
As low and wailing, yet clear the notes, rising and falling,
      flooding the night,
Sadly sinking and fainting, as warning and warning, and yet
      again bursting with joy,   190
Covering the earth and filling the spread of the heaven,
As that powerful psalm in the night I heard from recesses,
Passing, I leave thee lilac with heart-shaped leaves,
I leave thee there in the dooryard, blooming, returning with
      spring.

I cease from my song for thee,   195
From my gaze on thee in the west, fronting the west, com-
      muning with thee,
O comrade lustrous with silver face in the night.

Yet each to keep and all, retrievements out of the night,
The song, the wondrous chant of the gray-brown bird,

And the tallying chant, the echo arous'd in my soul,   200
With the lustrous and drooping star with the countenance
        full of woe,
With the holders holding my hand nearing the call of the
        bird,
Comrades mine and I in the midst, and their memory ever to
        keep, for the dead I loved so well,
For the sweetest, wisest soul of all my days and lands—and this
        for his dear sake,
Lilac and star and bird twined with the chant of my soul,   205
There in the fragrant pines and the cedars dusk and dim.

Matthew Arnold (1822-1888)

DOVER BEACH

The sea is calm to-night.
The tide is full, the moon lies fair
Upon the straits; on the French coast the light
Gleams and is gone; the cliffs of England stand,
Glimmering and vast, out in the tranquil bay.   5
Come to the window, sweet is the night-air!
Only, from the long line of spray
Where the sea meets the moon-blanched land,
Listen! you hear the grating roar
Of pebbles which the waves draw back, and fling,   10
At their return, up the high strand,
Begin, and cease, and then again begin,
With tremulous cadence slow, and bring
The eternal note of sadness in.

Sophocles long ago   15
Heard it on the Ægæan, and it brought
Into his mind the turbid ebb and flow
Of human misery; we
Find also in the sound a thought,
Hearing it by this distant northern sea.   20

The Sea of Faith
Was once, too, at the full, and round earth's shore
Lay like the folds of a bright girdle furled.
But now I only hear

Its melancholy, long, withdrawing roar,   25
Retreating, to the breath
Of the night-wind, down the vast edges drear
And naked shingles of the world.

Ah, love, let us be true
To one another! for the world, which seems   30
To lie before us like a land of dreams,
So various, so beautiful, so new,
Hath really neither joy, nor love, nor light,
Nor certitude, nor peace, nor help for pain;
And we are here as on a darkling plain   35
Swept with confused alarms of struggle and flight,
Where ignorant armies clash by night.

Emily Dickinson (*1830–1886*)

THE DAY CAME SLOW, TILL FIVE O'CLOCK

The day came slow, till five o'clock,
Then sprang before the hills
Like hindered rubies, or the light
A sudden musket spills.

The purple could not keep the east,   5
The sunrise shook from fold,
Like breadths of topaz, packed a night,
The lady just unrolled.

The happy winds their timbrels took;
The birds, in docile rows,   10
Arranged themselves around their prince
(The wind is prince of those).

The orchard sparkled like a Jew—
How mighty 'twas, to stay
A guest in this stupendous place,   15
The parlor of the day!

GLEE! THE GREAT STORM IS OVER

Glee! the great storm is over!
Four have recovered the land;

Forty gone down together
Into the boiling sand.

Ring, for the scant salvation!   5
Toll, for the bonnie souls,—
Neighbor and friend and bridegroom,
Spinning upon the shoals!

How they will tell the shipwreck
When winter shakes the door,   10
Till the children ask, "But the forty?
Did they come back no more?"

Then a silence suffuses the story,
And a softness the teller's eye;
And the children no further question,   15
And only the waves reply.

MUCH MADNESS IS DIVINEST SENSE

Much madness is divinest sense
To a discerning eye;
Much sense the starkest madness.
'T is the majority
In this, as all, prevails.   5
Assent, and you are sane;
Demur,—you're straightway dangerous,
And handled with a chain.

A NARROW FELLOW IN THE GRASS

A narrow fellow in the grass
Occasionally rides;
You may have met him—did you not?
His notice sudden is.

The grass divides as with a comb,   5
A spotted shaft is seen;
And then it closes at your feet
And opens further on.

He likes a boggy acre,
A floor too cool for corn.   10
Yet when a child, and barefoot,
I more than once, at morn,

Have passed, I thought, a whip-lash
Unbraiding in the sun—
When, stooping to secure it,   15
It wrinkled, and was gone.

Several of nature's people
I know, and they know me;
I feel for them a transport
Of cordiality;   20

But never met this fellow,
Attended or alone,
Without a tighter breathing,
And zero at the bone.

ON SUCH A NIGHT, OR SUCH A NIGHT

On such a night, or such a night,
Would anybody care
If such a little figure
Slipped quiet from its chair,

So quiet, oh, how quiet!   5
That nobody might know
But that the little figure
Rocked softer, to and fro?

On such a dawn, or such a dawn,
Would anybody sigh   10
That such a little figure
Too sound asleep did lie

For chanticleer to wake it—
Or stirring house below,
Or giddy bird in orchard,   15
Or early task to do?

There was a little figure plump
For every little knoll,
Busy needles, and spools of thread,
And trudging feet from school.   20

Playmates, and holidays, and nuts,
And visions vast and small.
Strange that the feet so precious charged
Should reach so small a goal!

A PRECIOUS, MOULDERING PLEASURE 'TIS

A precious, mouldering pleasure 't is
To meet an antique book,
In just the dress his century wore;
A privilege, I think,

His venerable hand to take,   5
And warming in our own,
A passage back, or two, to make
To times when he was young.

His quaint opinions to inspect,
His knowledge to unfold   10
On what concerns our mutual mind,
The literature of old;

What interested scholars most,
What competitions ran
When Plato was a certainty,   15
And Sophocles a man;

When Sappho was a living girl,
And Beatrice wore
The gown that Dante deified.
Facts, centuries before,   20

He traverses familiar,
As one should come to town
And tell you all your dreams were true:
He lived where dreams were born.

His presence is enchantment,   25
You beg him not to go;
Old volumes shake their vellum heads
And tantalize, just so.

THE ROSE DID CAPER ON HER CHEEK

The rose did caper on her cheek,
Her bodice rose and fell,
Her pretty speech, like drunken men,
Did stagger pitiful.

Her fingers fumbled at her work,—   5
Her needle would not go;

What ailed so smart a little maid
It puzzled me to know,

Till opposite I spied a cheek
That bore another rose;   10
Just opposite, another speech
That like the drunkard goes;

A vest that, like the bodice, danced
To the immortal tune,—
Till those two troubled little clocks   15
Ticked softly into one.

SAFE IN THEIR ALABASTER CHAMBERS

Safe in their alabaster chambers,
Untouched by morning and untouched by noon,
Sleep the meek members of the resurrection,
Rafter of satin, and roof of stone.

Light laughs the breeze in her castle of sunshine;   5
Babbles the bee in a stolid ear;
Pipe the sweet birds in ignorant cadence—
Ah, what sagacity perished here!

Grand go the years in the crescent above them;
Worlds scoop their arcs, and firmaments row,   10
Diadems drop and Doges surrender,
Soundless as dots on a disk of snow.

THE SOUL SELECTS HER OWN SOCIETY

The soul selects her own society,
Then shuts the door;
On her divine majority
Obtrude no more.

Unmoved, she notes the chariot's pausing   5
At her low gate;
Unmoved, an emperor is kneeling
Upon her mat.

I've known her from an ample nation
Choose one;   10
Then close the valves of her attention
Like stone.

THERE'S A CERTAIN SLANT OF LIGHT

There's a certain slant of light,
On winter afternoons,
That oppresses, like the weight
Of cathedral tunes.

Heavenly hurt it gives us;   5
We can find no scar,
But internal difference
Where the meanings are.

None may teach it anything,
'Tis the seal, despair—   10
An imperial affliction
Sent us of the air.

When it comes, the landscape listens,
Shadows hold their breath;
When it goes, 'tis like the distance   15
On the look of death.

TO FIGHT ALOUD IS VERY BRAVE

To fight aloud is very brave,
But gallanter, I know,
Who charge within the bosom,
The cavalry of woe.

Who win, and nations do not see,   5
Who fall, and none observe,
Whose dying eyes no country
Regards with patriot love.

We trust, in plumed procession,
For such the angels go,   10
Rank after rank, with even feet
And uniforms of snow.

William McGonagall (1830–1902)

ATTEMPTED ASSASSINATION OF THE QUEEN

God prosper long our noble Queen,
    And long may she reign!

Maclean he tried to shoot her,
 But it was all in vain.

For God He turned the ball aside   5
 Maclean aimed at her head;
And he felt very angry
 Because he didn't shoot her dead.

There's a divinity that hedgeth a king,
 And so it does seem,   10
And my opinion is, it has hedged
 Our most gracious Queen.

Maclean must be a madman,
 Which is obvious to be seen,
Or else he wouldn't have tried to shoot   15
 Our most beloved Queen.

Victoria is a good Queen,
 Which all her subjects know,
And for that God has protected her
 From all her deadly foes.   20

She is noble and generous,
 Her subjects must confess;
There hasn't been her equal
 Since the days of good Queen Bess.

Long may she be spared to roam   25
 Among the bonnie Highland floral,
And spend many a happy day
 In the palace of Balmoral.

Because she is very kind
 To the old women there,   30
And allows them bread, tea, and sugar,
 And each one to get a share.

And when they know of her coming,
 Their hearts feel overjoy'd,
Because, in general, she finds work   35
 For men that's unemploy'd.

And she also gives the gipsies money
 While at Balmoral, I've been told,
And, mind ye, seldom silver,
 But very often gold.   40

I hope God will protect her
 By night and by day,

> At home and abroad
>> When she's far away.

> May He be as a hedge around her,   45
>> As He's been all along,
> And let her live and die in peace
>> Is the end of my song.

Gerard Manley Hopkins (*1844–1889*)

THE BUGLER'S FIRST COMMUNION

A bugler boy from barrack (it is over the hill
There)—boy bugler, born, he tells me, of Irish
>> Mother to an English sire (he
Shares their best gifts surely, fall how things will),

This very very day came down to us after a boon he on   5
My late being there begged of me, overflowing
>> Boon in my bestowing,
Came, I say, this day to it—to a First Communion.

Here he knelt then ín regimental red.
Forth Christ from cupboard fetched, how fain I of feet   10
>> To his youngster take his treat!
Low-latched in leaf-light housel his too huge godhead.

There! and your sweetest sendings, ah divine,
By it, heavens, befall him! as a heart Christ's darling,
>> dauntless;
>> Tongue true, vaunt- and tauntless;   15
Breathing bloom of a chastity in mansex fine.

Frowning and forefending angel-warder
Squander the hell-rook ranks sally to molest him;
>> March, kind comrade, abreast him;
Dress his days to a dexterous and starlight order.   20

How it dóes my heart good, visiting at that bleak hill,
When limber liquid youth, that to all I teach
>> Yields tender as a pushed peach,
Hies headstrong to its wellbeing of a self-wise self-will!

Then though I should tread tufts of consolation   25
Dáys áfter, só I in a sort deserve to

And do serve God to serve to
Just such slips of soldiery Christ's royal ration.

Nothing élse is like it, no, not all so strains
Us: fresh youth fretted in a bloomfall all portending   30
          That sweet's sweeter ending;
Realm both Christ is heir to and thére réigns.

O now well work that sealing sacred ointment!
O for now charms, arms, what bans off bad
          And locks love ever in a lad!   35
Let mé though see no more of him, and not disappointment

Those sweet hopes quell whose least me quickenings lift,
In scarlet or somewhere of some day seeing
          That brow and bead of being,
An our day's God's own Galahad. Though this child's drift   40

Seems by a divíne doom chánnelled, nor do I cry
Disaster there; but may he not rankle and roam
          In backwheels though bound home?—
That left to the Lord of the Eucharist, I here lie by;

Recorded only, I have put my lips on pleas   45
Would brandle adamantine heaven with ride and jar, did
          Prayer go disregarded:
Forward-like, but however, and like favourable heaven
          heard these.

THE LEADEN ECHO AND THE GOLDEN ECHO
(MAIDEN'S SONG FROM ST. WINEFRED'S WELL)

THE LEADEN ECHO

How to kéep—is there ány any, is there none such, nowhere
          known some, bow or brooch or braid or brace, láce,
          latch or catch or key to keep
Back beauty, keep it, beauty, beauty, beauty, . . . from van-
          ishing away?
Ó is there no frowning of these wrinkles, rankèd wrinkles deep,
Dówn? no waving off of these most mournful messengers,
          still messengers, sad and stealing messengers of grey?
No there's none, there's none, O no there's none,   5
Nor can you long be, what you now are, called fair,
Do what you may do, what, do what you may,
And wisdom is early to despair:

Be beginning; since, no, nothing can be done
To keep at bay   10
Age and age's evils, hoar hair,
Ruck and wrinkle, drooping, dying, death's worst, winding
    sheets, tombs and worms and tumbling to decay;
So be beginning, be beginning to despair.
O there's none; no no no there's none:
Be beginning to despair, to despair,   15
Despair, despair, despair, despair.

THE GOLDEN ECHO

    Spare!
There ís one, yes I have one (Hush there!);
Only not within seeing of the sun,
Not within the singeing of the strong sun,   20
Tall sun's tingeing, or treacherous the tainting of the earth's
    air,
Somewhere elsewhere there is ah well where! one,
Ońe. Yes I cán tell such a key, I dó know such a place,
Where whatever's prized and passes of us, everything that's
    fresh and fast flying of us, seems to us sweet of us and
    swiftly away with, done away with, undone,
Úndone, done with, soon done with, and yet dearly and
    dangerously sweet   25
Of us, the wimpled-water-dimpled, not-by-morning-match-
    èd face,
The flower of beauty, fleece of beauty, too too apt to, ah! to
    fleet,
Never fleets móre, fastened with the tenderest truth
To its own best being and its loveliness of youth: it is an ever-
    lastingness of, O it is an all youth!
Come then, your ways and airs and looks, locks, maiden gear,
    gallantry and gaiety and grace,   30
Winning ways, airs innocent, maiden manners, sweet looks,
    loose locks, long locks, lovelocks, gaygear, going gal-
    lant, girlgrace—
Resign them, sign them, seal them, send them, motion them
    with breath,
And with sighs soaring, soaring síghs deliver
Them; beauty-in-the-ghost, deliver it, early now, long before
    death
Give beauty back, beauty, beauty, beauty, back to God,
    beauty's self and beauty's giver.   35

See; not a hair is, not an eyelash, not the least lash lost; every
        hair
Is, hair of the head, numbered.
Nay, what we had lighthanded left in surly the mere mould
Will have waked and have waxed and have walked with the
        wind what while we slept,
This side, that side hurling a heavyheaded hundredfold   40
What while we, while we slumbered.
O then, weary then whý should we tread? O why are we so
      haggard at the heart, so care-coiled, care-killed, so fagged,
      so fashed, so cogged, so cumbered,
When the thing we freely fórfeit is kept with fonder a care,
Fonder a care kept than we could have kept it, kept
Far with fonder a care (and we, we should have lost it) finer,
        fonder   45
A care kept.—Where kept? Do but tell us where kept,
        where.—
Yonder.—What high as that! We follow, now we follow.—
        Yonder, yes yonder, yonder,
Yonder.

THE LOSS OF THE EURYDICE
FOUNDERED MARCH 24, 1878

The Eurydice—it concerned thee, O Lord:
Three hundred souls, O alas! on board,
      Some asleep unawakened, all un-
warned, eleven fathoms fallen

Where she foundered! One stroke   5
Felled and furled them, the hearts of oak!
      And flockbells off the aerial
Downs' forefalls beat to the burial.

For did she pride her, freighted fully, on
Bounden bales or a hoard of bullion?—   10
      Precious passing measure,
Lads and men her lade and treasure.

She had come from a cruise, training seamen—
Men, boldboys soon to be men:
      Must it, worst weather,   15
Blast bole and bloom together?

No Atlantic squall overwrought her
Or rearing billow of the Biscay water:

Home was hard at hand
And the blow bore from land.   20

And you were a liar, O blue March day.
Bright sun lanced fire in the heavenly bay;
    But what black Boreas wrecked her? he
Came equipped, deadly-electric,

A beetling baldbright cloud thorough England   25
Riding: there did storms not mingle? and
    Hailropes hustle and grind their
Heavengravel? wolfsnow, worlds of it, wind there?

Now Carisbrook keep goes under in gloom;
Now it overvaults Appledurcombe;   30
    Now near by Ventnor town
It hurls, hurls off Boniface Down.

Too proud, too proud, what a press she bore!
Royal, and all her royals wore.
    Sharp with her, shorten sail!   35
Too late; lost; gone with the gale.

This was that fell capsize.
As half she had righted and hoped to rise
    Death teeming in by her portholes
Raced down decks, round messes of mortals.   40

Then a lurch forward, frigate and men;
"All hands for themselves" the cry ran then;
    But she who had housed them thither
Was around them, bound them or wound them with her.

Marcus Hare, high her captain,   45
Kept to her—care-drowned and wrapped in
    Cheer's death, would follow
His charge through the champ-white water-in-a-wallow,

All under Channel to bury in a beach her
Cheeks: Right, rude of feature,   50
    He thought he heard say
"Her commander! and thou too, and thou this way."

It is even seen, time's something server,
In mankind's medley a duty-swerver,
    At downright "No or yes?"   55
Doffs all, drives full for righteousness.

Sydney Fletcher, Bristol-bred,
(Low lie his mates now on watery bed)

Takes to the seas and snows
As sheer down the ship goes.   60

Now her afterdraught gullies him too down;
Now he wrings for breath with the deathgush brown;
    Till a lifebelt and God's will
Land him a lift from the sea-swill.

Now he shoots short up to the round air;   65
Now he gasps, now he gazes everywhere;
    But his eye no cliff, no coast or
Mark makes in the rivelling snowstorm.

Him, after an hour of wintry waves,
A schooner sights, with another, and saves,   70
    And he boards her in Oh! such joy
He has lost count what came next, poor boy.—

They say who saw one sea-corpse cold
He was all of lovely manly mould,
    Every inch a tar,   75
Of the best we boast our sailors are.

Look, foot to forelock, how all things suit! he
Is strung by duty, is strained to beauty,
    And brown-as-dawning-skinned
With brine and shine and whirling wind.   80

O his nimble finger, his gnarled grip!
Leagues, leagues of seamanship
    Slumber in these forsaken
Bones, this sinew, and will nor waken.

He was but one like thousands more.   85
Day and night I deplore
    My people and born own nation,
Fast foundering own generation.

I might let bygones be—our curse
Of ruinous shrine no hand or, worse,   90
    Robbery's hand is busy to
Dress, hoar-hallowèd shrines unvisited;

Only the breathing temple and fleet
Life, this wildworth blown so sweet,
    These daredeaths, ay this crew, in   95
Unchrist, all rolled in ruin—

Deeply surely I need to deplore it,
Wondering why my master bore it,

    The riving off that race
So at home, time was, to his truth and grace   100

That a starlight-wender of ours would say
The marvellous Milk was Walsingham Way
    And one—but let be, let be:
More, more than was will yet be.—

O well wept, mother have lost son;   105
Wept, wife; wept, sweetheart would be one:
    Though grief yield them no good
Yet shed what tears sad truelove should.

But to Christ lord of thunder
Crouch; lay knee by earth low under: 110
    "Holiest, loveliest, bravest,
Save my hero, O Hero savest.

And the prayer thou hearst me making
Have, at the awful overtaking,
    Heard; have heard and granted   115
Grace that day grace was wanted."

Not that hell knows redeeming,
But for souls sunk in seeming
    Fresh, till doomfire burn all,
Prayer shall fetch pity eternal.   120

PIED BEAUTY

Glory be to God for dappled things—
    For skies of couple-colour as a brinded cow;
        For rose-moles all in stipple upon trout that swim;
Fresh-firecoal chestnut-falls; finches' wings;
    Landscape plotted and pieced—fold, fallow, and plough;   5
        And áll trádes, their gear and tackle and trim.
All things counter, original, spare, strange;
    Whatever is fickle, freckled (who knows how?)
        With swift, slow; sweet, sour; adazzle, dim;
He fathers-forth whose beauty is past change: 10
        Praise him.

THAT NATURE IS A HERACLITEAN FIRE AND OF THE
COMFORT OF THE RESURRECTION

Cloud-puffball, torn tufts, tossed pillows | flaunt forth, then
        chevy on an air-

built thoroughfare: heaven-roysterers, in gay-gangs ¦ they
          throng; they glitter in marches.
Down roughcast, down dazzling whitewash, ¦ wherever an
          elm arches,
Shivelights and shadowtackle in long ¦ lashes lace, lance, and
          pair.
Delightfully the bright wind boisterous ¦ ropes, wrestles,
          beats earth bare   5
Of yestertempest's creases; ¦ in pool and rut peel parches
Squandering ooze to squeezed ¦ dough, crust, dust; stanches,
          starches
Squadroned masks and manmarks ¦ treadmire toil there
Footfretted in it. Million-fuelèd, ¦ nature's bonfire burns on.
But quench her bonniest, dearest ¦ to her, her clearest-selvèd
          spark   10
Man, how fast his firedint, ¦ his mark on mind, is gone!
Both are in an unfathomable, all is in an enormous dark
Drowned. O pity and indig ¦ nation! Manshape, that shone
Sheer off, disseveral, a star, ¦ death blots black out; nor mark
          Is any of him at all so stark
But vastness blurs and time ¦ beats level. Enough! the Resur-
          rection,   15
A heart's-clarion! Away grief's gasping, ¦ joyless days, de-
          jection.
          Across my foundering deck shone
A beacon, an eternal beam. ¦ Flesh fade, and mortal trash
Fall to the residuary worm; ¦ world's wildfire, leave but ash:
          In a flash, at a trumpet crash,
I am all at once what Christ is, ¦ since he was what I am, and   20
This Jack, joke, poor potsherd, ¦ patch, matchwood, immortal
          diamond,
          Is immortal diamond.

THE WINDHOVER:
TO CHRIST OUR LORD

I caught this morning morning's minion, king-
          dom of daylight's dauphin, dapple-dawn-drawn Falcon,
          in his riding
     Of the rolling level underneath him steady air, and
          striding
High there, how he rung upon the rein of a wimpling wing
In his ecstasy! then off, off forth on swing,

As a skate's heel sweeps smooth on a bow-bend: the
     hurl and gliding   5
Rebuffed the big wind. My heart in hiding
Stirred for a bird,—the achieve of, the mastery of the thing!

Brute beauty and valor and act, oh, air, pride, plume, here
     Buckle! AND the fire that breaks from thee then, a billion
Times told lovelier, more dangerous, O my chevalier!   10

     No wonder of it: shéer plód makes plow down sillion
Shine, and blue-bleak embers, ah my dear,
     Fall, gall themselves, and gash gold-vermilion.

Edmund Gosse (1849–1928)

THE LOSS OF THE "EURYDICE"
MARCH 24, 1878

Tired with the toils that know no end,
     On wintry seas long doomed to roam,
They smiled to think that March could lend
     Such radiant winds to waft them home;
          Long perils overpast,   5
          They stood for port at last,
Close by the fair familiar waterway,
          And on their sunlit lee
          All hearts were glad to see
The crags of Culver through the shining day;   10
          While every white-winged bird,
          Whose joyous cry they heard,
Seemed wild to shout the welcome that it bore
          Of love from friends on shore.

Ah! brief their joy, as days are brief   15
     In March, that loves not joy nor sun;
O bitter to the heart of grief
     The port that never shall be won!
          Fair ship, with all sail set,
          Didst thou perchance forget   20
The changing times and treacherous winds of Spring?
          And could those headlands gray
          Rehearse no tale to-day

Of wrecks they have seen, and many a grievous thing?
        Thy towering cliff, Dunnose,   25
        Full many a secret knows,—
Cry out in warning voice! too much they dare;
        Death gathers in the air!

A wind blew sharp out of the north,
        And o'er the island ridges rose   30
A sound of tempest going forth,
        And murmur of approaching snows;
          Then through the sunlit air
          Streamed dark the lifted hair
Of storm-cloud, gathering for the light's eclipse,   35
          And fiercely rose and fell
          The shriek of waves, the knell
Of seamen, and the doom of wandering ships;
          As with an eagle's cry
          The mighty storm rushed by,   40
Trailing its robe of snow across the wave,
        And gulfed them like a grave.

It passed; it fell; and all was still;
        But, homebound wanderers, where were they?
The wind went down behind the hill,   45
        The sunset gilded half the bay;
          Ah! loud bewildered sea,
          Vain, vain our trust in thee
To bring our kinsfolk home, through storm and tide!
          So sharp and swift the blow,   50
          Thyself dost hardly know
Where now they rest whom thou didst bear and guide!
          Our human hearts may break,
          Cold Ocean, for thy sake,—
Thou not the less canst paint in colours fair   55
        The eve of our despair.

Not hard for heroes is the death
        That greets them from the cannon's lips,
When heaven is red with flaming breath,
        And shakes with roar of sundering ships: 60
          When through the thunder-cloud
          Sounds to them, clear and loud,
The voice of England calling them by name;
          And as their eyes grow dim
          They hear their nation's hymn,   65

And know the prelude of immortal fame;
    But sad indeed is this,
    The meed of war to miss,
To die for England, yet in dying know
    They leave no name but woe.   70

They cannot rest through coming years,
    In any ground that England owns,
And billows salter than our tears
    Wash over their unhonoured bones;
        Yet in our hearts they rest   75
        Not less revered and blest
Than those, their brothers, who in fighting fell;
    Nor shall our children hear
    Their name pronounced less dear,
When England's roll of gallant dead we tell;   80
    For ever shall our ships,
    There, at the Solent's lips,
Pass out to glory over their still bed,
    And praise the silent dead.

W. B. Yeats (1865–1939)

COOLE AND BALLYLEE, 1931

Under my window-ledge the waters race,
Otters below and moor-hens on the top,
Run for a mile undimmed in Heaven's face
Then darkening through "dark" Raftery's "cellar" drop,
Run underground, rise in a rocky place   5
In Coole demesne, and there to finish up
Spread to a lake and drop into a hole.
What's water but the generated soul?

Upon the border of that lake's a wood
Now all dry sticks under a wintry sun,   10
And in a copse of beeches there I stood,
For Nature's pulled her tragic buskin on
And all the rant's a mirror of my mood:
At sudden thunder of the mounting swan
I turned about and looked where branches break   15
The glittering reaches of the flooded lake.

Another emblem there! That stormy white
But seems a concentration of the sky;
And, like the soul, it sails into the sight
And in the morning's gone, no man knows why;   20
And is so lovely that it sets to right
What knowledge or its lack had set awry,
So arrogantly pure, a child might think
It can be murdered with a spot of ink.

Sound of a stick upon the floor, a sound   25
From somebody that toils from chair to chair;
Beloved books that famous hands have bound,
Old marble heads, old pictures everywhere;
Great rooms where travelled men and children found
Content or joy; a last inheritor   30
Where none has reigned that lacked a name and fame
Or out of folly into folly came.

A spot whereon the founders lived and died
Seemed once more dear than life; ancestral trees,
Or gardens rich in memory glorified   35
Marriages, alliances and families,
And every bride's ambition satisfied.
Where fashion or mere fantasy decrees
Man shifts about—all that great glory spent—
Like some poor Arab tribesman and his tent.   40

We were the last romantics—chose for theme
Traditional sanctity and loveliness;
Whatever's written in what poets name
The book of the people; whatever most can bless
The mind of man or elevate a rhyme;   45
But all is changed, that high horse riderless,
Though mounted in that saddle Homer rode
Where the swan drifts upon a darkening flood.

EASTER, 1916

I have met them at close of day
Coming with vivid faces
From counter or desk among grey
Eighteenth-century houses.
I have passed with a nod of the head   5
Or polite meaningless words,
Or have lingered awhile and said

Polite meaningless words,
And thought before I had done
Of a mocking tale or a gibe 10
To please a companion
Around the fire at the club,
Being certain that they and I
But lived where motley is worn:
All changed, changed utterly: 15
A terrible beauty is born.

That woman's days were spent
In ignorant good-will,
Her nights in argument
Until her voice grew shrill. 20
What voice more sweet than hers
When, young and beautiful,
She rode to harriers?
This man had kept a school
And rode our wingèd horse; 25
This other his helper and friend
Was coming into his force;
He might have won fame in the end,
So sensitive his nature seemed,
So daring and sweet his thought. 30
This other man I had dreamed
A drunken, vainglorious lout.
He had done most bitter wrong
To some who are near my heart,
Yet I number him in the song; 35
He, too, has resigned his part
In the casual comedy;
He, too, has been changed in his turn,
Transformed utterly:
A terrible beauty is born. 40

Hearts with one purpose alone
Through summer and winter seem
Enchanted to a stone
To trouble the living stream.
The horse that comes from the road, 45
The rider, the birds that range
From cloud to tumbling cloud,
Minute by minute they change;
A shadow of cloud on the stream
Changes minute by minute; 50

A horse-hoof slides on the brim,
And a horse plashes within it;
The long-legged moor-hens dive,
And hens to moor-cocks call;
Minute by minute they live: 55
The stone's in the midst of all.

Too long a sacrifice
Can make a stone of the heart.
O when may it suffice?
That is Heaven's part, our part   60
To murmur name upon name,
As a mother names her child
When sleep at last has come
On limbs that had run wild.
What is it but nightfall?   65
No, no, not night but death;
Was it needless death after all?
For England may keep faith
For all that is done and said.
We know their dream; enough   70
To know they dreamed and are dead;
And what if excess of love
Bewildered them till they died?
I write it out in a verse—
MacDonagh and MacBride   75
And Connolly and Pearse
Now and in time to be,
Whatever green is worn,
Are changed, changed utterly:
A terrible beauty is born.   80

A PRAYER FOR MY DAUGHTER

Once more the storm is howling, and half hid
Under this cradle-hood and coverlid
My child sleep on. There is no obstacle
But Gregory's wood and one bare hill
Whereby the haystack- and roof-levelling wind,   5
Bred on the Atlantic, can be stayed;
And for an hour I have walked and prayed
Because of the great gloom that is in my mind.

I have walked and prayed for this young child an hour
And heard the sea-wind scream upon the tower,   10
And under the arches of the bridge, and scream
In the elms above the flooded stream;
Imagining in excited reverie
That the future years had come,
Dancing to a frenzied drum,   15
Out of the murderous innocence of the sea.

May she be granted beauty and yet not
Beauty to make a stranger's eye distraught,
Or hers before a looking-glass, for such,
Being made beautiful overmuch,   20
Consider beauty a sufficient end,
Lose natural kindness and maybe
The heart-revealing intimacy
That chooses right, and never find a friend.

Helen being chosen found life flat and dull   25
And later had much trouble from a fool,
While that great Queen, that rose out of the spray,
Being fatherless could have her way
Yet chose a bandy-leggèd smith for man.
It's certain that fine women eat   30
A crazy salad with their meat
Whereby the Horn of Plenty is undone.

In courtesy I'd have her chiefly learned;
Hearts are not had as a gift but hearts are earned
By those that are not entirely beautiful;   35
Yet many, that have played the fool
For beauty's very self, has charm made wise,
And many a poor man that has roved,
Loved and thought himself beloved,
From a glad kindness cannot take his eyes.   40

May she become a flourishing hidden tree
That all her thoughts may like the linnet be,
And have no business but dispensing round
Their magnanimities of sound,
Nor but in merriment begin a chase,   45
Nor but in merriment a quarrel.
O may she live like some green laurel
Rooted in one dear perpetual place.

My mind, because the minds that I have loved,
The sort of beauty that I have approved,   50

Prosper but little, has dried up of late,
Yet knows that to be choked with hate
May well be of all evil chances chief.
If there's no hatred in a mind
Assault and battery of the wind   55
Can never tear the linnet from the leaf.

An intellectual hatred is the worst,
So let her think opinions are accursed.
Have I not seen the loveliest woman born
Out of the mouth of Plenty's horn,   60
Because of her opinionated mind
Barter that horn and every good
By quiet natures understood
For an old bellows full of angry wind?

Considering that, all hatred driven hence,   65
The soul recovers radical innocence
And learns at last that it is self-delighting,
Self-appeasing, self-affrighting,
And that its own sweet will is Heaven's will;
She can, though every face should scowl   70
And every windy quarter howl
Or every bellows burst, be happy still.

And may her bridegroom bring her to a house
Where all's accustomed, ceremonious;
For arrogance and hatred are the wares   75
Peddled in the thoroughfares
How but in custom and in ceremony
Are innocence and beauty born?
Ceremony's a name for the rich horn,
And custom for the spreading laurel tree.   80

THE SECOND COMING

Turning and turning in the widening gyre
The falcon cannot hear the falconer;
Things fall apart; the centre cannot hold;
Mere anarchy is loosed upon the world,
The blood-dimmed tide is loosed, and everywhere   5
The ceremony of innocence is drowned;
The best lack all conviction, while the worst
Are full of passionate intensity.

Surely some revelation is at hand;
Surely the Second Coming is at hand.   10
The Second Coming! Hardly are those words out
When a vast image out of *Spiritus Mundi*
Troubles my sight: somewhere in sands of the desert
A shape with lion body and the head of a man,
A gaze blank and pitiless as the sun,   15
Is moving its slow thighs, while all about it
Reel shadows of the indignant desert birds.
The darkness drops again; but now I know
That twenty centuries of stony sleep
Were vexed to nightmare by a rocking cradle,   20
And what rough beast, its hour come round at last,
Slouches towards Bethlehem to be born?

WHEN YOU ARE OLD

When you are old and grey and full of sleep,
And nodding by the fire, take down this book,
And slowly read, and dream of the soft look
Your eyes had once, and of their shadows deep;

How many loved your moments of glad grace,   5
And loved your beauty with love false or true,
But one man loved the pilgrim soul in you,
And loved the sorrows of your changing face;

And bending down beside the glowing bars,
Murmur, a little sadly, how Love fled   10
And paced upon the mountains overhead
And hid his face amid a crowd of stars.

THE WILD SWANS AT COOLE

The trees are in their autumn beauty,
The woodland paths are dry,
Under the October twilight the water
Mirrors a still sky;
Upon the brimming water among the stones   5
Are nine-and-fifty swans.

The nineteenth autumn has come upon me
Since I first made my count;
I saw, before I had well finished,

All suddenly mount   10
And scatter wheeling in great broken rings
Upon their clamorous wings.

I have looked upon those brilliant creatures,
And now my heart is sore.
All's changed since I, hearing at twilight,   15
The first time on this shore,
The bell-beat of their wings above my head,
Trod with a lighter tread.

Unwearied still, lover by lover,
They paddle in the cold   20
Companionable streams or climb the air;
Their hearts have not grown old;
Passion or conquest, wander where they will,
Attend upon them still.

But now they drift on the still water   25
Mysterious, beautiful;
Among what rushes will they build,
By what lake's edge or pool
Delight men's eyes when I awake some day
To find they have flown away?   30

Edwin Arlington Robinson (*1869–1935*)

THE MILL

The miller's wife had waited long,
    The tea was cold, the fire was dead;
And there might yet be nothing wrong
    In how he went and what he said:
"There are no millers any more,"   5
    Was all that she had heard him say;
And he had lingered at the door
    So long that it seemed yesterday.

Sick with a fear that had no form
    She knew that she was there at last;   10
And in the mill there was a warm
    And mealy fragrance of the past.

What else there was would only seem
    To say again what he had meant;
And what was hanging from a beam   15
    Would not have heeded where she went.

And if she thought it followed her,
    She may have reasoned in the dark
That one way of the few there were
    Would hide her and would leave no mark: 20
Black water, smooth above the weir
    Like starry velvet in the night,
Though ruffled once, would soon appear
    The same as ever to the sight.

Robert Frost (*1874–1963*)

DEPARTMENTAL: OR, MY ANT JERRY

An ant on the table-cloth
Ran into a dormant moth
Of many times his size.
He showed not the least surprise.
His business wasn't with such.   5
He gave it scarcely a touch,
And was off on his duty run.
Yet if he encountered one
Of the hive's enquiry squad
Whose work is to find out God   10
And the nature of time and space,
He would put him onto the case.
Ants are a curious race;
One crossing with hurried tread
The body of one of their dead   15
Isn't given a moment's arrest—
Seems not even impressed.
But he no doubt reports to any
With whom he crosses antennae,
And they no doubt report   20
To the higher up at court.
Then word goes forth in Formic:
"Death's come to Jerry McCormic,
Our selfless forager Jerry.

Will the special Janizary   25
Whose office it is to bury
The dead of the commissary
Go bring him home to his people.
Lay him in state on a sepal.
Wrap him for shroud in a petal.   30
Embalm him with ichor of nettle.
This is the word of your Queen."
And presently on the scene
Appears a solemn mortician;
And taking formal position   35
With feelers calmly atwiddle,
Seizes the dead by the middle,
And heaving him high in air,
Carries him out of there.
No one stands round to stare.   40
It is nobody else's affair.

It couldn't be called ungentle.
But how thoroughly departmental.

DESIGN

I found a dimpled spider, fat and white,
On a white heal-all, holding up a moth
Like a white piece of rigid satin cloth—
Assorted characters of death and blight
Mixed ready to begin the morning right,   5
Like the ingredients of a witches' broth—
A snow-drop spider, a flower like a froth,
And dead wings carried like a paper kite.

What had that flower to do with being white,
The wayside blue and innocent heal-all?   10
What brought the kindred spider to that height,
Then steered the white moth thither in the night?
What but design of darkness to appall?—
If design govern in a thing so small.

MOON COMPASSES

I stole forth dimly in the dripping pause
Between two downpours to see what there was.

And a masked moon had spread down compass rays
To a cone mountain in the midnight haze,
As if the final estimate were hers,   5
And as it measured in her calipers,
The mountain stood exalted in its place.
So love will take between the hands a face. . . .

"OUT, OUT—"

The buzz saw snarled and rattled in the yard
And made dust and dropped stove-length sticks of wood,
Sweet-scented stuff when the breeze drew across it.
And from there those that lifted eyes could count
Five mountain ranges one behind the other   5
Under the sunset far into Vermont.
And the saw snarled and rattled, snarled and rattled,
As it ran light, or had to bear a load.
And nothing happened: day was all but done.
Call it a day, I wish they might have said   10
To please the boy by giving him the half hour
That a boy counts so much when saved from work.
His sister stood beside them in her apron
To tell them "Supper." At the word, the saw,
As if to prove saws knew what supper meant,   15
Leaped out at the boy's hand, or seemed to leap—
He must have given the hand. However it was,
Neither refused the meeting. But the hand!
The boy's first outcry was a rueful laugh,
As he swung toward them holding up the hand   20
Half in appeal, but half as if to keep
The life from spilling. Then the boy saw all—
Since he was old enough to know, big boy
Doing a man's work, though a child at heart—
He saw all spoiled. "Don't let him cut my hand off—   25
The doctor, when he comes. Don't let him, sister!"
So. But the hand was gone already.
The doctor put him in the dark of ether.
He lay and puffed his lips out with his breath.
And then—the watcher at his pulse took fright.   30
No one believed. They listened at his heart.
Little—less—nothing!—and that ended it.
No more to build on there. And they, since they
Were not the one dead, turned to their affairs.

THE ROAD NOT TAKEN

Two roads diverged in a yellow wood,
And sorry I could not travel both
And be one traveler, long I stood
And looked down one as far as I could
To where it bent in the undergrowth;   5

Then took the other, as just as fair,
And having perhaps the better claim,
Because it was grassy and wanted wear;
Though as for that the passing there
Had worn them really about the same,   10

And both that morning equally lay
In leaves no step had trodden black.
Oh, I kept the first for another day!
Yet knowing how way leads on to way,
I doubted if I should ever come back.   15

I shall be telling this with a sigh
Somewhere ages and ages hence:
Two roads diverged in a wood, and I—
I took the one less traveled by,
And that has made all the difference.   20

THE SECRET SITS

We dance round in a ring and suppose,
But the Secret sits in the middle and knows.

STOPPING BY WOODS ON A SNOWY EVENING

Whose woods these are I think I know.
His house is in the village though;
He will not see me stopping here
To watch his woods fill up with snow.

My little horse must think it queer   5
To stop without a farmhouse near
Between the woods and frozen lake
The darkest evening of the years.

He gives his harness bells a shake
To ask if there is some mistake.   10

The only other sound's the sweep
Of easy wind and downy flake.

The woods are lovely, dark and deep,
But I have promises to keep,
And miles to go before I sleep,   15
And miles to go before I sleep.

THE WITCH OF COÖS

I staid the night for shelter at a farm
Behind the mountain, with a mother and son,
Two old-believers. They did all the talking.

Mother: Folks think a witch who has familiar spirits
She could call up to pass a winter evening,   5
But won't, should be burned at the stake or something.
Summoning spirits isn't "Button, button,
Who's got the button," I would have them know.

Son: Mother can make a common table rear
And kick with two legs like an army mule.   10

Mother: And when I've done it, what good have I done?
Rather than tip a table for you, let me
Tell you what Ralle the Sioux Control once told me.
He said the dead had souls, but when I asked him
How could that be—I though the dead were souls,   15
He broke my trance. Don't that make you suspicious
That there's something the dead are keeping back?
Yes, there's something the dead are keeping back.

Son: You wouldn't want to tell him what we have
Up attic, mother?   20

Mother: Bones—a skeleton.

Son: But the headboard of mother's bed is pushed
Against the attic door: the door is nailed.
It's harmless. Mother hears it in the night
Halting perplexed behind the barrier   25
Of door and headboard. Where it wants to get
Is back into the cellar where it came from.

Mother: We'll never let them, will we, son? We'll never!

Son: It left the celler forty years ago
And carried itself like a pile of dishes   30

Up one flight from the cellar to the kitchen,
Another from the kitchen to the bedroom,
Another from the bedroom to the attic,
Right past both father and mother, and neither stopped it.
Father had gone upstairs; mother was downstairs.   35
I was a baby: I don't know where I was.

Mother: The only fault my husband found with me—
I went to sleep before I went to bed,
Especially in winter when the bed
Might just as well be ice and the clothes snow.   40
The night the bones came up the cellar-stairs
Toffile had gone to bed alone and left me,
But left an open door to cool the room off
So as to sort of turn me out of it.
I was just coming to myself enough   45
To wonder where the cold was coming from,
When I heard Toffile upstairs in the bedroom
And thought I heard him downstairs in the cellar.
The board we had laid down to walk dry-shod on
When there was water in the cellar in spring   50
Struck the hard cellar bottom. And then someone
Began the stairs, two footsteps for each step,
The way a man with one leg and a crutch,
Or a little child, comes up. It wasn't Toffile:
It wasn't anyone who could be there.   55
The bulkhead double-doors were double-locked
And swollen tight and buried under snow.
The cellar windows were banked up with sawdust
And swollen tight and buried under snow.
It was the bones. I knew them—and good reason.   60
My first impulse was to get to the knob
And hold the door. But the bones didn't try
The door; they halted helpless on the landing,
Waiting for things to happen in their favor.
The faintest restless rustling ran all through them.   65
I never could have done the thing I did
If the wish hadn't been too strong in me
To see how they were mounted for this walk.
I had a vision of them put together
Not like a man, but like a chandelier.   70
So suddenly I flung the door wide on him.
A moment he stood balancing with emotion,
And all but lost himself. (A tongue of fire

Flashed out and licked along his upper teeth.
Smoke rolled inside the sockets of his eyes.)   75
Then he came at me with one hand outstretched,
The way he did in life once; but this time
I struck the hand off brittle on the floor,
And fell back from him on the floor myself.
The finger-pieces slid in all directions.   80
(Where did I see one of those pieces lately?
Hand me my button-box—it must be there.)
I sat up on the floor and shouted, "Toffile,
It's coming up to you." It had its choice
Of the door to the cellar or the hall.   85
It took the hall door for the novelty,
And set off briskly for so slow a thing,
Still going every which way in the joints, though,
So that it looked like lightning or a scribble,
From the slap I had just now given its hand.   90
I listened till it almost climbed the stairs
From the hall to the only finished bedroom,
Before I got up to do anything;
Then ran and shouted, "Shut the bedroom door,
Toffile, for my sake!" "Company," he said,   95
"Don't make me get up; I'm too warm in bed."
So lying forward weakly on the handrail
I pushed myself upstairs, and in the light
(The kitchen had been dark) I had to own
I could see nothing. "Toffile, I don't see it.   100
It's with us in the room though. It's the bones."
"What bones?" "The cellar bones—out of the grave."
That made him throw his bare legs out of bed
And sit up by me and take hold of me.
I wanted to put out the light and see   105
If I could see it, or else mow the room,
With our arms at the level of our knees,
And bring the chalk-pile down. "I'll tell you what—
It's looking for another door to try.
The uncommonly deep snow has made him think   110
Of his old song, *The Wild Colonial Boy*,
He always used to sing along the tote-road.
He's after an open door to get out-doors.
Let's trap him with an open door up attic."
Toffile agreed to that, and sure enough,   115

Almost the moment he was given an opening,
The steps began to climb the attic stairs.
I heard them. Toffile didn't seem to hear them.
"Quick!" I slammed to the door and held the knob.
"Toffile, get nails." I made him nail the door shut,   120
And push the headboard of the bed against it.
Then we asked was there anything
Up attic that we'd ever want again.
The attic was less to us than the cellar.
If the bones liked the attic, let them have it,   125
Let them stay in the attic. When they sometimes
Come down the stairs at night and stand perplexed
Behind the door and headboard of the bed,
Brushing their chalky skull with chalky fingers,
With sounds like the dry rattling of a shutter,   130
That's what I sit up in the dark to say—
To no one any more since Toffile died.
Let them stay in the attic since they went there.
I promised Toffile to be cruel to them
For helping them be cruel once to him.   135

Son: We think they had a grave down in the cellar.

Mother: We know they had a grave down in the cellar.

Son: We never could find out whose bones they were.

Mother: Yes, we could too, son. Tell the truth for once.
They were a man's his father killed for me.   140
I mean a man he killed instead of me.
The least I could do was to help dig their grave.
We were about it one night in the cellar.
Son knows the story: but 'twas not for him
To tell the truth, suppose the time had come.   145
Son looks surprised to see me end a lie
We'd kept all these years between ourselves
So as to have it ready for outsiders.
But tonight I don't care enough to lie—
I don't remember why I ever cared.   150
Toffile, if he were here, I don't believe
Could tell you why he ever cared himself . . .

She hadn't found the finger-bone she wanted
Among the buttons poured out in her lap.

I verified the name next morning: Toffile.
The rural letter-box said Toffile Lajway.

Carl Sandburg (*1878–1967*)

ELEPHANTS ARE DIFFERENT TO DIFFERENT PEOPLE

Wilson and Pilcer and Snack stood before the zoo elephant.

Wilson said, "What is its name? Is it from Asia or Africa? Who feeds it? Is it a he or a she? How old is it? Do they have twins? How much does it cost to feed? How much   5
does it weigh? If it dies how much will another one cost? If it dies what will they use the bones, the fat, and hide for? What use is it besides to look at?"

Pilcer didn't have any questions; he was murmuring to himself, "It's a house by itself, walls and windows, the ears   10
came from tall cornfields, by God; the architect of those legs was a workman, by God; he stands like a bridge out across deep water; the face is sad and the eyes are kind; I know elephants are good to babies."

Snack looked up and down and at last said to himself,   15
"He's a tough son-of-a-gun outside and I'll bet he's got a strong heart, I'll bet he's as strong as a copper-riveted boiler inside."

They didn't put up any arguments.

They didn't throw anything in each other's faces.   20

Three men saw the elephant three ways.

And let it go at that.

They didn't spoil a sunny Sunday afternoon;

"Sunday comes only once a week," they told each other.

PRAYERS OF STEEL

Lay me on an anvil, O God.
Beat me and hammer me into a crowbar.
Let me pry loose old walls.
Let me lift and loosen old foundations.

Lay me on an anvil, O God.   5
Beat me and hammer me into a steel spike.
Drive me into the girders that hold a skyscraper together.
Take red-hot rivets and fasten me into the central girders.
Let me be the great nail holding a skyscraper through blue
                nights into white stars.

James Joyce (*1882–1941*)

THE BALLAD OF PERSSHE O'REILLY

Have you heard of one Humpty Dumpty
How he fell with a roll and a rumble
And curled up like Lord Olofa Crumple
By the butt of the Magazine Wall,
        (Chorus) Of the Magazine Wall,   5
                Hump, helmet and all?

He was one time our King of the Castle
Now he's kicked about like a rotten old parsnip.
And from Green street he'll be sent by order of His Worship
To the penal jail of Mountjoy   10
        (Chorus) To the jail of Mountjoy!
                Jail him and joy.

He was fafafather of all schemes for to bother us
Slow coaches and immaculate contraceptives for the populace,
Mare's milk for the sick, seven dry Sundays a week,   15
Openair love and religion's reform,
        (Chorus) And religious reform,
                Hideous in form.

Arrah, why, says you, couldn't he manage it?
I'll go bail, my fine dairyman darling,   20
Like the bumping bull of the Cassidys
All your butter is in your horns.
        (Chorus) His butter is in his horns.
                Butter his horns!

(Repeat) Hurrah there, Hosty, frosty Hosty, change that
                shirt on ye,   25
Rhyme the rann, the king of all ranns!

Balbaccio, balbuccio!

We had chaw chaw chops, chairs, chewing gum, the chicken-
pox and china chambers
Universally provided by this soffsoaping salesman.
Small wonder He'll Cheat E'erawan our local lads nick-
named him
When Chimpden first took the floor   30
   (Chorus) With his bucketshop store
      Down Bargainweg, Lower.

So snug he was in his hotel premises sumptuous
But soon we'll bonfire all his trash, tricks and trumpery
And'tis short till sheriff Clancy'll be winding up his unlim-
ited company   35
With the bailiff's bom at the door,
   (Chorus) Bimbam at the door.
      Then he'll bum no more.

Sweet bad luck on the waves washed to our island
The hooker of that hammerfast viking   40
And Gall's curse on the day when Eblana bay
Saw his black and tan man-o'-war.
   (Chorus) Saw his man-o'-war.
      On the harbour bar.

Where from? roars Poolbeg. Cookingha'pence, he bawls
      Donnez-moi scampitle, wick an wipin'fam-
      piny   45
Fingal Mac Oscar Onesine Bargearse Boniface
Thok's min gammelhole Norveegickers moniker
Og as ay are at gammelhore Norveegickers cod.
   (Chorus) A Norwegian camel old cod.
      He is, begod.   50

Lift it, Hosty, lift it, ye devil ye! up with the rann, the rhym-
ing rann!

It was during some fresh water garden pumping
Or, according to the *Nursing Mirror*, while admiring the
monkeys
That our heavyweight heathen Humpharey
Made bold a maid to woo   55
   (Chorus) Woohoo, what'll she doo!
      The general lost her maidenloo!

He ought to blush for himself, the old hayheaded philosopher,
For to go and shove himself that way on top of her.

Begob, he's the crux of the catalogue   60
Of our antediluvial zoo,
  (Chorus) Messrs. Billing and Coo.
    Noah's larks, good as noo.

He was joulting by Wellinton's monument
Our rotorious hippopopopotamuns   65
When some bugger let down the backtrap of the omnibus
And he caught his death of fusiliers,
  (Chorus) With his rent in his rears.
    Give him six years.

'Tis sore pity for his innocent poor children   70
But look out for his missus legitimate!
When that frew gets a grip of old Earwicker
Won't there be earwigs on the green?
  (Chorus) Big earwigs on the green,
    The largest ever you seen.   75

  Suffoclose! Shikespower! Seudodanto! Anonymoses!

Then we'll have a free trade Gaels' band and mass meeting
For to sod the brave son of Scandiknavery.
And we'll bury him down in Oxmanstown
Along with the devil and Danes,   80
  (Chorus) With the deaf and dumb Danes,
    And all their remains.

And not all the king's men nor his horses
Will resurrect his corpus
For there's no true spell in Connacht or hell   85
  (bis) That's able to raise a Cain.

James Stephens (*1882–1950*)

A GLASS OF BEER

The lanky hank of a she in the inn over there
Nearly killed me for asking the loan of a glass of beer;
May the devil grip the whey-faced slut by the hair,
And beat bad manners out of her skin for a year.

That parboiled ape, with the toughest jaw you will see   5
On virtue's path, and a voice that would rasp the dead,

Came roaring and raging the minute she looked at me,
And threw me out of the house on the back of my head!

If I asked her master he'd give me a cask a day;
But she, with the beer at hand, not a gill would arrange!   10
May she marry a ghost and bear him a kitten, and may
The High King of Glory permit her to get the mange.

William Carlos Williams (*1883–1963*)

A MARRIAGE RITUAL

1928
                    Above
the darkness of a river, upon
winter's icy sky,
dreams the silhouette of the city:

This is my own! a flower,   5
a fruit, an animal by itself—

It does not recognize me
and never will. Still, it is my own
and my heart goes out to it
dumbly—   10

                    But eloquently in
my own breast for you whom I love
—and cannot express what
my love is, how it varies, though
I waste it—   15

                    It is
a river flowing through refuse
the dried sticks of weeds
and falling shell-ice lilac
from above as if with thoughts   20
of you—

This is my face and its moods
my moods, a riffled whiteness
shaken by the flow
that's constant in its swiftness   25
as a pool—

A Polack in
the stinging wind, her arms
wrapped to her breast
comes shambling near. To look   30
at what? downstream. It is
an old world flavor: the poor
the unthrifty, passionately biased
by what errors of conviction—

Now a boy   35
is rolling a stout metal drum
up from below the river bank.
The woman and the boy, two
thievish figures, struggle with
the object . . in this light!   40

And still
there is one leafless tree
just at the water's edge and—

my face
constant to you!   45

THE POOR

It's the anarchy of poverty
delights me, the old
yellow wooden house indented
among the new brick tenements

Or a cast iron balcony   5
with panels showing oak branches
in full leaf. It fits
the dress of the children

reflecting every stage and
custom of necessity—   10
Chimneys, roofs, fences of
wood and metal in an unfenced

age and enclosing next to
nothing at all: the old man
in a sweater and soft black   15
hat who sweeps the sidewalk—

his own ten feet of it—
in a wind that fitfully

turning his corner has
overwhelmed the entire city   20

Ezra Pound (*1885–*   )

THE RIVER-MERCHANT'S WIFE:
A LETTER

While my hair was still cut straight across my forehead
I played about the front gate, pulling flowers.
You came by on bamboo stilts, playing horse,
You walked about my seat, playing with blue plums.
And we went on living in the village of Chokan: 5
Two small people, without dislike or suspicion.

At fourteen I married My Lord you.
I never laughed, being bashful.
Lowering my head, I looked at the wall.
Called to, a thousand times, I never looked back.   10

At fifteen I stopped scowling,
I desired my dust to be mingled with yours
Forever and forever and forever.
Why should I climb the look out?

At sixteen you departed,   15
You went into far Ku-to-yen, by the river of swirling
                    eddies,
And you have been gone five months.
The monkeys make sorrowful noise overhead.

You dragged your feet when you went out.
By the gate now, the moss is grown, the different mosses,   20
Too deep to clear them away!
The leaves fall early this autumn, in wind.
The paired butterflies are already yellow with August
Over the grass in the West garden;
They hurt me. I grow older.   25
If you are coming down through the narrows of the river
                    Kiang,
Please let me know beforehand,
And I will come out to meet you
                    As far as Cho-fu-Sa.

By Rihaku

Elinor Wylie (*1885–1928*)

THE EAGLE AND THE MOLE

Avoid the reeking herd,
Shun the polluted flock,
Live like that stoic bird,
The eagle of the rock.

The huddled warmth of crowds   5
Begets and fosters hate;
He keeps, above the clouds,
His cliff inviolate.

When flocks are folded warm,
And herds to shelter run,   10
He sails above the storm,
He stares into the sun.

If in the eagle's track
Your sinews cannot leap,
Avoid the lathered pack,   15
Turn from the steaming sheep.

If you would keep your soul
From spotted sight or sound,
Live like the velvet mole;
Go burrow underground   20

And there hold intercourse
With roots of trees and stones,
With rivers at their source,
And disembodied bones.

John Gould Fletcher (*1886–1950*)

EVENING SKY

The Sky spreads out its poor array
Of tattered flags,
Saffron and rose
Over the weary huddle of housetops
Smoking their evening pipes in silence.   5

Marianne Moore (*1887–*   )

COMBAT CULTURAL

One likes to see a laggard rook's high
speed at sunset to outfly the dark,
    or a mount well schooled for a medal—
front legs tucked under for the barrier,
    or team of leapers turned aerial.   5

I recall a documentary
of Cossacks: a visual figure, a mist
    of swords that seemed to sever
heads from bodies—feet stepping as through
    harp-strings in a scherzo. However,   10

the quadrille of Old Russia for me:
with aimlessly drooping handkerchief
    snapped like the crack of a whip;
a deliriously spun-out-level
    frock-coat skirt, unswirled and a-droop   15

in remote promenade. Let me see . . .
Old Russia, did I say? Cold Russia
    this time: the prize bunnyhug
and platform-piece of experts in the
    trip-and-slug of wrestlers in a rug.   20

"Sacked" and ready for bed apparently—
with a jab, a kick, pinned to the wall,
    they work toward the edge and stick;
stagger off, and one is victim of a
    flipflop—leg having circled leg as thick.   25

Some art, because of high quality,
is unlikely to command high sales;
    yes, no doubt; but here, oh no;
not with the frozen North's Nan-ai-ans
    of the sack in their tight touch-and-go.   30

These battlers, dressed identically—
just one person—may, by seeming twins,
    point a moral, should I confess;
we must cement the parts of any
    objective symbolic of *sagesse*.   35

Edwin Muir (*1887–1959*)

THE ANIMALS

They do not live in the world,
Are not in time and space.
From birth to death hurled
No word do they have, not one
To plant a foot upon,   5
Were never in any place.

For with names the world was called
Out of the empty air,
With names was built and walled,
Line and circle and square,   10
Dust and emerald;
Snatched from deceiving death
By the articulate breath.

But these have never trod
Twice the familiar track,   15
Never never turned back
Into the memoried day.
All is new and near
In the unchanging Here
Of the fifth great day of God,   20
That shall remain the same,
Never shall pass away.

On the sixth day we came.

T. S. Eliot (*1888–1965*)

BURNT NORTON

I

Time present and time past
Are both perhaps present in time future,
And time future contained in time past.
If all time is eternally present
All time is unredeemable.   5

What might have been is an abstraction
Remaining a perpetual possibility
Only in a world of speculation.
What might have been and what has been
Point to one end, which is always present.   10
Footfalls echo in the memory
Down the passage which we did not take
Towards the door we never opened
Into the rose-garden. My words echo
Thus, in your mind.   15
                    But to what purpose
Disturbing the dust on a bowl of rose-leaves
I do not know.
                    Other echoes
Inhabit the garden. Shall we follow?   20
Quick, said the bird, find them, find them,
Round the corner. Through the first gate,
Into our first world, shall we follow
The deception of the thrush? Into our first world.
There they were, dignified, invisible,   25
Moving without pressure, over the dead leaves,
In the autumn heat, through the vibrant air,
And the bird called, in response to
The unheard music hidden in the shrubbery,
And the unseen eyebeam crossed, for the roses   30
Had the look of flowers that are looked at.
There they were as our guests, accepted and accepting.
So we moved, and they, in a formal pattern,
Along the empty alley, into the box circle,
To look down into the drained pool.   35
Dry the pool, dry concrete, brown edged,
And the pool was filled with water out of sunlight,
And the lotos rose, quietly, quietly,
The surface glittered out of heart of light,
And they were behind us, reflected in the pool.   40
Then a cloud passed, and the pool was empty.
Go, said the bird, for the leaves were full of children,
Hidden excitedly, containing laughter.
Go, go, go, said the bird: human kind
Cannot bear very much reality.   45
Time past and time future
What might have been and what has been
Point to one end, which is always present.

II

Garlic and sapphires in the mud
Clot the bedded axle-tree.   50
The trilling wire in the blood
Sings below inveterate scars
And reconciles forgotten wars.
The dance along the artery
The circulation of the lymph   55
Are figured in the drift of stars
Ascend to summer in the tree
We move above the moving tree
In light upon the figured leaf
And hear upon the sodden floor   60
Below, the boarhound and the boar
Pursue their pattern as before
But reconciled among the stars.

At the still point of the turning world. Neither flesh nor
                                    fleshless;
Neither from nor towards; at the still point, there the dance is,   65
But neither arrest nor movement. And do not call it fixity,
Where past and future are gathered. Neither movement
                                    from nor towards,
Neither ascent nor decline. Except for the point, the still
                                    point,
There would be no dance, and there is only the dance.
I can only say, *there* we have been: but I cannot say where.   70
And I cannot say, how long, for that is to place it in time.

The inner freedom from the practical desire,
The release from action and suffering, release from the inner
And the outer compulsion, yet surrounded
By a grace of sense, a white light still and moving,   75
Erhebung without motion, concentration
Without elimination, both a new world
And the old made explicit, understood
In the completion of its partial ecstasy,
The resolution of its partial horror.   80
Yet the enchainment of past and future
Woven in the weakness of the changing body,
Protects mankind from heaven and damnation
Which flesh cannot endure.
                                    Time past and time future   85
Allow but a little consciousness.

To be conscious is not to be in time
But only in time can the moment in the rose-garden,
The moment in the arbour where the rain beat,
The moment in the draughty church at smokefall   90
Be remembered; involved with past and future.
Only through time time is conquered.

III

Here is a place of disaffection
Time before and time after
In a dim light: neither daylight   95
Investing form with lucid stillness
Turning shadow into transient beauty
With slow rotation suggesting permanence
Nor darkness to purify the soul
Emptying the sensual with deprivation   100
Cleansing affection from the temporal.
Neither plenitude nor vacancy. Only a flicker
Over the strained time-ridden faces
Distracted from distraction by distraction
Filled with fancies and empty of meaning   105
Tumid apathy with no concentration
Men and bits of paper, whirled by the cold wind
That blows before and after time,
Wind in and out of unwholesome lungs
Time before and time after.   110
Eructation of unhealthy souls
Into the faded air, the torpid
Driven on the wind that sweeps the gloomy hills of London,
Hampstead and Clerkenwell, Campden and Putney,
Highgate, Primrose and Ludgate. Not here   115
Not here the darkness, in this twittering world.

Descend lower, descend only
Into the world of perpetual solitude,
World not world, but that which is not world,
Internal darkness, deprivation   120
And destitution of all property,
Desiccation of the world of sense,
Evacuation of the world of fancy,
Inoperancy of the world of spirit;
This is the one way, and the other   125
Is the same, not in movement
But abstention from movement; while the world moves

In appetency, on its metalled ways
Of time past and time future.

IV

Time and the bell have buried the day,   130
The black cloud carries the sun away.
Will the sunflower turn to us, will the clematis
Stray down, bend to us; tendril and spray
Clutch and cling?
Chill   135
Fingers of yew be curled
Down on us? After the kingfisher's wing
Has answered light to light, and is silent, the light is still
At the still point of the turning world.

V

Words move, music moves   140
Only in time; but that which is only living
Can only die. Words, after speech, reach
Into the silence. Only by the form, the pattern,
Can words or music reach
The stillness, as a Chinese jar still   145
Moves perpetually in its stillness.
Not the stillness of the violin, while the note lasts,
Not that only, but the co-existence,
Or say that the end precedes the beginning,
And the end and the beginning were always there   150
Before the beginning and after the end.
And all is always now. Words strain,
Crack and sometimes break, under the burden,
Under the tension, slip, slide, perish,
Decay with imprecision, will not stay in place,   155
Will not stay still. Shrieking voices
Scolding, mocking, or merely chattering,
Always assail them. The Word in the desert
Is most attacked by voices of temptation,
The crying shadow in the funeral dance,   160
The loud lament of the disconsolate chimera.

The detail of the pattern is movement,
As in the figure of the ten stairs.
Desire itself is movement
Not in itself desirable;   165
Love is itself unmoving,

Only the cause and end of movement,
Timeless, and undesiring
Except in the aspect of time
Caught in the form of limitation   170
Between un-being and being.
Sudden in a shaft of sunlight
Even while the dust moves
There rises the hidden laughter
Of children in the foliage   175
Quick now, here, now, always—
Ridiculous the waste sad time
Stretching before and after.

THE LOVE SONG OF J. ALFRED PRUFROCK

S'io credesse che mia riposta fosse
A persona che mai tornasse al mondo,
Questa fiamma staria senza piu scosse.
Ma perciocche giammai di questo fondo
Non torno vivo alcun, s'i'odo il vero,
Senza tema d'infamia ti rispondo.

Let us go then, you and I,
When the evening is spread out against the sky
Like a patient etherised upon a table;
Let us go, through certain half-deserted streets,
The muttering retreats   5
Of restless nights in one-night cheap hotels
And sawdust restaurants with oyster-shells:
Streets that follow like a tedious argument
Of insidious intent
To lead you to an overwhelming question . . .   10
Oh, do not ask, "What is it?"
Let us go and make our visit.

In the room the women come and go
Talking of Michelangelo.

The yellow fog that rubs its back upon the window-
                                    panes   15
The yellow smoke that rubs its muzzle on the window-panes
Licked its tongue into the corners of the evening,
Lingered upon the pools that stand in drains,
Let fall upon its back the soot that falls from chimneys,

Slipped by the terrace, made a sudden leap,   20
And seeing that it was a soft October night,
Curled once about the house, and fell asleep.

    And indeed there will be time
For the yellow smoke that slides along the street,
Rubbing its back upon the window-panes;   25
There will be time, there will be time
To prepare a face to meet the faces that you meet;
There will be time to murder and create,
And time for all the works and days of hands
That lift and drop a question on your plate;   30
Time for you and time for me,
And time yet for a hundred indecisions,
And for a hundred visions and revisions,
Before the taking of a toast and tea.

    In the room the women come and go   35
Talking of Michelangelo.

    And indeed there will be time
To wonder, "Do I dare?" and, "Do I dare?"
Time to turn back and descend the stair,
With a bald spot in the middle of my hair—   40
[They will say: "How his hair is growing thin!"]
My morning coat, my collar mounting firmly to the chin,
My necktie rich and modest, but asserted by a simple pin—
[They will say: "But how his arms and legs are thin!"]
Do I dare   45
Disturb the universe?
In a minute there is time
For decisions and revisions which a minute will reverse.

    For I have known them all already, known them all:—
Have known the evenings, mornings, afternoons,   50
I have measured out my life with coffee spoons;
I know the voices dying with a dying fall
Beneath the music from a farther room.
    So how should I presume?

And I have known the eyes already, known them all—   55
The eyes that fix you in a formulated phrase,
And when I am formulated, sprawling on a pin,
When I am pinned and wriggling on the wall,
Then how should I begin

To spit out all the butt-ends of my days and ways? 60
    And how should I presume?
    And I have known the arms already, known them all—
Arms that are braceleted and white and bare
[But in the lamplight, downed with light brown hair!]
Is it perfume from a dress 65
That makes me so digress?
Arms that lie along a table, or wrap about a shawl.
    And should I then presume?
    And how should I begin?

      .   .   .   .   .

Shall I say, I have gone at dusk through narrow streets 70
And watched the smoke that rises from the pipes
Of lonely men in shirt-sleeves, leaning out of windows?

    I should have been a pair of ragged claws
Scuttling across the floors of silent seas.

      .   .   .   .   .

And the afternoon, the evening, sleeps so peacefully! 75
Smoothed by long fingers,
Asleep ... tired ... or it malingers,
Stretched on the floor, here beside you and me.
Should I, after tea and cakes and ices,
Have the strength to force the moment to its crisis? 80
But though I have wept and fasted, wept and prayed,
Though I have seen my head [grown slightly bald] brought in
    upon a platter,
I am no prophet—and here's no great matter;
I have seen the moment of my greatness flicker,
And I have seen the eternal Footman hold my coat, and
            snicker, 85
And in short, I was afraid.

    And would it have been worth it, after all,
After the cups, the marmalade, the tea,
Among the porcelain, among some talk of you and me,
Would it have been worth while, 90
To have bitten off the matter with a smile,
To have squeezed the universe into a ball
To roll it toward some overwhelming question,
To say: "I am Lazarus, come from the dead,
Come back to tell you all, I shall tell you all"— 95
If one, settling a pillow by her head,

Should say: "That is not what I meant at all.
That is not it, at all."

And would it have been worth it, after all,
Would it have been worth while,   100
After the sunsets and the dooryards and the sprinkled streets,
After the novels, after the teacups, after the skirts that trail
    along the floor—
And this, and so much more?—
It is impossible to say just what I mean!
But as if a magic lantern threw the nerves in patterns on a
    screen: 105
Would it have been worth while
If one, settling a pillow or throwing off a shawl,
And turning toward the window, should say:
  "That is not it at all,
  That is not what I meant, at all."   110

    . . . . .

No! I am not Prince Hamlet, nor was meant to be;
Am an attendant lord, one that will do
To swell a progress, start a scene or two,
Advise the prince; no doubt, an easy tool,
Deferential, glad to be of use,   115
Politic, cautious, and meticulous;
Full of high sentence, but a bit obtuse;
At times, indeed, almost ridiculous—
Almost, at times, the Fool.

  I grow old . . . I grow old . . .   120
I shall wear the bottoms of my trousers rolled.

  Shall I part my hair behind? Do I dare to eat a peach?
I shall wear white flannel trousers, and walk upon the beach.
I have heard the mermaids singing, each to each.

  I do not think that they will sing to me.   125

  I have seen them riding seaward on the waves
Combing the white hair of the waves blown back
When the wind blows the water white and black.

  We have lingered in the chambers of the sea
By sea-girls wreathed with seaweed red and brown   130
Till human voices wake us, and we drown.

Archibald MacLeish (*1892–*   )

YOU, ANDREW MARVELL

And here face down beneath the sun
And here upon earth's noonward height
To feel the always coming on
The always rising of the night

To feel creep up the curving east   5
The earthly chill of dusk and slow
Upon those under lands the vast
And ever-climbing shadow grow

And strange at Ecbatan the trees
Take leaf by leaf the evening strange   10
The flooding dark about their knees
The mountains over Persia change

And now at Kermanshah the gate
Dark empty and the withered grass
And through the twilight now the late   15
Few travelers in the westward pass

And Baghdad darken and the bridge
Across the silent river gone
And through Arabia the edge
Of evening widen and steal on   20

And deepen on Palmyra's street
The wheel rut in the ruined stone
And Lebanon fade out and Crete
High through the clouds and overblown

And over Sicily the air   25
Still flashing with the landward gulls
And loom and slowly disappear
The sails above the shadowy hulls

And Spain go under and the shore
Of Africa the gilded sand   30
And evening vanish and no more
The low pale light across that land

Nor now the long light on the sea—

And here face downward in the sun
To feel how swift how secretly   35
The shadow of the night comes on . . .

E. E. Cummings (*1894–1962*)

IN JUST-SPRING

in Just-
spring   when the world is mud-
luscious the little
lame balloonman

whistles   far   and wee   5

and eddieandbill come
running from marbles and
piracies and it's
spring

when the world is puddle-wonderful   10

the queer
old balloonman whistles
far   and   wee
and bettyandisbel come dancing

from hop-scotch and jump-rope and   15

it's
spring
and
      the

            goat-footed   20

balloonMan   whistles
far
and
wee

MAGGIE AND MILLY AND MOLLY AND MAY

maggie and milly and molly and may
went down to the beach(to play one day)

and maggie discovered a shell that sang
so sweetly she couldn't remember her troubles,and

milly befriended a stranded star   5
whose rays five languid fingers were;

and molly was chased by a horrible thing
which raced sideways while blowing bubbles:and

may came home with a smooth round stone
as small as a world and as large as alone.   10

For whatever we lose(like a you or a me)
it's always ourselves we find in the sea

MY FATHER MOVED THROUGH DOOMS OF LOVE

my father moved through dooms of love
through sames of am through haves of give,
singing each morning out of each night
my father moved through depths of height

this motionless forgetful where   5
turned at his glance to shining here;
that if(so timid air is firm)
under his eyes would stir and squirm

newly as from unburied which
floats the first who,his april touch   10
drove sleeping selves to swarm their fates
woke dreamers to their ghostly roots

and should some why completely weep
my father's fingers brought her sleep:
vainly no smallest voice might cry   15
for he could feel the mountains grow.

Lifting the valleys of the sea
my father moved through griefs of joy;
praising a forehead called the moon
singing desire into begin   20

joy was his song and joy so pure
a heart of star by him could steer
and pure so now and now so yes
the wrists of twilight would rejoice

keen as midsummer's keen beyond   25
conceiving mind of sun will stand,
so strictly(over utmost him
so hugely)stood my father's dream

his flesh was flesh his blood was blood:
no hungry man but wished him food;   30

no cripple wouldn't creep one mile
uphill to only see him smile.

Scorning the pomp of must and shall
my father moved through dooms of feel;
his anger was as right as rain   35
his pity was as green as grain

septembering arms of year extend
less humbly wealth to foe and friend
than he to foolish and to wise
offered immeasurable is   40

proudly and(by octobering flame
beckoned)as earth will downward climb,
so naked for immortal work
his shoulders marched against the dark

his sorrow was as true as bread: 45
no liar looked him in the head;
if every friend became his foe
he'd laugh and build a world with snow.

My father moved through theys of we,
singing each new leaf out of each tree   50
(and every child was sure that spring
danced when she heard my father sing)

then let men kill which cannot share,
let blood and flesh be mud and mire,
scheming imagine,passion willed,   55
freedom a drug that's bought and sold

giving to steal and cruel kind,
a heart to fear,to doubt a mind,
to differ a disease of same,
conform the pinnacle of am   60

though dull were all we taste as bright,
bitter all utterly things sweet,
maggoty minus and dumb death
all we inherit,all bequeath

and nothing quite so least as truth   65
—i say though hate were why men breathe—
because my father lived his soul
love is the whole and more than all

PITY THIS BUSY MONSTER, MANUNKIND

pity this busy monster,manunkind,

not. Progress is a comfortable disease:
your victim(death and life safely beyond)

plays with the bigness of his littleness
—electrons deify one razorblade   5
into a mountainrange;lenses extend

unwish through curving wherewhen till unwish
returns on its unself.
                              A world of made
is not a world of born—pity poor flesh   10

and trees,poor stars and stones,but never this
fine specimen of hypermagical

ultraomnipotence. We doctors know

a hopeless case if—listen:there's a hell
of a good universe next door;let's go   15

SOMEWHERE I HAVE NEVER TRAVELLED

somewhere i have never travelled,gladly beyond
any experience,your eyes have their silence:
in your most frail gesture are things which enclose me,
or which i cannot touch because they are too near

your slightest look easily will unclose me   5
though i have closed myself as fingers,
you open always petal by petal myself as Spring opens
(touching skilfully,mysteriously)her first rose

or if your wish be to close me,i and
my life will shut very beautifully,suddenly,   10
as when the heart of this flower imagines
the snow carefully everywhere descending;

nothing which we are to perceive in this world equals
the power of your intense fragility:whose texture
compels me with the colour of its countries,   15
rendering death and forever with each breathing

(i do not know what it is about you that closes
and opens;only something in me understands

the voice of your eyes is deeper than all roses)
nobody,not even the rain,has such small hands   20

THAT MELANCHOLY

that melancholy

fellow'll play
his handorgan
until you say

"i want a fortune"   5

.At which(smiling)he stops:
& pick
ing up a magical stick
t,a,p,s

this dingy cage:then with a ghost   10

's rainfaint windthin
voice-which-is
no-voice sobcries

"paw?lee"

—whereupon out(SlO   15
wLy)steps(to
mount the wand)a by no
means almost

white morethanPerson;who

(riding through space   20
to diminutive this
opened drawer)tweak

S with his brutebeak

one fatal faded(pinkish or
yellowish maybe)piece   25
of pitiful paper—
but now,as Mr bowing Cockatoo

proffers the meaning of the stars

14th st dis(because my tears
are full of eyes)appears. Because   30
only the truest things always

are true because they can't be true

Allen Tate (*1899–   *)

ODE TO THE CONFEDERATE DEAD

Row after row with strict impunity
The headstones yield their names to the element,
The wind whirrs without recollection;
In the riven troughs the splayed leaves
Pile up, of nature the casual sacrament   5
To the seasonal eternity of death;
Then driven by the fierce scrutiny
Of heaven to their election in the vast breath,
They sough the rumor of mortality.

Autumn is desolation in the plot   10
Of a thousand acres where these memories grow
From the inexhaustible bodies that are not
Dead, but feed the grass row after rich row.
Think of the autumns that have come and gone!—
Ambitious November with the humors of the year   15
With a particular zeal for every slab,
Staining the uncomfortable angels that rot
On the slabs, a wing chipped here, an arm there:
The brute curiosity of an angel's stare
Turns you, like them, to stone,   20
Transforms the heaving air
Till plunged to a heavier world below
You shift your sea-space blindly
Heaving, turning like the blind crab.

    Dazed by the wind, only the wind   25
    The leaves flying, plunge

You know who have waited by the wall
The twilight certainty of an animal,
Those midnight restitutions of the blood
You know—the immitigable pines, the smoky frieze   30
Of the sky, the sudden call: you know the rage,
The cold pool left by the mounting flood,
Of muted Zeno and Parmenides.
You who have waited for the angry resolution
Of those desires that should be yours tomorrow,   35
You know the unimportant shrift of death
And praise the vision

And praise the arrogant circumstance
Of those who fall
Rank upon rank, hurried beyond decision—   40
Here by the sagging gate, stopped by the wall.

    Seeing, seeing only the leaves
    Flying, plunge and expire

Turn your eyes to the immoderate past,
Turn to the inscrutable infantry rising   45
Demons out of the earth—they will not last.
Stonewall, Stonewall, and the sunken fields of hemp,
Shiloh, Antietam, Malvern Hill, Bull Run.
Lost in that orient of the thick and fast
You will curse the setting sun.   50

    Cursing only the leaves crying
    Like an old man in a storm

You hear the shout, the crazy hemlocks point
With troubled fingers to the silence which
Smothers you, a mummy, in time.   55
                        The hound bitch
Toothless and dying, in a musty cellar
Hears the wind only.
                    Now that the salt of their blood
Stiffens the saltier oblivion of the sea,   60
Seals the malignant purity of the flood,
What shall we who count our days and bow
Our heads with a commemorial woe
In the ribboned coats of grim felicity,
What shall we say of the bones, unclean,   65
Whose verdurous anonymity will grow?

The ragged arms, the ragged heads and eyes
Lost in these acres of the insane green?
The gray lean spiders come, they come and go;
In a tangle of willows without light   70
The singular screech-owl's tight
Invisible lyric seeds the mind
With the furious murmur of their chivalry.

    We shall say only the leaves
    Flying, plunge and expire   75

We shall say only the leaves whispering
In the improbable mist of nightfall

That flies on multiple wing:
Night is the beginning and the end

And in between the ends of distraction   80
Waits mute speculation, the patient curse
That stones the eyes, or like the jaguar leaps
For his own image in a jungle pool, his victim.

What shall we say who have knowledge
Carried to the heart? Shall we take the act   85
To the grave? Shall we, more hopeful, set up the grave
In the house? The ravenous grave?

                                   Leave now
The shut gate and the decomposing wall:
The gentle serpent, green in the mulberry bush,
Riots with his tongue through the hush—   90
Sentinel of the grave who counts us all!

Langston Hughes (*1902–1967*)

MORNING AFTER

I was so sick last night I
Didn't hardly know my mind.
So sick last night I
Didn't know my mind.
I drunk some bad licker that   5
Almost made me blind.

Had a dream last night I
Thought I was in hell.
I drempt last night I
Thought I was in hell.   10
Woke up and looked around me—
Babe, your mouth was open like a well.

I said, Baby! Baby!
Please don't snore so loud.
Baby! Please!   15
Please don't snore so loud.
You jest a little bit o' woman but you
Sound like a great big crowd.

Merrill Moore (*1903–1957*)

WARNING TO ONE

Death is the strongest of all living things
And when it happens do not look in the eyes
For a dead fire or a lack-luster there,
But listen for the words that fall from lips
Or do not fall. Silence is not death;   5
It merely means that the one who is conserving breath
Is not concerned with tattle and small quips.

Watch the quick fingers and the way they move
During unguarded moments—words of love
And love's caresses may be cold as ice   10
And cold the glitter of engagement rings;
Death is the sword that hangs on a single hair,
And that thin tenuous hair is no more than love
And yours is the silly head it hangs above.

Richard Eberhart (*1904–   *)

BOSTON

Some of the best Bostonians were truck drivers.
Packy came across the river daily, year to year,
With a load of goods and passed the time of day
In the shipping room. In a stand-up at the corner
One took the gossip of the street with a coke and frank.   5
The Custom House Tower was our Rialto.

While the head walked daily up Franklin Street
In all seasons, in every kind of weather,
Without the slightest ability to change his ways,
To sit primly on a round stool at Thompson's Spa,   10
The ritual lunch and talk with singular friends.
His observations were objective, brittle, realistic.

There were the old days on Atlantic Avenue
When the Eastern Steamship Company vessel left at five,
Blasts reverberating out across Boston Harbor,   15

With folk for Maine. Good meals and the receiving sea,
A comfortable rest, and in cold morning light
To be put down on your own island or point of mainland,

Dark Harbor, Leadbetter Narrows, Blake's Point, Cape
            Rosier
And to see your wife and children waving greetings,   20
A week-end of pleasure in store, before taking the boat
Monday southwest Boston bound, back to Broad Street.
Each sea voyage was potential danger. Vessels
Disappeared in sudden storms never to be seen again.

Once there on the wharf on a cold winter day   25
A man fell off the dock, the icy waters dragged at him,
But his winter overcoat held him up somewhat.
A life line reached him and they pulled him in.
Shivering with exposure, calling at taxi cabs,
None would stop for a wet and ludicrous man.   30

A police car stopped and took him in.
By now chattering and somewhat incoherent
When he reached the desk and asked for a blanket
This old descendant of the earliest settlers
Was asked his name and address, then his religion,   35
At which he jumped, "Can't you see that I am a Baptist?"

The dead are safest in their graves off Tremont Street.
Some stop to read, most pass to live their days,
History is visible on the stones and in the faces.
We think nothing of reducing Scollay Square,   40
Gone are the smoky jokes and highjinks of the Old Howard.
Will we not some day tear up the holy gravestones?

The city is violated of its intimate past
To make way for public transportation high above it
As if a city were only to get in and out of,   45
Cars go under the Common where cows used to graze,
Or at least once a year to keep it common property.
The present highest building would be called Prudential.

The enticing light on the Charles in early Spring,
Only navigable to Watertown, too dirty to swim in,   50
As in other seasons ennobles the hill and the dome,
Gay boats in the limited contention of the basin,
Lovers believing on the banks along by the Boat House,
Young mothers sporting new babies by hand or in pram.

While up the river beyond the halls of conclamant Harvard   55
The typical dump heap of American enterprise

Smoulders and smokes, tyrannizing Mount Auburn Cemetery
Where rest the just and the unjust, ancient corpses and new
ones,
Including Henry James, and Mary Baker Eddy
With a telephone in her pergola to call us if need be.   60

The old English faces are disappearing,
The Saltonstall look gives way to Irish Kennedy,
Small prankster Ciardi dodged the cops of Medford Square,
John Brooks Wheelwright's father built the Pepper Pot
bridge,
John was killed in a taxi crossing from M.I.T. to Marlborough
Street.   65
Phelps Putnam passed smutty postcards in a bar on Mass.
Avenue

After the first reading of Robert Lowell—he was T.S. then.
And when Dylan Thomas came to town
He practically knocked over Matty's grandfather clock
On Louisburg Square. Our wives, custodial, had to   70
Pull off his pants and put him to bed like a baby
At Mrs. Tremble's Faculty Guest House at two in the morning.

City of the swanboats, the Abolitionists, Bunker Hill,
Back to the time beyond us when Leif Erickson
Was supposed to have voyaged up the Charles River.   75
Whether he did so or not is unknown, is misty still.
The sea ever intrigued the skins of Bostonians,
Many a smart vessel docked and sailed, Dana sailed to fame.

The new city cannot remember the old Boston
Of Revere. It cannot remember the Boston Massacre   80
Walking over the place on casual errands.
It has saved at least, thus far, Fanueil Hall.
The new dynamism is less of individualism,
More of the touch of the whole of America.

Planes drop in from India and Africa.   85
Art flourishes and the universities inquire.
Dark beer is still the best at Jakey Wirth's.
At the Athens Olympia George serves shishkebab,
Who served the same in nineteen thirty-five.
But hide-bound elders still decline to bless   90

The marriage of their daughters with another race
Than theirs. In this they have lost the race.
As yet no curfew keeps the young indoors at home,
Although crime finds its way about the town at night.

And how many, in the business and press of the day,   95
Think of the forward look of William James, of Emerson?

The Irish mayor took lessons in Harvard English,
Kept the Grotonian President waiting at Commencement.
I beheld bow-legged President Lowell at eighty
Walking on Commonwealth, death-dealer to edge trimmer,   100
Fish peddler. The bad, the good, the weak and the best
Have trod the cow paths, ridden the sea ways.

And who shall stand up with fearless eye
Warning of sin like Jonathan Edwards?
Where is the taut character in modern Boston?   105
The tea party was itself a kind of family trust,
Now we imagine psychedelic trips, and lust
For invention of new kinds of truths and thrusts.

The future holds the past awry and askance.
I remember an elderly lady of stately grace   110
Reclining in bed at the end of her life
Pay old English respect to the art, not the person,
Who gave me the kind command, "Read, poet."
What do we do with our old histories?

In Minnesota where I came from the streams were clear,   115
Then they became more psychic in their flow.
The Cam was one such, after which came the Charles.
Now I live on an esker by the Connecticut.
I dream back to the Cedar River of my youth
My beginnings far inland, far away from Boston.   120

W. H. Auden (*1907–*   )

From KAIROS AND LOGOS

Around them boomed the rhetoric of time,
The smells and furniture of the known world
Where conscience worshipped an aesthetic order
And what was unsuccessful was condemned;
And, at the centre of its vast self-love,   5
The emperor and his pleasures, dreading death.

In lovely verse that military order,
Transferring its obsession onto time,

Besieged the body and cuckolded love;
Puzzling the boys of an athletic world,   10
These only feared another kind of Death
To which the time-obsessed are all condemned.

Night and the rivers sang a chthonic love,
Destroyer of cities and the daylight order,
But seemed to them weak arguments for death;   15
The apple tree that cannot measure time
Might taste the apple yet not be condemned;
They, to enjoy it, must renounce the world.

Friendly to what the sensual call death,
Placing their lives below the dogs who love   20
Their fallen masters and are not condemned,
They came to life within a dying order;
Outside the sunshine of its civil world
The savage waited their appointed time.

Its brilliant self-assertions were condemned   25
To interest the forest and draw death
On aqueducts and learning; yet the world
Through them, had witnessed, when predestined love
Fell like a daring meteor into time,
The condescension of eternal order.   30

So, sown in little clumps about the world,
The fair, the faithful and the uncondemned
Broke out spontaneously all over time,
Setting against the random facts of death
A ground and possibility of order,   35
Against defeat the certainty of love.

And never, like its own, condemned the world
Or hated time, but sang until their death:
"O Thou who lovest, set its love in order."

Theodore Roethke (*1908–1963*)

HER LONGING

Before this longing,
I lived serene as a fish,
At one with the plants in the pond,

The mare's tail, the floating frogbit,
Among my eight-legged friends,   5
Open like a pool, a lesser parsnip,
Like a leech, looping myself along,
A bug-eyed edible one,
A mouth like a stickleback,—
A thing quiescent!   10

But now—
The wild stream, the sea itself cannot contain me:
I dive with the black hag, the cormorant,
Or walk the pebbly shore with the humpbacked heron,
Shaking out my catch in the morning sunlight,   15
Or rise with the gar-eagle, the great-winged condor,
Floating over the mountains,
Pitting my breast against the rushing air,
A phoenix, sure of my body,
Perpetually rising out of myself,   20
My wings hovering over the shorebirds,
Or beating against the black clouds of the storm,
Protecting the sea-cliffs.

IN A DARK TIME

In a dark time, the eye begins to see,
I meet my shadow in the deepening shade;
I hear my echo in the echoing wood—
A lord of nature weeping to a tree.
I live between the heron and the wren,   5
Beasts of the hill and serpents of the den.

What's madness but nobility of soul
At odds with circumstance? The day's on fire!
I know the purity of pure despair,
My shadow pinned against a sweating wall.   10
That place among the rocks—is it a cave,
Or winding path? The edge is what I have.

A steady storm of correspondences!
A night flowing with birds, a ragged moon,
And in broad day the midnight come again!   15
A man goes far to find out what he is—
Death of the self in a long, tearless night,
All natural shapes blazing unnatural light.

Dark, dark my light, and darker my desire.
My soul, like some heat-maddened summer fly,   20
Keeps buzzing at the sill. Which I is *I*?
A fallen man, I climb out of my fear.
The mind enters itself, and God the mind,
And one is One, free in the tearing wind.

JOURNEY TO THE INTERIOR

I

In the long journey out of the self,
There are many detours, washed-out interrupted raw places
Where the shale slides dangerously
And the back wheels hang almost over the edge
At the sudden veering, the moment of turning.   5
Better to hug close, wary of rubble and falling stones.
The arroyo cracking the road, the wind-bitten buttes, the
                                canyons,
Creeks swollen in midsummer from the flash-flood roaring
                        into the narrow valley.
Reeds beaten flat by wind and rain,
Gray from the long winter, burnt at the base in late summer.   10
—Or the path narrowing,
Winding upward toward the stream with its sharp stones,
The upland of alder and birchtrees,
Through the swamp alive with quicksand,
The way blocked at last by a fallen fir-tree,   15
The thickets darkening,
The ravines ugly.

II

I remember how it was to drive in gravel,
Watching for dangerous down-hill places, where the wheels
                        whined beyond eighty—
When you hit the deep pit at the bottom of the swale,   20
The trick was to throw the car sideways and charge over the
                        hill, full of the throttle.
Grinding up and over the narrow road, spitting and roaring.
A chance? Perhaps. But the road was part of me, and its
                        ditches,
And the dust lay thick on my eyelids,—Who ever wore
                        goggles?—

Always a sharp turn to the left past a barn close to the roadside,   25
To a scurry of small dogs and a shriek of children,
The highway ribboning out in a straight thrust to the North,
To the sand dunes and fish flies, hanging, thicker than moths,
Dying brightly under the street lights sunk in coarse concrete,
The towns with their high pitted road-crowns and deep
        gutters,   30
Their wooden stores of silvery pine and weather-beaten red
        courthouses,
An old bridge below with a buckled iron railing, broken by
        some idiot plunger;
Underneath, the sluggish water running between weeds,
        broken wheels, tires, stones.
And all flows past—
The cemetery with two scrubby trees in the middle of the
        prairie,   35
The dead snakes and muskrats, the turtles gasping in the
        rubble,
The spikey purple bushes in the winding dry creek bed—
The floating hawks, the jackrabbits, the grazing cattle—
I am not moving but they are,
And the sun comes out of a blue cloud over the Tetons,   40
While, farther away, the heat-lightning flashes.
I rise and fall in the slow sea of a grassy plain,
The wind veering the car slightly to the right,
Whipping the line of white laundry, bending the cotton-
        woods apart,
The scraggly wind-break of a dusty ranch-house.   45
I rise and fall, and time folds
Into a long moment;
And I hear the lichen speak,
And the ivy advance with its white lizard feet—
On the shimmering road,   50
On the dusty detour.

III

I see the flower of all water, above and below me, the never
        receding,
Moving, unmoving in a parched land, white in the moonlight:
The soul at a still-stand,
At ease after rocking the flesh to sleep,   55
Petals and reflections of petals mixed on the surface of a glassy
        pool,

And the waves flattening out when the fishermen drag their
                    nets over the stones.

In the moment of time when the small drop forms, but does
                    not fall,
I have known the heart of the sun,—
In the dark and light of a dry place,   60
In a flicker of fire brisked by a dusty wind.
I have heard, in a drip of leaves,
A slight song,
After the midnight cries.
I rehearse myself for this: 65
The stand at the stretch in the face of death,
Delighting in surface change, the glitter of light on waves,
And I roam elsewhere, my body thinking,
Turning toward the other side of light,
In a tower of wind, a tree idling in air,   70
Beyond my own echo,
Neither forward nor backward,
Unperplexed, in a place leading nowhere.

As a blind man, lifting a curtain, knows it is morning,
I know this change: 75
On one side of silence there is no smile;
But when I breathe with the birds,
The spirit of wrath becomes the spirit of blessing,
And the dead begin from their dark to sing in my sleep.

THE MEADOW MOUSE

I

In a shoe box stuffed in an old nylon stocking
Sleeps the baby mouse I found in the meadow,
Where he trembled and shook beneath a stick
Till I caught him up by the tail and brought him in,
Cradled in my hand,   5
A little quaker, the whole body of him trembling,
His absurd whiskers sticking out like a cartoon-mouse,
His feet like small leaves,
Little lizard-feet,
Whitish and spread wide when he tried to struggle away,   10
Wriggling like a miniscule puppy.

Now he's eaten his three kinds of cheese and drunk from his
                    bottle-cap watering-trough—

So much he just lies in one corner,
His tail curled under him, his belly big
As his head; his bat-like ears   15
Twitching, tilting toward the least sound.

Do I imagine he no longer trembles
When I come close to him?
He seems no longer to tremble.

II

But this morning the shoe-box house on the back porch is
                     empty.   20
Where has he gone, my meadow mouse,
My thumb of a child that nuzzled in my palm?—
To run under the hawk's wing,
Under the eye of the great owl watching from the elm-tree,
To live by courtesy of the shrike, the snake, the tom-cat.   25

I think of the nestling fallen into the deep grass,
The turtle gasping in the dusty rubble of the highway,
The paralytic stunned in the tub, and the water rising,—
All things innocent, hapless, forsaken.

ROOT CELLAR

Nothing would sleep in that cellar, dank as a ditch,
Bulbs broke out of boxes hunting for chinks in the dark,
Shoots dangled and drooped,
Lolling obscenely from mildewed crates,
Hung down long yellow evil necks, like tropical snakes.   5
And what a congress of stinks!—
Roots ripe as old bait,
Pulpy stems, rank, silo-rich,
Leaf-mold, manure, lime, piled against slippery planks.
Nothing would give up life: 10
Even the dirt kept breathing a small breath.

THE SEQUEL

I

Was I too glib about eternal things,
An intimate of air and all its songs?
Pure aimlessness pursued and yet pursued
And all wild longings of the insatiate blood

Brought me down to my knees. O who can be   5
Both moth and flame? The weak moth blundering by.
Whom do we love? I thought I knew the truth;
Of grief I died, but no one knew my death.

II

I saw a body dancing in the wind,
A shape called up out of my natural mind;   10
I heard a bird stir in its true confine;
A nestling sighed—I called that nestling mine;
A partridge drummed; a minnow nudged its stone;
We danced, we danced, under a dancing moon;
And on the coming of the outrageous dawn,   15
We danced together, we danced on and on.

III

Morning's a motion in a happy mind:
She stayed in light, as leaves live in the wind,
Swaying in air, like some long water weed.
She left my body, lighter than a seed;   20
I gave her body full and grave farewell.
A wind came close, like a shy animal.
A light leaf on a tree, she swayed away
To the dark beginnings of another day.

IV

Was nature kind? The heart's core tractable?   25
All waters waver, and all fires fail.
Leaves, leaves, lean forth and tell me what I am;
This single tree turns into purest flame.
I am a man, a man at intervals
Pacing a room, a room with dead-white walls;   30
I feel the autumn fail—all that slow fire
Denied in me, who has denied desire.

WISH FOR A YOUNG WIFE

My lizard, my lively writher,
May your limbs never wither,
May the eyes in your face
Survive the green ice
Of envy's mean gaze;   5
May you live out your life
Without hate, without grief,

And your hair ever blaze,
In the sun, in the sun,
When I am undone,   10
When I am no one.

Stephen Spender (*1909–*   )

THE EXPRESS

After the first powerful plain manifesto
The black statement of pistons, without more fuss
But gliding like a queen, she leaves the station.
Without bowing and with unrestrained concern
She passes the houses which humbly crowd outside,   5
The gasworks and at last the heavy page
Of death, printed by gravestones in the cemetery.
Beyond the town there lies the open country
Where, gathering speed, she acquires mystery,
The luminous self-possession of ships on ocean.   10
It is now she begins to sing—at first quite low
Then loud, and at last with a jazzy madness—
The song of her whistle screaming at curves,
Of deafening tunnels, brakes, innumerable bolts.
And always light, aerial, underneath   15
Goes the elate meter of her wheels.
Steaming through metal landscape on her lines
She plunges new eras of wild happiness
Where speed throws up strange shapes, broad curves
And parallels clean like the steel of guns.   20
At last, further than Edinburgh or Rome,
Beyond the crest of the world, she reaches night
Where only a low streamline brightness
Of phosphorus on the tossing hills is white.
Ah, like a comet through flames she moves entranced   25
Wrapped in her music no bird song, no, nor bough
Breaking with honey buds, shall ever equal.

THE LANDSCAPE NEAR AN AERODROME

More beautiful and soft than any moth
With burring furred antennae feeling its huge path
Through dusk, the air-liner with shut-off engines

Glides over suburbs and the sleeves set trailing tall
To point the wind. Gently, broadly, she falls   5
Scarcely disturbing charted currents of air.

Lulled by descent, the travellers across sea
And across feminine land indulging its easy limbs
In miles of softness, now let their eyes trained by watching
Penetrate through dusk the outskirts of this town   10
Here where industry shows a fraying edge.
Here they may see what is being done.

Beyond the winking masthead light
And the landing-ground, they observe the outposts
Of work: chimneys like lank black fingers   15
Or figures frightening and mad: and squat buildings
With their strange air behind trees, like women's faces
Shattered by grief. Here where few houses
Moan with faint light behind their blinds
They remark the unhomely sense of complaint, like a dog   20
Shut out and shivering at the foreign moon.

In the last sweep of love, they pass over fields
Behind the aerodrome, where boys play all day
Hacking dead grass: whose cries, like wild birds,
Settle upon the nearest roofs   25
But soon are hid under the loud city.

Then, as they land, they hear the tolling bell
Reaching across the landscape of hysteria
To where, larger than all the charcoaled batteries
And imaged towers against that dying sky,   30
Religion stands, the church blocking the sun.

Charles Olson (*1910–1970*)

LETTER 3

Tansy buttons, tansy
for my city
Tansy for their noses

Tansy for them,
tansy for Gloucester to take the smell   5
of all owners,
the smell

Tansy
for all of us

        Let those who use words cheap, who use us cheap   10
        take themselves out of the way
        Let them not talk of what is good for the city

        Let them free the way for me, for the men of the
                Fort
        who are not hired, who buy the white houses

        Let them cease putting out words in the public print.   15
        so that any of us have to leave, so that my Portuguese
                leave,
        leave the Lady they gave us, sell their schooners
        with the greyhounds aft, the long Diesels
        they put their money in, leave Gloucester
        in the present shame of,   20
        the wondership stolen by,
        ownership

Tansy from Cressy's
I rolled in as a boy
and didn't know it was   25
tansy

   1

Did you know, she sd, growing up there,
how rare it was? And it turned out later she meant exactly the
            long field
drops down from Ravenswood where the land abrupts,
this side of Fresh Water Cove, and throws out   30
that wonder of my childhood, the descending green does run
so,
by the beach

        where they held the muster Labor Day, and the
              engine teams
        threw such arcs of water   35

                    runs with summer with
tansy

   2

I was not born there, came, as so many of the people came,
from elsewhere. That is, my father did. And not from the
        Provinces,

not from Newfoundland. But we came early enough. When
                              he came,   40
there were three hundred sail could fill the harbor,
if they were all in, as for the Races, say
Or as now the Italians are in, for San Pietro,
and the way it is from Town Landing, all band-concert,
and fireworks   45

So I answered her: Yes,
I knew (I had that to compare to it,
was Worcester)

As the people of the earth are now, Gloucester
is heterogeneous, and so can know polis   50
not as localism, not that mu-sick (the trick
of corporations, newpapers, slick magazines, movie houses,
the ships, even the wharves, absentee-owned

they whine to my people, these entertainers, sellers

they play upon their bigotries (upon their fears   55
these   they have the nerve
to speak of that lovely hour
the Waiting Station, 5 o'clock, the Magnolia bus, Al Levy
on duty (the difference
from 1 o'clock, all the women getting off   60
the Annisquam-Lanesville,
and the letter carriers

5:40, and only the lollers
in front of the shoe-shine parlor

these, right in the people's faces (and not at all as the gulls do it,   65
who do it straight, do it all over the "Times" blowing
the day after, or the "Summer Sun" catching on pilings,
                              floating
off the Landing, the slime
the low tide reveals, the smell
then   70

3

The word does intimidate. The pay-check does.
But to use either, as cheap men

o tansy city, root city
let them not make you
as the nation is   75

I speak to any of you, not to you all, to no group, not to you
        as citizens
as my Tyrian might have. Polis now
is a few, is a coherence not even yet new (the island of this city
is a mainland now of who? who can say who are
citizens?   80

Only a man or a girl who hear a word
and that word meant to mean not a single thing the least more
        than
what it does mean (not at all to sell any one anything, to keep
        them anywhere,

not even
in this rare place   85

        Root person in root place, hear one tansy-covered
            boy tell you
what any knowing man of your city might, a letter carrier,
        say,
or that doctor—if they dared afford to take the risk, if they
        reminded themselves
that you should not be played with, that you deserve . . .
        they'd tell you
the condition of the under-water, the cut-water of anyone,
        including those   90
who take on themselves
to give you advice,
to tell you, for example,
what not to read

        They'd tell you, because they know (know as the
            house knows,   95
wearing its white face, its clapboard mask) who there is will
        not outrage you
in the next edition, who'll not seek, even knowingly, to make
        you
slave

as he is slave
whom you read   100
as the bus starts off

            whose slaver
            would keep you off the sea, would keep you
                local,

> my Nova Scotians,
> Newfoundlanders,   105
> Sicilianos,
> Isolatos

4

Isolated person in Gloucester, Massachusetts, I, Maximus,
            address you
you islands
of men and girls   110

Brother Antoninus (William Everson) (*1912–*   )

A CANTICLE TO THE WATERBIRDS
WRITTEN FOR THE FEAST OF ST. FRANCIS OF ASSISI, 1950

Clack your beaks you cormorants and kittiwakes,
North on those rockcroppings fingerjutted into the rough
            Pacific surge;
You migratory terns and pipers who leave but the temporal
            claw-track written on sandbars there of
            your presence;
Grebes and pelicans; you comber-picking scoters and you
            shore-long gulls;
All you keepers of the coastline north of here to the Men-
            docino beaches;   5
All you beyond upon the cliff-face thwarting the surf at
            Hecate Head,
Hovering the under-surge where the cold Columbia grap-
            ples at the bar;
North yet to the Sound, whose islands float like a sown flurry
            of chips upon the sea:
Break wide your harsh and salt-encrusted beaks unmade for
            song
And say a praise up to the Lord.   10

And you freshwater egrets east in the flooded marshlands
            skirting the sea-level rivers, white one-leg-
            ged watchers of shallows;
Broadheaded kingfishers minnow-hunting from willow
            stems on meandering valley sloughs;

You too, you herons, blue and supple-throated, stately,
        taking the air majestical in the sunflooded
        San Joaquin,
Grading down on your belted wings from the upper lights
        of sunset,
Mating over the willow clumps or where the flatwater rice-
        fields shimmer;   15
You killdeer, high night criers, far in the moon-suffusion sky;
Bitterns, sandwaders, all shorewalkers, all roostkeepers,
Populates of the 'dobe cliffs of the Sacramento:
Open your waterdartling beaks,
And make a praise up to the Lord.   20

For you hold the heart of His mighty fastnesses,
And shape the life of His indeterminate realms.
You are everywhere on the lonesome shores of His wide
        creation.
You keep seclusion where no man may go, giving Him
        praise;
Nor may a woman come to lift like your cleaving flight her
        clear contralto song   25
To honor the spindrift gifts of His soft abundance.
You sanctify His hermitage rocks where no holy priest may
        kneel to adore, nor holy nun assist;
And where his true communion-keepers are not enabled to
        enter.
And well may you say His praises, birds, for your ways
Are verved with the secret skills of His inclinations,   30
And your habits plaited and rare with the subdued elab-
        oration of His intricate craft;
Your days intent with the direct astuteness needful for His
        outworking,
And your nights alive with the dense repose of His infinite
        sleep.
You are His secretive charges and you serve His secretive
        ends,
In His clouded mist-conditioned stations, in His murk,   35
Obscure in your matted nestings, immured in His limitless
        ranges.
He makes you penetrate through dark interstitial joinings
        of His thicketed kingdoms,
And keep your concourse in the deeps of His shadowed
        world.

Your ways are wild but earnest, your manners grave,
Your customs carefully schooled to the note of His serious
                mien.   40
You hold the prime condition of His clean creating,
And the swift compliance with which you serve His minor
                means
Speaks of the constancy with which you hold Him.
For what is your high flight forever going home to your first
                beginnings,
But such a testament to your devotion?   45
You hold His outstretched world beneath your wings, and
                mount upon His storms,
And keep your sheer wind-lidded sight upon the vast per-
                spectives of His mazy latitudes.

But mostly it is your way you bear existence wholly within
                the context of His utter will and are un-
                troubled.
Day upon day you do not reckon, nor scrutinize tomorrow,
                nor multiply the nightfalls with a rash
                concern,
But rather assume each instant as warrant sufficient of His
                final seal.   50
Wholly in Providence you spring, and when you die you
                look on death in clarity unflinched,
Go down, a clutch of feather ragged upon the brush;
Or drop on water where you briefly lived, found food,
And now yourselves made food for His deep current-
                keeping fish, and then are gone:
Is left but the pinion feather spinning a bit on the uproil   55
Where lately the dorsal cut clear air.

You leave a silence. And this for you suffices, who are not of
                the ceremonials of man,
And hence are not made sad to now forgo them.
Yours is of another order of being, and wholly it compels.
But may you, birds, utterly seized in God's supremacy,   60
Austerely living under His austere eye—
Yet may you teach a man a necessary thing to know,
Which has to do of the strict conformity that creaturehood
                entails,
And constitutes the prime commitment all things share.
For God has given you the imponderable grace to *be* His
                verification,   65

Outside the mulled incertitude of our forensic choices;
That you, our lessers in the rich hegemony of Being,
May serve as testament to what a creature is,
And what creation owes.

Curlews, stilts and scissortails, beachcomber gulls;   70
Wave-haunters, shore-keepers, rockhead-holders, all cape-
                                        top vigilantes,
Now give God praise.
Send up the strict articulation of your throats,
And say His name.

Robert Hayden (*1913–*   )

THE BALLAD OF SUE ELLEN WESTERFIELD
(FOR CLYDE)

She grew up in bedeviled southern wilderness,
but had not been a slave, she said,
because her father wept and set her mother free.
She hardened in perilous rivertowns
and after The Surrender,   5
went as maid upon the tarnished Floating Palaces.
Rivermen reviled her for the rankling cold
sardonic pride
that gave a knife-edge to her comeliness.

When she was old, her back still straight,   10
her hair still glossy black,
she'd talk sometimes
of dangers lived through on the rivers.
But never told of him,
whose name she'd vowed she would not speak again   15
till after Jordan.
Oh, he was nearer nearer now
than wearisome kith and kin.
His blue eyes followed her
as she moved about her tasks upon the *Memphis Rose.*   20
He smiled and joshed, his voice quickening her.
She cursed the circumstance. . . .

The crazing horrors of that summer night,
the swifting flames, he fought his way to her,
the savaging panic, and helped her swim to shore.   25
The steamer like besieged Atlanta blazing,
the cries, the smoke and bellowing flames,
the flamelit thrashing forms in hellmouth water,
and he swimming out to them,
leaving her dazed and lost.   30
A woman screaming under the raddled trees—
Sue Ellen felt it was herself who screamed.
The moaning of the hurt, the terrified—
she held off shuddering despair
and went to comfort whom she could.   35

Wagons torches bells
and whimpering dusk of morning
and blankness lostness nothingness for her
until his arms had lifted her
into wild and secret dark.   40

How long how long was it they wandered,
loving fearing loving,
fugitives whose dangerous only hidingplace
was love?
How long was it before she knew   45
she could not forfeit what she was,
even for him—could not, even for him,
forswear her pride?
They kissed and said farewell at last.
He wept as had her father once.   50
They kissed and said farewell.
Until her dying-bed,
she cursed the circumstance.

Karl Shapiro (*1913–*   )

I'M WRITING THIS POEM FOR SOMEONE TO SEE

I'm writing this poem for someone to see when I'm not
    looking. This is an open book. I want to be careful to
    startle you gently. The poem is about your looking at it,

as one looks at a woman covertly. (I wonder what she's
doing in this town; it's a long way from the look in her   5
eyes.) The rings of my big notebook stand open like
the rib cage of a baracuda. Careful with your fingers.

I'm writing this poem for an after-dinner friend who's using
my pipe tobacco or my pen. I'd like some phrase to
catch his eye. I'd like some phrase to wake him up in   10
the early hours, as one wakes up with a fragment of
tune in his head (the melody for the day). The toilet
bowls glow graciously and there's a box of the best
Kleenex on the sink. I'm writing this poem for hos-
pitality. I can't stand people who say Help Yourself.   15
That always means Don't Be a Pig. Tired of picking
the locks of poems I leave this one for all and sundry.
To put your name in it would be a dirty trick.

Younger I dreamed of being a poet whose trash basket was
rifled by scholars. I learned to write trash-basket poems.   20
But this is closer to my real desire. I'm writing this
poem as much for you as a poem is possible. It stands
there like a half-filled glass, both coming and going.
I'm a bad host. The drinks are too strong; I don't know
how to carve (I say with a grin, I'm left-handed). This   25
is a poem to sneak at a glance. (I'm writing it to mean,
not be.)

John Berryman (*1914–*   )

WINTER LANDSCAPE

The three men coming down the winter hill
In brown, with tall poles and a pack of hounds
At heel, through the arrangement of the trees
Past the five figures at the burning straw,
Returning cold and silent to their town,   5

Returning to the drifted snow, the rink
Lively with children, to the older men,
The long companions they can never reach,
The blue light, men with ladders, by the church
The sledge and shadow in the twilit street,   10

Are not aware that in the sandy time
To come, the evil waste of history
Outstretched, they will be seen upon the brow
Of that same hill: when all their company
Will have been irrecoverably lost,   15

These men, this particular three in brown
Witnessed by birds will keep the scene and say
By their configuration with the trees,
The small bridge, the red houses and the fire,
What place, what time, what morning occasion   20

Sent them into the wood, a pack of hounds
At heel and the tall poles upon their shoulders,
Thence to return as now we see them and
Ankle-deep in snow down the winter hill
Descend, while three birds watch and the fourth flies.   25

Dylan Thomas (*1914–1953*)

IF I WERE TICKLED BY THE RUB OF LOVE

If I were tickled by the rub of love,
A rooking girl who stole me for her side,
Broke through her straws, breaking my bandaged string,
If the red tickle as the cattle calve
Still set to scratch a laughter from my lung,   5
I would not fear the apple nor the flood
Nor the bad blood of spring.

Shall it be male or female? say the cells,
And drop the plum like fire from the flesh.
If I were tickled by the hatching hair,   10
The winging bone that sprouted in the heels,
The itch of man upon the baby's thigh,
I would not fear the gallows nor the axe
Nor the crossed sticks of war.

Shall it be male or female? say the fingers   15
That chalk the walls with green girls and their men.
I would not fear the muscling-in of love
If I were tickled by the urchin hungers

Rehearsing heat upon a raw-edged nerve.
I would not fear the devil in the loin   20
Nor the outspoken grave.

If I were tickled by the lovers' rub
That wipes away not crow's-foot nor the lock
Of sick old manhood on the fallen jaws,
Time and the crabs and the sweethearting crib   25
Would leave me cold as butter for the flies,
The sea of scums could drown me as it broke
Dead on the sweethearts' toes.

This world is half the devil's and my own,
Daft with the drug that's smoking in a girl   30
And curling round the bud that forks her eye.
An old man's shank one-marrowed with my bone,
And all the herrings smelling in the sea,
I sit and watch the worm beneath my nail
Wearing the quick away.   35

And that's the rub, the only rub that tickles.
The knobbly ape that swings along his sex
From damp love-darkness and the nurse's twist
Can never raise the midnight of a chuckle,
Nor when he finds a beauty in the breast   40
Of lover, mother, lovers, or his six
Feet in the rubbing dust.

And what's the rub? Death's feather on the nerve?
Your mouth, my love, the thistle in the kiss?
My Jack of Christ born thorny on the tree?   45
The words of death are dryer than his stiff,
My wordy wounds are printed with your hair.
I would be tickled by the rub that is:
Man be my metaphor.

Peter Viereck (*1916–*   )

TO A SINISTER POTATO

O vast earth-apple, waiting to be fried,
Of all the starers the most many-eyed,
What furtive purpose hatched you long ago
In Indiana or in Idaho?

In Indiana and in Idaho   5
Snug underground, the great potatoes grow,
Puffed up with secret paranoias unguessed
By all the duped and starch-fed Middle West.

Like coiled-up springs or like a will-to-power
The fat and earthy lurkers bide their hour,   10
The silent watchers of our raucous show
In Indiana or in Idaho.

"They deem us dull, a food and not a flower.
Wait! We'll outshine all roses in our hour.
Not wholesomeness but mania swells us so   15
In Indiana and in Idaho.

"In each Kiwanis Club on every plate
So bland and health-exuding do we wait
That Indiana never, never knows
How much we envy stars and hate the rose."   20

Some doom will strike (as all potatoes know)
When—once too often mashed in Idaho—
From its cocoon the drabbest of earth's powers
Rises and is a star.
                              And shines.   25
                              And lours.

Gwendolyn Brooks (1917–   )

THE BALLAD OF RUDOLPH REED

Rudolph Reed was oaken.
His wife was oaken too.
And his two good girls and his good little man
Oakened as they grew.

"I am not hungry for berries.   5
I am not hungry for bread.
But hungry hungry for a house
Where at night a man in bed

"May never hear the plaster
Stir as if in pain.   10
May never hear the roaches
Falling like fat rain.

"Where never wife and children need
Go blinking through the gloom.
Where every room of many rooms   15
Will be full of room.

"Oh my home may have its east or west
Or north or south behind it.
All I know is I shall know it,
And fight for it when I find it."   20

It was in a street of bitter white
That he made his application.
For Rudolph Reed was oakener
Than others in the nation.

The agent's steep and steady stare   25
Corroded to a grin.
Why, you black old, tough old hell of a man,
Move your family in!

Nary a grin grinned Rudolph Reed,
Nary a curse cursed he,   30
But moved in his House. With his dark little wife,
And his dark little children three.

A neighbor would *look*, with a yawning eye
That squeezed into a slit.
But the Rudolph Reeds and the children three   35
Were too joyous to notice it.

For were they not firm in a home of their own
With windows everywhere
And a beautiful banistered stair
And a front yard for flowers and a back yard for grass? 40

The first night, a rock, big as two fists.
The second, a rock big as three.
But nary a curse cursed Rudolph Reed.
(Though oaken as man could be.)

The third night, a silvery ring of glass.   45
Patience ached to endure.
But he looked, and lo! small Mabel's blood
Was staining her gaze so pure.

Then up did rise our Rudolph Reed
And pressed the hand of his wife,   50
And went to the door with a thirty-four
And a beastly butcher knife.

He ran like a mad thing into the night.
And the words in his mouth were stinking.
By the time he had hurt his first white man   55
He was no longer thinking.

By the time he had hurt his fourth white man
Rudolph Reed was dead.
His neighbors gathered and kicked his corpse.
"Nigger—" his neighbors said.   60

Small Mabel whimpered all night long,
For calling herself the cause.
Her oak-eyed mother did no thing
But change the bloody gauze.

Robert Lowell (*1917–*   )

FOR THE UNION DEAD
"RELINQUUNT OMNIA SERVARE REM PUBLICAM."

The old South Boston Aquarium stands
in a Sahara of snow now. Its broken windows are boarded.
The bronze weathervane cod has lost half its scales.
The airy tanks are dry.

Once my nose crawled like a snail on the glass;   5
my hand tingled
to burst the bubbles
drifting from the noses of the cowed, compliant fish.

My hand draws back. I often sigh still
for the dark downward and vegetating kingdom   10
of the fish and reptile. One morning last March,
I pressed against the new barbed and galvanized

fence on the Boston Common. Behind their cage,
yellow dinosaur steamshovels were grunting
as they cropped up tons of mush and grass   15
to gouge their underworld garage.

Parking spaces luxuriate like civic
sandpiles in the heart of Boston.
A girdle of orange, Puritan-pumpkin colored girders
braces the tingling Statehouse,   20

shaking over the excavations, as it faces Colonel Shaw
and his bell-cheeked Negro infantry
on St. Gaudens' shaking Civil War relief,
propped by a plank splint against the garage's earthquake.

Two months after marching through Boston,   25
half the regiment was dead;
at the dedication,
William James could almost hear the bronze Negroes breathe.

Their monument sticks like a fishbone
in the city's throat.   30
Its Colonel is as lean
as a compass-needle.

He has an angry wrenlike vigilance,
a greyhound's gentle tautness;
he seems to wince at pleasure,   35
and suffocate for privacy.

He is out of bounds now. He rejoices in man's lovely,
peculiar power to choose life and die—
when he leads his black soldiers to death,
he cannot bend his back.   40

On a thousand small town New England greens,
the old white churches hold their air
of sparse, sincere rebellion; frayed flags
quilt the graveyards of the Grand Army of the Republic.

The stone statues of the abstract Union Soldier   45
grow slimmer and younger each year—
wasp-waisted, they doze over muskets
and muse through their sideburns . . .

Shaw's father wanted no monument
except the ditch,   50
where his son's body was thrown
and lost with his "niggers."

The ditch is nearer.
There are no statues for the last war here;
on Boylston Street, a commercial photograph   55
shows Hiroshima boiling

over a Mosler Safe, the "Rock of Ages"
that survived the blast. Space is nearer.
When I crouch to my television set,
the drained faces of Negro school-children rise like balloons.   60

Colonel Shaw
is riding on his bubble,
he waits
for the blessèd break.

The Aquarium is gone. Everywhere,   65
giant finned cars nose forward like fish;
a savage servility
slides by on grease.

John Bennett (*1920–*   )

ON D. H. LAWRENCE AND HIS SNAKE

New-born to brightness, free from his old skin
that rustled near him in the crinkling wind,
a huge bull blacksnake dozed where April's sun
poured warmth into a random cul-de-sac
of stones tipped vaguely from our orchard wall.   5

A boy in April, filled with April blood,
I saw him there and aped the hunter's crouch,
crept slowly near and slowly near, and then,
in primitive aggression, quick as snakes,
my hand leaped for his throat and grabbed him tight   10
and grabbed him tighter yet at his wild thresh.

His eyes remained sheer glints of anthracite,
unchanged, impassive, arrogant as bombs.
His jaws gaped useless just above my thumb,
his tongue flicked out to taste my human voice,   15
his scutes bit gently at the sudden sweat
that lifted on my hand, and his long flesh
coiled backward blindly round my lower arm.

I had the snake. He was as much possessed
as any snake could ever be. I felt   20
his cold dry anger squeeze around my skin,
I felt his muscles slide along their coils,
I looked into his black, slit-irised eyes
and held his head beyond my wincing fist.

I had him purely in my grasp, and then,   25
with care and by the purest choice, I leaned
and dropped him sideways down and free. He whirled
his hurdled length pell-mell along itself
down into granite chambers while I stood
in the green whelm of April.   30

                        And I knew,
come fresh from his long verse three days before,
that Lawrence talked too subtly of the snake
he learned to call a king (too late! too late!)
as it was sipping at the water trough.   35
He never truly knew that snake as snake:
he never held it in outrageous hands,
forcing its jaws to mouth the empty air,
nor ever, as he thought, gave his dark king
the deepest insult one might offer kings,   40
letting it go unhurt to its dark earth.

Howard Nemerov (1920–   )

SARAJEVO

In the summer, when the Archduke dies
Past the year's height, after the burning wheel
Steadies and plunges down the mountainside,
The days' succession fails from one to one
Still great as kings, whose shock troops in the field   5
Begin to burnish their green shoots to gold.

That undeclared war always takes the field
In the summer, when the Archduke dies,
And the blind spills buried beneath the wheel
Are risen, spears bespoken through earth's side   10
To sacrifice their fast and turning gold
In ransom for the blood of all in one.

Now that blood will be redeemed for gold
Eagle and crown aglitter in the wheel,
In the summer, when the Archduke dies,   15
Europe divides and fuses, side and side,
Ranging the human filings on the field
Of force, held by the magnet, not yet one.

Still empty of its food the battle field
Waits on the harvest and the great wain's wheel,   20
The vessels wait at hearth and harborside.
In the summer, when the Archduke dies,
Fate and the fortune of the game are one,
The green time turns to a heavy red, to gold.

And now responsible men on either side   25
Acknowledge their allegiance to the One
God of battles whose name is writ in gold,
The same whose coin, that cruelly blazing wheel,
In the summer, when the Archduke dies,
Buys earth as though it were a peasant's field.   30

The wildly streaming past now falls to one
Plunge on the oldest number of the wheel,
The zero twice redeemed in suicide,
Last blood sport of the green civilian field
Where the old world's sun went down in gold   35
In the summer when the Archduke died.

Hilary Corke (*1921–*   )

HIEROSULEM

In a fourth-floor flat in Hierosulem
A rabbi and the rabbi's rabbi son
Sit in their black hats at the breakfast table.
They nibble matzos. Underneath their elbows
The plywood surface sadly bends and creaks.   5
The rabbi looks towards his son and speaks:

"This world, an onion, is a holy bulb
That may be peeled to Hierosulem;
And in that skin called Hierosulem
Lie smaller tighter skins that may be peeled;   10
And we shall find when the last peeling's done
Myself (a rabbi) you (a rabbi's son).

It is an onion or a clock with wheels,
Wheel within wheel or sphere within gaseous sphere,"
The rabbi says. "Within His brooding will   15
We are the crystal pinion. It is so.

If we should nod, the whole thing's down the sink:
We are God's watchspring, making the round world go."

The rabbi hands his son a cup:
The young man looks into the cup and sees   20
All the poor pelting villages of Pripet,
Dumb walls of Spanish ghettos, Lombard street,
Shylock at 'change, a pawnshop in Odessa,
And Rothschild with a mink rug over his knees.

The room is dark, the curtains being drawn,   25
The window closed behind them. It has never
Been opened, that window. The rabbi sighs and rises:
"You were never like the others, Reb Yisroel:
Ephraim and Menachem never cared.
No doubt the One prepares them dark surprises."   30

A dying fly prays in the window frame.
He puts the matzos on the German sideboard,
Which also serves as Ark. Safe lodged within
His tattered tallith and phylacteries;
The holy Torah in its bag of silk   35
Burns in that darkness like a mildewed flame.

                    .   .   .

Outside in the damned hot streets of Jerusalem
Yisroel's uncle sweats and wipes his warts;
Young Ephraim and Menachem twirl their racquets
Discussing likely favorites for the sports;   40
And cousin Aaron on his bicycle
Whistles at Goyim girls in shirts and shorts.

Edgar Simmons (*1921–*   )

FAULKNER

I

Having often gone privately
through woods and swamp lands near Oxford,
having often trailed in at night through his mother's parlor
in dirty duck pants and muddy sneakers, furtively bobbing

to aunts and spinster librarians lifting in the light   5
warm muffins —with sweat on him going past
the parlor lamp, going privately and steadily to his room
his heart topsy turvy
with pine pitch & Negroes in the boiling sun—
the shrieking birds, the slick coon hounds   10
resounding in his blood
inveigling in him a grand privacy

such good hostelry often repeated and privately magnified
the elements breaking and burning
beginning a pattern   15
the words finally lighting him
like the sun lighting the courthouse in Oxford.

II

—Days and nights of spidery calligraphy, exquisite as a
                    monk's,
jesus corporals gliding from his pen—
Faulkner's private   20
hot line, his mammy, nanny, his fine rockabye,
his fingers funding the vast rubble of time, the hiss of con-
                    trols
working, his face slightly swaying & downed with a lichen
                    that
fringes the slowly turning turret of his face,
the carp-like threads of the thrusting face in a lean to the
                    paper—   25
he is the ecstatic fox running under the Pleiades,
moustache bristling like a toucan, moist lips making vowels
of agreement—mind, fingers & face dancing so as not to fall,
lips asserting private zonal priorities over the old
irrational cry: Faulkner assimilating Adam and his tree   30
branching the apples of vision, becoming the grease and
                    shine
of amplitude, providing beneath the jelly
red horns   red cloven feet
                              wearing finally only the figleaf
of language, knowing that to have moved at all   35
was to have begun this necessitous rattley dance
this silent private flit through the plot of old thorns:

bard, scop, skald, trouvère
                              this slight Celtic minstrel
—this Falconer—armored—tussling with his bird.   40

Richard Wilbur (*1921–*)

LOVE CALLS US TO THE THINGS
OF THIS WORLD

The eyes open to a cry of pulleys,
And spirited from sleep, the astounded soul
Hangs for a moment bodiless and simple
As false dawn.
              Outside the open window   5
The morning air is all awash with angels.

   Some are in bed-sheets, some are in blouses,
Some are in smocks: but truly there they are.
Now they are rising together in calm swells
Of halcyon feeling, filling whatever they wear   10
With the deep joy of their impersonal breathing;

   Now they are flying in place, conveying
The terrible speed of their omnipresence, moving
And staying like white water; and now of a sudden
They swoon down into so rapt a quiet   15
That nobody seems to be there.
                     The soul shrinks

   From all that it is about to remember,
From the punctual rape of every blessèd day,
And cries,   20
       "Oh, let there be nothing on earth but laundry,
Nothing but rosy hands in the rising steam
And clear dances done in the sight of heaven."

   Yet, as the sun acknowledges
With a warm look the world's hunks and colors,   25
The soul descends once more in bitter love
To accept the waking body, saying now
In a changed voice as the man yawns and rises,

   "Bring them down from their ruddy gallows;
Let there be clean linen for the backs of thieves;   30
Let lovers go fresh and sweet to be undone,
And the heaviest nuns walk in a pure floating
Of dark habits,
          keeping their difficult balance."

THEN

Then when the ample season
Warmed us, waned and went,
We gave to the leaves no graves,
To the robin gone no name,
Nor thought at the birds' return   5
Of their sourceless dim descent,
And we read no loss in the leaf,
But a freshness ever the same.

The leaf first learned of years
One not forgotten fall;   10
Of lineage now, and loss
These latter singers tell,
Of a year when birds now still
Were all one choiring call
Till the unreturning leaves   15
Imperishably fell.

James Dickey (*1923–   *)

CHERRYLOG ROAD

Off Highway 106
At Cherrylog Road I entered
The '34 Ford without wheels,
Smothered in kudzu,
With a seat pulled out to run   5
Corn whiskey down from the hills,

And then from the other side
Crept into an Essex
With a rumble seat of red leather
And then out again, aboard   10
A blue Chevrolet, releasing
The rust from its other color,

Reared up on three building blocks.
None had the same body heat;
I changed with them inward, toward   15

The weedy heart of the junkyard,
For I knew that Doris Holbrook
Would escape from her father at noon

And would come from the farm
To seek parts owned by the sun   20
Among the abandoned chassis,
Sitting in each in turn
As I did, leaning forward
As in a wild stock-car race

In the parking lot of the dead.   25
Time after time, I climbed in
And out the other side, like
An envoy or movie star
Met at the station by crickets.
A radiator cap raised its head,   30

Become a real toad or a kingsnake
As I neared the hub of the yard,
Passing through many states,
Many lives, to reach
Some grandmother's long Pierce-Arrow   35
Sending platters of blindness forth

From its nickel hubcaps
And spilling its tender upholstery
On sleepy roaches,
The glass panel in between   40
Lady and colored driver
Not all the way broken out,

The back-seat phone
Still on its hook.
I got in as though to exclaim,   45
"Let us go to the orphan asylum,
John; I have some old toys
For children who say their prayers."

I popped with sweat as I thought
I heard Doris Holbrook scrape   50
Like a mouse in the southern-state sun
That was eating the paint in blisters
From a hundred car tops and hoods.
She was tapping like code,

Loosening the screws,   55
Carrying off headlights,
Sparkplugs, bumpers,

Cracked mirrors and gear-knobs,
Getting ready, already,
To go back with something to show   60

Other than her lips, new trembling
I would hold to me soon, soon,
Where I sat in the ripped back seat
Talking over the interphone,
Praying for Doris Holbrook   65
To come from her father's farm

And to get back there
With no trace of me on her face
To be seen by her red-haired father
Who would change, in the squalling barn,   70
Her back's pale skin with a strop,
Then lay for me

In a bootlegger's roasting car
With a string-triggered 12-gauge shotgun
To blast the breath from the air.   75
Not cut by the jagged windshields,
Through the acres of wrecks she came
With a wrench in her hand,

Through dust where the blacksnake dies
Of boredom, and the beetle knows   80
The compost has no more life.
Someone outside would have seen
The oldest car's door inexplicably
Close from within:

I held her and held her and held her,   85
Convoyed at terrific speed
By the stalled, dreaming traffic around us,
So the blacksnake, stiff
With inaction, curved back
Into life, and hunted the mouse,   90

With deadly overexcitement,
The beetles reclaimed their field
As we clung, glued together,
With the hooks of the seat springs
Working through to catch us red-handed   95
Amidst the gray, breathless batting

That burst from the seat at our backs.
We left by separate doors
Into the changed, other bodies

Of cars, she down Cherrylog Road   100
And I to my motorcycle
Parked like the soul of the junkyard

Restored, a bicycle fleshed
With power, and tore off
Up Highway 106, continually   105
Drunk on the wind in my mouth,
Wringing the handlebar for speed,
Wild to be wreckage forever.

Alan Dugan (*1923–*   )

LOVE SONG: I AND THOU

Nothing is plumb, level or square:
     the studs are bowed, the joists
are shaky by nature, no piece fits
     any other piece without a gap
or pinch, and bent nails   5
     dance all over the surfacing
like maggots. By Christ
     I am no carpenter. I built
the roof for myself, the walls
     for myself, the floors   10
for myself, and got
     hung up in it myself. I
danced with a purple thumb
     at this house-warming, drunk
with my prime whiskey: rage.   15
     Oh I spat rage's nails
into the frame-up of my work:
     it held. It settled plumb,
level, solid, square and true
     for that great moment. Then   20
it screamed and went on through,
     skewing as wrong the other way.
God damned it. This is hell,
     but I planned it, I sawed it,
I nailed it, and I   25
     will live in it until it kills me.

I can nail my left palm
    to the left-hand cross-piece but
I can't do everything myself.
    I need a hand to nail the right,   30
a help, a love, a you, a wife.

Daniel Hoffman (*1923–*   )

ON THE INDUSTRIAL HIGHWAY

Approaching the Walt
Whitman Bridge you pass
an affluent world—

a subculture of spouts,
nozzles, ducts, a host   5
of snakes and ladders

in nests and thickets
or by tribes, laying
dinosaur farts

against the sun.   10
I drive slowly through the
stink and gawk at

shapes that no
familiarity breeds,
a ghostless city   15

called "gas works," never
meant for death or living.
A pipe pulses

flame in secret
code on the gashed sky.   20
Here are things

whose archetypes
have not yet been dreamed.
There's no more perfect

duct than these   25
ducts, pipes, facts
burdened with nothing

anticipating
unhappened memories,
visionary things.   30

Sy Kahn (*1924–*   )

POET ON TOUR

Wing down, world up,
The poets are moving around
These days, like birds,
Mr. Shelley, like moles,
Mr. Poe, emerging   5
From the underground—
Singing from city to city,
Mr. Whitman, counterpointing
Your songs.

They move through the gardens   10
Of flower children and
Occasional beds of pansies.
They cause doubt
In the minds of senior girls
About to marry safely.   15
They are spoilers. Watch out
Mr. College President and Mr. Dean—
The troubadour has often
Stolen the queen
And left a muddled maiden's head.   20

They move in the cross winds
Of the continent,
Alight on the campus,
Sometimes create a draft
That chills,   25
But does not kill.

Watch out, Mr. Sociologist—
Watch out, Mr. Psychologist—
He has no identity crisis;
He has lain on the bed of Isis,   30

Tasted the jelly of the stars—
He'd rather kiss than confess.

Watch out, Mr. Historian,
He doesn't believe your fictions—
Watch out, you Dean of Ladies,   35
He doesn't believe in constrictions.

Glory be to God for dappled things,
The poets are moving, Mr. Hopkins,
Singing their mottled songs,
The dark and light octaves   40
Of their voices making a thin
Chorus, taking on airs,
Mr. Yeats, singing old songs.

Sometimes the rooms are lonely,
Mr. Robinson, after the songs   45
Are sung and the people
Go back to the late show.
And the cigaretts taste bad,
Mr. Bukowski, at three
O'clock in the morning.   50

But the poets are moving
Around these days,
Around these days,
Around,
And faster than sound.   55

In the belly of birds
They fashion new songs;
They are writing their notes
In the air. High bravery
At Hattaras at last, Mr. Crane.   60
The poets are moving around.

Do you hear, Mr. Cummings,
In your fresh sod, do you
Hear Mr. Frost, in the rain—
Do you know, Mr. Fearing,   65
In spite of your leering,
Your ominous, seering refrain?
The poets are moving,
From inn to inn,
From court to court,   70
Do you hear, Mr. Bloat-belly

Powerful Thomas?
It's a force, Dylan,
The force that drives the flower.
Thou should'st be with us at this hour.   75

Allen Ginsberg (*1926–*   )

THE SHROUDED STRANGER

Bare skin is my wrinkled sack
When hot Apollo humps my back
When Jack Frost grabs me in these rags
I wrap my legs with burlap bags

My flesh is cinder my face is snow   5
I walk the railroad to and fro
When city streets are black and dead
The railroad embankment is my bed

I sup my soup from old tin cans
And take my sweets from little hands   10
In Tiger Alley near the jail
I steal away from the garbage pail

In darkest night where none can see
Down in the bowels of the factory
I sneak barefoot upon stone   15
Come and hear the old man groan

I hide and wait like a naked child
Under the bridge my heart goes wild
I scream at a fire on the river bank
I give my body to an old gas tank   20

I dream that I have burning hair
Boiled arms that claw the air
The torso of an iron king
And on my back a broken wing

Who'll go out whoring into the night   25
On the eyeless road in the skinny moonlight
Maid or dowd or athlete proud
May wanton with me in the shroud

Who'll come lay down in the dark with me
Belly to belly and knee to knee   30
Who'll look into my hooded eye
Who'll lay down under my darkened thigh?

SUNFLOWER SUTRA

I walked on the banks of the tincan banana dock and sat down
    under the huge shade of a Southern Pacific locomotive to
    look at the sunset over the box house hills and cry.
Jack Kerouac sat beside me on a busted rusty iron pole,
    companion, we thought the same thoughts of the soul,
    bleak and blue and sad-eyed, surrounded by the gnarled
    steel roots of trees of machinery.
The oily water on the river mirrored by the red sky, sun sank
    on top of final Frisco peaks, no fish in that stream, no
    hermit in those mounts, just ourselves rheumy-eyed and
    hungover like old bums on the riverbank, tired and wily.
Look at the Sunflower, he said, there was a dead gray shadow
    against the sky, big as a man, sitting dry on top of a pile
    of ancient sawdust—
—I rushed up enchanted—it was my first sunflower, memories
    of Blake—my visions—Harlem   5
and Hells of the Eastern rivers, bridges clanking, Joes Greasy
    Sandwiches, dead baby carriages, black treadless tires for-
    gotten and unretreaded, the poem of the riverbank, con-
    doms & pots, steel knives, nothing stainless, only the
    dank muck and the razor sharp artifacts passing into the
    past—
and the gray Sunflower poised against the sunset, crackly
    bleak and dusty with the smut and smog and smoke of
    olden locomotives in its eye—
corolla of bleary spikes pushed down and broken like a bat-
    tered crown, seeds fallen out of its face, soon-to-be-
    toothless mouth of sunny air, sunrays obliterated on its
    hairy head like a dried wire spiderweb,
leaves stuck out like arms out of the stem, gestures from the
    sawdust root, broke pieces of plaster fallen out of the
    black twigs, a dead fly in its ear,
Unholy battered old thing you were, my sunflower O my
    soul, I loved you then!   10
The grime was no man's grime but death and human locomo-
    tives,

all that dress of dust, that veil of darkened railroad skin, that
smog of cheek, that eyelid of black mis'ry, that sooty
hand or phallus or protuberance of artificial worse-than-
dirt—industrial—modern—all that civilization spotting
your crazy golden crown—

and those blear thoughts of death and dusty loveless eyes and
ends and withered roots below, in the home-pile of sand
and sawdust, rubber dollar bills, skin of machinery, the
guts and innards of the weeping coughing car, the empty
lonely tincans with their rusty tongues alack, what more
could I name, the smoked ashes of some cock cigar, the
cunts of wheelbarrows and the milky breasts of cars,
wornout asses out of chairs & sphincters of dynamos—
all these

entangled in your mummied roots—and you there standing
before me in the sunset, all your glory in your form!

A perfect beauty of a sunflower! a perfect excellent lovely
sunflower existence! a sweet natural eye to the new hip
moon, woke up alive and excited grasping in the sunset
shadow sunrise golden monthly breeze!   15

How many flies buzzed round you innocent of your grime,
while you cursed the heavens of the railroad and your
flower soul?

Poor dead flower? when did you forget you were a flower?
when did you look at your skin and decide you were an
impotent dirty old locomotive? the ghost of a locomo-
tive? the specter and shade of a once powerful mad
American locomotive?

You were never no locomotive, Sunflower, you were a sun-
flower!

And you Locomotive, you are a locomotive, forget me
not!

So I grabbed up the skeleton thick sunflower and stuck it at
my side like a scepter,   20

and deliver my sermon to my soul, and Jack's soul too, and
anyone who'll listen,

—We're not our skin of grime, we're not our dread bleak
dusty imageless locomotive, we're all beautiful golden
sunflowers inside, we're blessed by our own seed &
golden hairy naked accomplishment-bodies growing
into mad black formal sunflowers in the sunset, spied on
by our eyes under the shadow of the mad locomotive
riverbank sunset Frisco hilly tincan evening sitdown
vision.

Alastair Reid (*1926–*   )

CALENTURE

He never lives to tell,
but other men bring back the tale

of how, after days of gazing at the sea
unfolding itself incessantly and greenly—
hillsides of water, crested with clouds of foam—   5
he, heavy with a fading dream of home,
clambers aloft one morning, and, looking down,
cries out at seeing a different green,
farms, woods, grasslands, an extending plain,
hazy meadows, a long tree-fledged horizon,   10
swallows flashing in the halcyon sun,
his ship riding deep in rippled grain,
the road well-known to him, the house, the garden,
figures at the gate; and, lost in his passion,
he suddenly climbs down and begins to run.   15
Dazed by his joy, the others watch him drown.

Such calenture, they say,
is not unknown in lovers long at sea

yet such a like fever did she make in me
this green-leaved summer morning, that I,   20
seeing her confirm a wish made lovingly,
felt gate, trees, grass, birds, garden glimmer over,
a ripple cross her face, the sky quiver,
the cropped lawn sway in waves, the house founder,
the light break into flecks, the path shimmer,   25
till, finding her eyes clear and true at the centre,
I walked toward her on the flowering water.

Jascha Kessler (*1929–*   )

A WIFE'S LAMENT
FOR JULIA

Three April weeks had washed Manhattan clean when
I was born. Crawstuffed, the gulls paddled placid
on the East River brack; cats snoozed among begonias

on brownstone sills; contented peasant nations lulled
at night on that shore of slums. My father watched
stars flare from rivet pots to sky scaffolds; in my
mother's breast I heard faint mandolins, cries of lovers,
ponies' hooves drumming Magyar plains.
A mild, generous spring.

My hair sprung thick, black and long. My brows
arched in the high Romany cast over a hooked nose.
My small breasts shaped late, and my round belly,
firm sides, my deep waist, long back, and heavy pear
of buttocks are fleshed lightest olive yet darker
than cream. Full thighs and straight, fleet in
shin, ankle, foot. A tall thin girl with the
proud, Czardas head. And since my youth is proud
I dream no dreams: my eyes change with the seasons . . .

My parents were simple lovers, chaste, good:
I knew nothing of life. My first friend died,
a soldier, in that gray erupting time when the
armored winds shuddered overhead and flung down
in our laps the torn, naked parts of young men.
What more was to be known? I saw common crowds
of sterile men. I walked among millions in steel
gardens of the torrid town, among faces of glass,
of stone. I waited; others went mad.

Then I married—a man of restless dreams,
full of words, all truth, all lies, who because
born beneath November's ashen rains can never
forgive that season's wrack. He is doomed
not to be mine: for he cannot see time confounds
even the subtle music of the flesh which, in its choosings,
marks us heroes with love's sad beauty, and will not know
that sons of the cannibal earth, eating and eaten,
are fruitful and multiply.

Though men tie and sunder with the hot breath
of killing joy in the open woman, though the best
are ignorant conquerors of a land they never know,
seeking the golden knot which binds her drabbest
elements (and the worst rape what she cannot give,
the heart of her pride, sense of her love), still
the power to storm is theirs, and we must hear, wait,
bear them . . . for men make music when the wind has blown,
and we lie in the savage arms of men.

5

10

15

20

25

30

35

40

45

Ted Hughes (*1930–*   )

HER HUSBAND

Comes home dull with coal-dust deliberately
To grime the sink and foul towels and let her
Learn with scrubbing brush and scrubbing board
The stubborn character of money.

And let her learn through what kind of dust   5
He has earned his thirst and the right to quench it
And what sweat he has exchanged for his money
And the blood-weight of money. He'll humble her

With new light on her obligations.
The fried, woody chips, kept warm two hours in the oven,   10
Are only part of her answer.
Hearing the rest, he slams them to the fire back

And is away round the house-end singing
"Come back to Sorrento" in a voice
Of resounding corrugated iron.   15
Her back has bunched into a hump as an insult.

For they will have their rights.
Their jurors are to be assembled
From the little crumbs of soot. Their brief
Goes straight up to heaven and nothing more is heard of it.   20

Paris Leary (*1931–*   )

VIEWS OF THE OXFORD COLLEGES

There are no red leaves in yellow Oxford,
no acrid scent of red leaves burning
on wet grass waiting to be brown.
At night the coal-smoke settling on the town
brought the small sky closer, and the turning   5
of the earth numbed the keys in awkward locks.

Moisture logs the print of Christ's scorched shadow
sagging from the frost-crippled altar
where the breath rimes the chalice with a touch

of cold humanity and snaps with such   10
frozen Amens that fingers smart and falter
in their chilled blessing over silent bread.

A ragged cat with yellow dignity
moves like a stone along a ragged wall
and vanishes from sight by standing still.   15
But the season will not change for me until
I walk ankle-deep through the blazing fall
and watch the wind blow the sun away.

For though the summer rose in me in Ludlow,
and though a second autumn pales me here,   20
yet always it is Tilbury Town that rises
around me where the Cherwell and the Isis
swell gently with the custom of the year.
It is too many years until the snow.

Christ in sacrifice leans dangerously   25
from the chipped wall, his broken nose
and powdered eyes brutal with centuries.
Leaves drop like jaundiced blood from chestnut trees
but, falling where the feeble morning rose,
scatter mercy down the thin lame street—   30

and in that part of mind where I am youngest
sumac bleeds and crimson cracks like thunder
through maples incandescent with the reason
there are no red leaves this yellow season;
and I, admiring Magdalen Tower, wonder   35
how the age has scraped Christ's blood from everything.

Sylvia Plath (1932–1963)

THE APPLICANT

First, are you our sort of a person?
Do you wear
A glass eye, false teeth or a crutch,
A brace or a hook,
Rubber breasts or a rubber crotch,   5

Stitches to show something's missing? No, no? Then
How can we give you a thing?
Stop crying.

Open your hand.
Empty? Empty. Here is a hand   10

To fill it and willing
To bring teacups and roll away headaches
And do whatever you tell it.
Will you marry it?
It is guaranteed   15

To thumb shut your eyes at the end
And dissolve of sorrow.
We make new stock from the salt.
I notice you are stark naked.
How about this suit—   20

Black and stiff, but not a bad fit.
Will you marry it?
It is waterproof, shatterproof, proof
Against fire and bombs through the roof.
Believe me, they'll bury you in it.   25

Now your head, excuse me, is empty.
I have the ticket for that.
Come here, sweetie, out of the closet.
Well, what do you think of *that*?
Naked as paper to start   30

But in twenty-five years she'll be silver,
In fifty, gold.
A living doll, everywhere you look.
It can sew, it can cook,
It can talk, talk, talk.   35

It works, there is nothing wrong with it.
You have a hole, it's a poultice.
You have an eye, it's an image.
My boy, it's your last resort.
Will you marry it, marry it, marry it.   40

Suzanne Gross (*1933–*   )

THE VINE

Whenever I was small, a child,
a little girl, there was doubt then
if some of those beings we saw

in microscopes if we saw them
at all, belonged in the kingdom   5

of plants, or with the animals,
their bodies and their lives looked so
complete and simple. Grown woman
as I am, yet I cannot tell
if these bacteria, all these   10

seeming self-sufficient cells still
go homeless in taxonomy;
but I have learned from cells that make
my veins and are the blood that beats
in them, as from the cells that are   15

my bowels as they are my food,
my love, what kingdom they are in.
Tell me what kingdom this vine's is,
here in the middle of winter,
that hugs the bricks, the mortar,   20

so hard with its red, shockingly
five-fingered hands. I call them so
as they recall my own and have
the beautiful color of blood
like mine; but I remember more   25

how hard I cling to horses, men,
the very trunks of trees, even
such a rasping wall as this is,
with fingers as red as the vine
has, and as the naked vine does,   30

only to live. Do not the hawks
have hands and fly with them as well
as we? I know I have the bones
of birds and am the fishes' child.
Someday the water will leach me   35

home to their bodies: then lions
maned with the lightning and mares limbed
in the splendor of night shall come
be my soaring, my song. Salmon
and harp seal and hooded merganser   40

shall come be a body for me;
neither now shall any show me
where that careful point or plane is
that my life is not mine any
more but another's beginning.   45

Rod McKuen (*1933–*   )

BEFORE THE MONKEYS CAME

We'll go wild into the noon
to find what love there is to find
an angel on the bedpost
or a demon in the mind
and we'll be happy as we were   5
before the monkeys came
and put the flowers into pots
and gave love sinful names.

when apple trees were apple trees
and not the curse of man   10
and all the mountains piled high
were only heaps of sand
there were no yellow roses then
the roses all were red
and lovers slept on grassy banks   15
and never knew a bed.

We'll go wild into the noon
and try to be the same
the way we were awhile ago
before the monkeys came   20
when every street was Eden street
and Man our only name
that was oh so long ago
before the monkeys came.

Ronald Gross (*1935–*   )

SIZE OF BREASTS IS OF NO IMPORTANCE

Some women with small breasts
                              assume
That they will be less able
                    to produce milk
                    in sufficient quantity.   5
There is probably little basis
                    for this belief.

When a woman is not pregnant
                              and not nursing,
The glandular tissue is quiescent   10
And constitutes only a minor part
                              of the breast.
The greater part is composed
                              of fat tissue,
Which is apparently concentrated there   15
                                   for purposes
                                   of beauty.

Don L. Lee (*1942–*)

THE DEATH DANCE
FOR MAXINE

my empty steps mashed
your face in a mad
rhythm of happiness.
as if i was just learning to
boo-ga-loo.   5

my mother took the
"b" train to the loop
to seek work & was laughed at by
some dumb, eye-less image maker as
she scored idiot on "your" i. Q. test.   10

i watched mom;
an ebony mind
on a yellow frame.
"i got work son, go back to school."
(she was placed according to her   15
intelligence into some honkie's kitchen)

i thought & my steps
took on a hip be-bop beat
on your little brain
trying to reach any of   20
your senseless senses.

mom would come home late
at night & talk sadtalk

or funny sadtalk, she talked
about a pipe smoking sissy   25
who talked sissy-talk & had
sissy sons who were forever playing
sissy games with themselves
 & then she would say,
"son you is a man, a black man."   30

i was now tapdancing on your
balls & you felt no pain.
my steps were beating a staccato
message that told of the past 400 years.

the next day mom cried &   35
sadtalked me. she talked about
the eggs of maggot colored,
gaunt creatures from europe
who came here/put on pants, stopped eating with their hands
stole land, massacred indians,   40
hid from the sun, enslaved blacks &
thought that they were substitutes
for gods. she talked about a
faggot who grabbed her ass as
she tried to get out of the   45
backdoor of his kitchen & she said,
"son you is a man, a black man."

the African ballet
was now my guide; a teacher of self &
the dance of a people.   50
a dance of concept & essence.
i grew.

mom stayed home & the
ADC became my father/in projects without
backdoors/"old grand dad" over   55
the cries of bessie smith/
until pains didn't pain anymore.

i began to dance dangerous steps,
warrior's steps.
my steps took on a cadence with other blk/brothers   60
& you could hear the cracking of
gun shots in them & we said that,
"we were men, black men."

i took the "b" train to the loop &
you SEE me coming,   65

you don't like it,
you can't hide &
you can't stop me.
you will not laugh this time.
you know,   70
that when i dance again
it will be the
Death Dance.

James Tate (*1943–*   )

COMING DOWN CLEVELAND AVENUE

The fumes from all kinds
of machines have dirtied
the snow. You propose
to polish it, the miles
between home and wherever   5
you and your lily
of a woman might go. You
go, pail, brush, and
suds, scrubbing down
Cleveland Avenue   10
toward the Hartford Life
Insurance Company. No
one appreciates your
effort and one important
character calls you   15
a baboon. But pretty
soon your darling jumps
out of an elevator
and kisses you and you
sing and tell her to   20
walk the white plains
proudly. At one point
your even lay down
your coat, and she, in
turn, puts hers down for   25
you. And you put your
shirt down, and she, her

blouse, and your pants,
and her skirt, shoes—
removes her lavender   30
underwear and you slip
into her proud, white skin.

Traditional Ballads[1]

LORD RANDAL

"O where ha you been, Lord Randal, my son?
And where ha you been, my handsome young man?"
"I ha been at the greenwood; mother, mak my bed soon,
For I'm wearied wi hunting, and fain wad lie down."

"An wha met ye there, Lord Randal, my son?   5
An wha met you there, my handsome young man?"
"O I met wi my true-love; mother, mak my bed soon,
For I'm wearied wi huntin, an fain wad lie down."

"And what did she give you, Lord Randal, my son?
And what did she give you, my handsome young man?"   10
"Eels fried in a pan; mother, mak my bed soon,
For I'm wearied wi huntin, and fain wad lie down."

"And wha gat your leavings, Lord Randal, my son?
And wha gat your leavings, my handsome young man?"
"My hawks and my hounds; mother, mak my bed soon,   15
For I'm wearied wi hunting, and fain wad lie down."

"And what becam of them, Lord Randal, my son?
And what becam of them, my handsome young man?"
"They stretched their legs out an died; mother, mak my bed
            soon,
For I'm wearied wi huntin, and fain wad lie down."   20

"O I fear you are poisoned, Lord Randal, my son!
I fear you are poisoned, my handsome young man!"
"O yes, I am poisoned; mother, mak my bed soon,
For I'm sick at the heart, and I fain wad lie down."

---

[1]"Lord Randal" is British. The text of "Our Goodman" given here is a New England version of a British ballad. "Stagolee" and "Jim Haggerty's Story" originated in the United States.

"What d'ye leave to your mother, Lord Randal, my son?   25
What d'ye leave to your mother, my handsome young man?"
"Four and twenty milk kye; mother, mak my bed soon,
For I'm sick at the heart, and I fain wad lie down."

"What d'ye leave to your sister, Lord Randal, my son?
What d'ye leave to your sister, my handsome young man?"   30
"My gold and my silver; mother, mak my bed soon,
For I'm sick at the heart, an I fain wad lie down."

"What d'ye leave to your brother, Lord Randal, my son?
What d'ye leave to your brother, my handsome young
          man?"
"My houses and my lands; mother, mak my bed soon,   35
For I'm sick at the heart, and I fain wad lie down."

"What d'ye leave to your true-love, Lord Randal, my son?
What d'ye leave to your true-love, my handsome young
          man?"
"I leave her hell and fire; mother, mak my bed soon,
For I'm sick at the heart, and I fain wad lie down."   40

OUR GOODMAN

Last night when I came home
As drunk as I could be
I thought I saw another hat
Where my hat ought to be.

"O dear wife   O fond wife   5
O darling wife says I
Whose hat is that hat
With the gautlet gloves near by?"

"O you big fool   you old fool
You're drunk as drunk can be   10
It's nothing but a stewing pot
My mother sent to me."

"O dear wife   O fond wife
I've travelled the wide world o'er
But a stew pot with a lining in   15
I never saw before"

Last night when I came home
As drunk as I could be
I thought I saw another coat
Where my coat ought to be   20

"O dear wife   O fond wife
O darling wife says I
Whose coat is that coat
With the stirrup boots near by"

"O you big fool   you old fool   25
You're drunk as drunk can be
It's nothing but a dinny bag
My father sent to me."

"O dear wife   O fond wife
I've travelled the wide world o'er   30
But a dinny bag with a collar on
I never saw before."

Last night when I came home
As drunk as I could be
I thought I saw another horse   35
Where my horse ought to be

"O dear wife   O fond wife
O darling wife says I
Whose horse is that horse
What made my horse to shy"   40

"You big fool   you old fool
You're drunk as drunk can be
It's only that old muley cow
My brother sent to me"

"O dear wife   O fond wife   45
I've travelled the wide world o'er
But a muley cow with a saddle on
I never saw before."

Last night when I came home
As drunk as drunk could be   50
I thought I saw another head
Laid where my head should be.

"O dear wife   O fond wife
O darling wife says I
Whose head is that head   55
Where my head ought to lie"

You big fool   you old fool
You're drunk as drunk can be
It's nothing but dear sister's head
Who's come to visit me."   60

O dear wife   O fond wife
I've travelled the wide world o'er
Your sister with a mustache on
I never saw before."

STAGOLEE

Stagolee, Stagolee, what's dat in yo' grip?
Nothin' but my Sunday clothes, I'm goin' to take a trip,
O dat man, bad man, Stagolee done come.

Stagolee, Stagolee, where you been so long?
I been out on de battle fiel' shootin' an' havin' fun,   5
O dat man, bad man, Stagolee done come.

Stagolee was a bully man, an' ev'ybody knowed,
When dey seed Stagolee comin', to give Stagolee de road,
O dat man, bad man, Stagolee done come.

Stagolee started out, he give his wife his han',   10
"Good-by darlin', I'm goin' to kill a man."
O dat man, bad man, Stagolee done come.

Stagolee killed a man an' laid him on de flo',
What's dat he kill him wid? Dat same ole fohty-fo'
O dat man, bad man, Stagolee done come.   15

Stagolee killed a man an' laid him on his side,
What's dat he kill him wid? Dat same ole fohty-five.
O dat man, bad man, Stagolee done come.

Out of house an' down de street Stagolee did run,
In his hand he held a great big smokin' gun.   20
O dat man, bad man, Stagolee done come.

Stagolee, Stagolee, I'll tell you what I'll do,
If you'll git me out'n dis trouble I'll do as much for you.
O dat man, bad man, Stagolee done come.

Ain't it a pity, ain't it a shame?   25
Stagolee was shot, but he don't want no name.
O dat man, bad man, Stagolee done come.

Stagolee, Stagolee, look what you done done,
Killed de best ole citerzen; now you'll hav' to be hung.
O dat man, bad man, Stagolee done come.   30

Stagolee cried to de jury an' to de judge: Please don't take my life.
I have only three little children an' one little lovin' wife,
O dat man, bad man, Stagolee done come.

JIM HAGGERTY'S STORY

In the shade of a tree, we two sat, him and me,
Where the Badger Hills slope to the rift,
While our ponies browsed around, reins a-dragging the ground.
Then he looked at me funny and laughed.

"Do you see that there town?" he inquired, pointing down   5
To some shacks sprawled about in the heat.
When I opined that I did, then he shifted his quid,
After drownding a tumblebug neat.

Then he looked at me square, "There's a man waitin' there,
That the sheep-men have hired to get me.   10
Are you game to go down to that jerk-water town
Just to see what the hell you will see?"

Then we rode down the hill, each a-puffin' a pill
To the shacks sprawled around in the heat,
And we stopped at a shack that was leanin' its back   15
'Gainst the side of the cowboys' retreat.

Just inside of the door, with one foot on the floor
And the other hist up on a rail,
Stood a big rawboned guy, with the oneriest eye
That I ever saw out of a jail.   20

By his side stood a girl, that sure looked like a pearl
That the Bible guy cast before swine.
She was pleadin' with him, her eyes all teary and dim,
As I high-signed the barkeep for mine.

Then the door swung again and my pal he stepped in,   25
And the look in his eyes was sure bad,
And the Big Guy, he wheeled, and the gal there, she squealed,
"Oh, for God's sake, don't shoot, Bill, that's Dad."

Now the thing that she saw was Bill reach for his draw,
When the guy she called Dad drew on Bill.   30
Dad was my pal, with his eyes on the gal,
And her eyes on his gun, standin' still.

Then the big raw-boned guy, with the onery eye,
Up and shot my pal dead in the door,
And right there Bill Baker went back to his Maker,   35
He won't take the advantage no more.

The list below is highly selective, containing only those terms most frequently used in discussing and analyzing poetry. The definitions are as brief as clarity will permit.

Page references are given when a term is defined in the text. If there are several references, the most important is in **boldface** type.

Allegory. A complex form of metaphor in which abstract concepts are represented by persons, creatures, things, or situations (e.g., Five-Wits in *Everyman* and the Slough of Despond in *Pilgrim's Progress*).

Alliteration, 47, 50, 62

Allusion, 96–97, 103–4, 117–18

Ambiguity. A statement capable of more than one meaning. Often used by poets to create greater richness and intensity.

Amphibrach. A metrical foot of three syllables, with the second stressed ($\smile$ / $\smile$).

Glossary

of

Terms

Amphimac, Amphimacer. Metrical foot of three syllables with the first and third stressed (/ $\smile$ /).

Anacrusis. Prefixing one or two unstressed syllables to a line of verse beginning with a stressed syllable.

Analogy. An elaborate form of simile, in which one thing is explained in terms of another. Often used to present abstract ideas in terms of familiar experiences.

Anapest, Anapestic. Metrical foot ($\smile \smile \diagup$). 66, **70–71**

Apostrophe. Figure of speech in which someone absent is addressed as though he were present, or a thing or quality is addressed as though alive.

Approximate Rhyme. (*See* Half Rhyme)

Archaism, 17–18

Assonance, 48, 50

Ballad, 63–64, **78**

Blank verse, 66–67, 87

Catalexis. Omission of the final unstressed syllable in a line of verse; sometimes also applied to omission of unstressed syllables at beginning of line.

Cesura. Pause in a line of poetry (most often near the middle).

Comparison, 28–32

Connotation, 9–22

Consonance, 49–50

Consonants, 53–58

Context, 15

Couplet, 76, 87–88

Dactyl, Dactylic, 70–71

Denotation, 9–22

Diction, 9–22

Didactic Poetry. Poetry designed to teach a lesson or win the reader over to a viewpoint.

Dimeter. Two-foot line.

Double Rhyme. (*See* Feminine Rhyme)

Double (Duple) Rhythm, 71

Duration (as basis of rhythm), 59–60

Elegy. In English poetry, originally any serious meditative poem. The term is now usually restricted to poems dealing with the death of any individual, or death collectively.

End-Stopped Line, 76

English Sonnet. (*See* Shakespearean Sonnet)

Enjambement, 76

Epic. Long narrative poem, usually written in an elevated style, and dealing with a hero associated with a particular nation, people, or religion.

Falling Rhythm, 71

Feminine Rhyme, 48

Figure Of Speech. Language used in various nonliteral ways (*e.g.*, simile, metaphor, metonymy).

Foot. Basic unit in line of poetry—iambic, dactylic, etc. 59–60, **64–65**

Form, 75–91

Free Association, 98–103

Free verse, 71–73, 86–87

French Forms, 82–83

Half Rhyme, 48–50

Heptameter. Seven-foot line.

Hexameter. Six-foot line.

Heroic Couplet, 76

Hyperbole. Extreme exaggeration, for special literary effects.

Iamb, Iambic, Iambus. Metrical foot (˘ ´). 66–68

Image, Imagery. Words used for connotative appeal to the senses; vividly descriptive language.

Imperfect Rhyme. (*See* Half Rhyme)

Incongruity, 110

Irony, 25–28

Italian Sonnet. (*See* Petrarchan sonnet)

Limerick, 83

Lyric. Originally, in Greek poetry, a song meant to be sung to the accompaniment of a lyre. Now used for a short, non-narrative poem. Sometimes extended to take in odes and elegies.

Masculine Rhyme, 48

Metaphor. A comparison in which *like*, etc., is omitted (*e.g.* "He is a beast" instead of "He is like a beast").

Meter, 59

Metonymy. Figure of speech in which a part stands for the whole (*e.g.*, "The bottle was his undoing").

Mock-Heroic. A poem using the lofty language and structure of the heroic narrative or epic, but dealing with trivial or absurd subject matter.

Monometer. One-foot line.

Near-Rhyme. (*See* Half Rhyme)

Octometer. Eight-foot line.

Ode. A term loosely applied to a poem usually of medium length and having a certain elevation of tone; often it is addressed to a particular person or persons.

Old English Rhythm, 59–60, **62–65**

Onomatopoeia, 58

Orthographical Rhyme, 48

Ottava Rima, 78–79

Oxymoron. Figure of speech in which apparently contradictory words are juxtaposed (*e.g.*, "gentle homicide").

Paradox, 23–25, 114

Paraphrase. Restatement of the meaning of a poem in prose.

Pentameter. Five-foot line.

Petrarchan Sonnet, 84–85

Personification. Treating non-human objects as though they had human traits.

Stream of Consciousness. (*See* Free Association)

Stress, 59–61, **62–64**

Symbol, 29–33

Synonym, 9–12

Tercet. Three-line stanza.

Terza Rima, 80

Tetrameter. Four-foot line.

Theme. Idea embodied in a poem.

Tone, 25, 150–56

Trimeter. Three-foot line.

Triolet. One of the "French forms." 82

Triple Rhyme. Three syllables rhyming (*e.g.*, easily-breezily).

Triple Rhythm. Feet containing three syllables each (*e.g.*, anapestic, dactylic).

Trochaic, Trochee. Metrical foot (/ ⌣). 66, **69–71**

Verse. As constrasted to prose—language used with a definite and regular formal structure such as meter.

Vowels, 52, 53–58

Index
of
Authors
and
Titles

Included are all selections in the text as well as in the section of Additional Poems. Italic page references indicate the poem. An asterisk (*) after a page reference refers to a discussion.